2021
2022
年度実施

The United Nations Association's Test of English

国連英検
過去問題集

公益財団法人
日本国際連合協会 編著

UNA-JAPAN

特A級

SANSHUSHA

はじめに
英語コミュニケーション能力の測定と国連英検

国連英検統括監修官　服部孝彦

国連英検は，英語コミュニケーション能力を測るためのテストです。ひとくちにコミュニケーション能力をテストするといっても，「コミュニケーション能力」という概念は複雑です。ここでは，コミュニケーション能力の理論的枠組みをできる限り明らかにし，コミュニケーション能力をより的確に測るためのテストとしての国連英検のあり方について論じます。

1960年代以降に言語研究に科学的な手法が求められるようになり，「コミュニケーション能力」という概念が生まれました。コミュニケーション能力の概念を最初に示したのはハイムズ（Hymes, 1972）ですが，それ以前に彼は，能力（competence）と運用（performance）の概念を提唱したチョムスキー（Chomsky, 1965）から大きな影響を受けたため，まずチョムスキーの言語理論から考察することにします。

チョムスキーは，従来の学習を習慣形成による刺激と反応の結合が発達したもの，すなわち練習と強化によって形成された習慣とみなす行動主義（behaviorism）の考え方に異論を唱えました。彼は「具体的状況における実際の言語使用」(the actual use of language in concrete situation）を運用（performance）とし，それを「話者―聴者の言語の知識」(the speaker-hearer's knowledge of his language）である能力（competence）と区別しました。

ハイムズはチョムスキーの能力（competence）の概念を発展させ，コミュニケーション能力（communicative competence）の概念を示しました。ハイムズは，文法的な意味に限定したチョムスキーの能力（competence）は不十分であるとし，能力を社会的文化的に拡張すると主張しました。ハイムズのコミュニケーション能力は次の4つに分類されます。

(1) Whether (and to what degree) something is formally possible;
(2) Whether (and to what degree) something is feasible in virtue of the means of implementation available;
(3) Whether (and to what degree) something is appropriate (adequate, happy, successful) in relation to a context in which it is used and evaluated;
(4) Whether (and to what degree) something is in fact done, actually performed, and what its doing entails.

ハイムズは，文法的に正しいのか，発話することが現実的に可能か，社会的に適切であるか，実際に遂行されているのか，といった４つの基準を示したわけです。前者２つが文法に関するもので，後者２つが発話としての容認性に関するものであるといえます。

ハイムズのコミュニケーション能力は，ウィドウソン（Widdowson, 1983），バックマン（Bachman, 1990），さらにはバックマンとパーマー（Bachman and Palmer, 1996）へと引き継がれました。「コミュニケーション能力」という用語は，communicative competence, communicative language ability, language ability と表記が変わり，定義も見直されました。コミュニケーション能力理論で最も新しいものは，バックマンの論理，およびバックマンとパーマーの理論です。バックマンとパーマー（Bachman and Palmer, 1996）の理論は，バックマン（Bachman, 1990）の理論を踏襲した改訂版で，テスティングのための理論という色彩を強めたものです。この２つの理論は現在，コミュニケーション理論の中で最も信頼のおけるものとして，言語教育で受け入れられています。

バックマンとパーマーは，コミュニケーション能力に language ability という用語を用いています。そして，その language ability の中にハイムズやカネールとスウェインなどが言う communicative competence の構成要素をすべて含んだ言語知識（language knowledge）という概念を設けました。バックマンとパーマーの言語知識は，組織的知識（organizational knowledge）と語用論的知識（pragmatic knowledge）に分けられます。組織的知識はさらに，文法的知識（grammatical knowledge）とテキスト的知識（textual knowledge）に分類されます。語用論的知識は，機能的知識

(functional knowledge) と社会言語学的知識 (sociolinguistic knowledge) に分類されます。バックマンとパーマーは，言語知識以外にトピック知識 (topical knowledge) や個人的特徴 (personal characteristics) なども language ability の中に含まれる要素としており，これらすべてを結びつける能力として方略的能力 (strategic competence) を挙げています。

バックマンとパーマーは次のように述べ，自分たちが提示したコミュニケーションのモデルはテスト開発のためのものである，としています。

> We would note that we conceive of this not as a working model of language processing, but rather as a conceptual basis for organizing our thinking about the test development process.

バックマンとパーマーは，心理的な意味での言語処理モデルではなく，テスト開発のための概念的な枠組みを設定したといえます。

バックマンとパーマーの language ability 理論の基礎になったのが，バックマン (Bachman, 1990) の communicative language ability 理論です。バックマンは，知識 (knowledge) ではなく能力 (competence) という用語を用いて，語用論的能力 (pragmatic competence) と組織的能力 (organizational competence) について，次のように述べています。

> Pragmatic competence includes the types of knowledge which, in addition to organization competence, are employed in the contexturalized performance and interpretation of socially appropriate illocutionary acts in discourse.

ここでバックマンは，語用論的能力／語用論的知識は，組織的能力／組織的知識の基盤の上にできあがるものであることを示しました。また，語用論的能力／語用論的知識は，テキストを構成しない一文単位でも発揮されるということを考えますと，組織的能力／組織的知識の中心は文法的能力／文法的知識であることがわかります。

以上のコミュニケーション能力理論に基づき，国連英検では以下のように出題されています。高等学校で学習する英語の範囲内で出題されるＣ級は，語用論的知識に先行して学習する必要のある組織的知識について問い，加えて組織的知識の基礎となる文法的知識を中心として出題しています。B級では，組織的知識の中の文法的知識に加え，英文エッセイをテーマに沿って“書く”問題も出題され，組織的知識の中のもう1つの力であるテキスト的知識も問われます。さらに，国連英検の特徴である国連に対する理解についての設問も出されます。特A級とA級では，1次試験の筆記試験で文法的知識とテキスト的知識および国連に関する知識が問われ，1次試験合格者を対象に実施される2次試験の面接テストでは，これらに加えて語用論的知識である機能的知識と社会言語学的知識，言語力の要素を統合させる方略的能力，さらには国際事情についての知識も問われます。

以上のように，国連英検ではコミュニケーション能力の研究成果を踏まえ，コミュニケーション能力の基盤をなす力を下の級で測定し，上の級ではそれらの基盤的な力の測定に加え，語用論的な力とメタ認知方略に関する力も測定しています。特に最上級の特A級では，良識ある国際人として持つべき国際常識や国際適応能力についてもテストされます。国連英検は，まさしく総合的英語コミュニケーション能力を測定する試験であるといえます。

参考文献

Bachman, L. F. (1990). *Fundamental considerations in language testing*. Oxford: Oxford University Press.

Bachman, L. F & Palmer, A. S. (1996). *Language testing in practice*. Oxford: Oxford University Press.

Canale, M. (1983). On some dimensions of language proficiency. In J. Oller (Ed.) *Issues in language testing research*. (pp. 333 387). Massachusetts: Newburry House.

Canale, M. & Swain, M. (1980). Theoretical bases of communicative approaches to second language teaching and testing. *Applied Linguistics, 1* (1), 1-47.

Chomsky, N. (1965). *Aspects of the theory of syntax*. Cambridge, M.A.: The MIT Press.

Hymes, D. (1972). On communicative competence. In J. Pride & J. Holmes (Eds.) *Sociolinguistics: Selected readings*. (pp. 269-293). Harmondsworth: Penguin.

Widdowson, H. G. (1983). *Learning purpose and language use*. Oxford: Oxford University Press.

国連英検過去問題集　特A級（2021-2022実施）

目次

※本書は，実際の検定試験で使用された試験問題に基づいて編集されておりますが，一部修正されている場合があります。

国連英検とは

■「国連英検」(国際連合公用語英語検定試験)は，1981 年に始まり，長い歴史を持つ英語検定試験です。試験は年に 2 回，全国主要都市で実施されます。特 A 級から E 級まで全部で 6 つの級があり(注：現在 D 級・E 級は休止中)，中学生から社会人，シニアエイジまでの幅広い層を対象とし，受験資格は特になく，どなたでも受験できます。

試験を主催するのは，外務省の外郭団体としてスタートした公益財団法人日本国際連合協会です。日本国際連合協会は，国連の A 級諮問民間団体である「国連協会世界連盟」(WFUNA)の有力メンバーで，国内外での国連普及活動を積極的に行っています。

国連英検も国連普及活動の一環として実施されており，国連の理念である「国際協力」「国際理解」をコンセプトに，「真に役立つグローバルコミュニケーション能力」の育成を目標としています。試験内容は国連の活動に沿って，世界平和，地球環境，世界政治，世界経済から，人権，食品，医療などの世界情勢，国際時事問題まで幅広く出題されるため，今まさに地球上で問われている問題を認識し，自分の考えや解決策を論理的に伝達する表現力が求められます。単なる語学力の判定にとどまらず，総合的な国際コミュニケーションスキルが問われます。

■ 国連英検は，資格として多角的にアピールできる検定試験です。多くの大学で推薦入試・編入試験の評価資格として認められ，B 級以上の合格を単位認定している大学もあります。

特 A 級は，成績優秀者に外務大臣賞が授与されるほか，合格者には外務省国際機関人事センターが実施している「JPO 派遣候補者選考試験」において加点が行われます。

この JPO は，国際公務員(国連職員・ユネスコ職員など)になるための登竜門と言えるもので，2 年間の海外派遣を経て国際公務員試験に挑戦できる制度です。

A 級は成績優秀者に国連協会会長賞が授与されます。

C 級以上の合格者は，文部科学省より，高等学校卒業程度認定規則において，英語資格としてレベル認定されています。

また，国際協力機構（JICA）では，C 級以上の合格者を，応募の際に必要となる語学力の評価基準をクリアしたものと認定しています。

なお，警視庁では警察官採用試験（1 次試験）に「資格経歴等の評定」を導入していますが，国連英検 C 級以上の合格者については，1 次試験の成績の一部として評価しています。

■ 国連英検は，コミュニケーションを重視した試験です。B 級〜 E 級で出題されるリスニング問題のウェイトは 40％と高く，また B 級以上は国際時事問題をテーマとした英作文（ウェイト 20％）が設けられています。A 級以上は 2 次試験で面接試験を実施し，ネイティブスピーカーと国際時事問題について討論を行います。さらに特 A 級については，ネイティブスピーカーに加え，元外務省大使など外交実務経験者や国際関係を研究する大学教授を面接官として，より深い議論を行います。

●国連英検 D 級・E 級の開催休止について
国連英検では昨今の英語教育における新学習指導要領の大幅な改定に鑑み，主に中学生〜高校生を受験対象としている D 級・E 級の試験実施を 2023 年度より休止しています。再開時期・受験形式等は，決定次第国連英検のホームページにて広報致します。

●国連英検受験のための指定テキストについて
国連英検は国連に関する基礎知識を学習するための教材として『新 わかりやすい国連の活動と世界』（三修社）を指定テキストとし，特 A 級〜 C 級の出題にも使用しています。級により出題範囲が異なりますので，事前にホームページで確認することをお勧めします。

● 特A級のレベルと審査基準および問題の傾向と対策 ●

レベルと審査基準

日本で行われている英語検定試験の中で最高水準にあると見なされ，種々の状況に対応できる英語力ばかりでなく，国際的に通用する常識も要求されます。具体的には，文化背景を異にする様々な国籍の人々と政治，経済，社会などの幅広い分野における諸問題について，英語で自由に討論できる能力があるかどうかが問われます。さらに，常識，マナー，判断力などの点で，真に国際人と呼ぶにふさわしい水準に達しているかどうかも審査基準になっています。

問題の傾向と対策

1次試験は，マークシートによる客観テスト（80点）と英作文（20点）から成り立っています（リスニングテストはありません）。

客観テストでは8題の大問が出され，各題ともほとんどが読解力だけでなく，表現力や総合力をも試すように工夫されています。各題の英文の長さは1000語を超えるものもありますので，速読力が求められます。トピックとしては，国連・国際事情に絡んだ政治，経済，外交，歴史，文化，科学や小説などから幅広く出題されます。

また，最初の大問は国連に関する知識を問うものです。そのため，指定テキストの『新 わかりやすい国連と活動の世界』*New Today's Guide to the United Nations*（三修社）を読んで理解した上で，自分の言葉で論じることができるようにしておくことが必要です。各級の指定テキストからの出題範囲は国連英検のホームページに掲載されています。

英作文では，約200～250語程度の小論文を作成できる知識・思考力・表現力が要求され，受験者の説得力ある意見の有無も考慮されます。

2次試験は1次試験合格者が対象の面接試験で，約15分間，ネイティブスピーカーおよび元大使や大学教授とディスカッションを行います。

面接でカバーされるトピックは主に，国連の理念と活動，時事問題，受験者の専門分野や仕事についてで，発音や文法のチェック，知識，判断力，表現力，マナーなどが審査されます。実施の詳細はp.240をご参照ください。

2021年

第1回試験

問題

特Ａ級第１次試験問題用紙

特Ａ級

外務省後援

２０２１年度第１回国際連合公用語

英語検定試験（120分）

受験上の注意

１．問題用紙は試験開始の合図があるまで開いてはいけません。その間に、この**受験上の注意を熟読しておいてください。**

２．**受験番号と氏名を解答用紙（マークシートと作文用紙）**に記入してください。

３．解答用紙の配布は１人１部のみです。複数の配布は致しません。

４．試験開始前は、答案への解答記入は禁止です。

５．マークシートの記入は、１～100までの記入箇所がありますが、この級では１～80までを使います。

６．マークシートの記入は、必ずＨＢ以上の濃い鉛筆を使って該当箇所を黒く塗りつぶしてください。書き間違いの場合は「アト」が残らないように消してください。マークシートは絶対に折ったり曲げたりしないでください。

７．受験級、受験地区、会場番号、受験番号のマークシートへの記入は監督者の指示に従い、間違いなく記入してください。**(裏表紙の「マークシート記入例」参照)**

８．作文は、⑴読みやすい文字をペン、ボールペンまたはＨＢ以上の濃い鉛筆で書いてください。⑵使用語数の200～250語を目安にしてください。

９．試験問題についての質問は、印刷が不鮮明な場合を除き、一切受けつけません。

10．中途退室の際は、マークシートと作文用紙を持って監督者に渡し、他の受験者の迷惑にならないように静かに退室してください。中途退室後の再入室はできません。

11．試験中は他の受験者の妨げとなる行動は慎んでください。また携帯電話等の電源はお切りください。

12．マークシートと作文用紙は監督者に提出し、問題用紙はご自由にお持ち帰りください。

＊試験問題の複製や転載、インターネットへのアップロード等、いかなる媒体への転用を禁止します。

試験結果について

１．第１次試験の結果は2021年６月30日㈬頃に受験申込書に記載された住所に郵送で通知します。

２．その間に住所変更をされた方は、郵便局へ住所変更の届け出を忘れずに行ってください。

３．発表前の試験結果のお問合せには応じられません。

第２次試験について

１．第１次試験合格者には、試験結果発表と同時に試験日時、会場を指定して通知します。

２．第２次試験は2021年７月11日㈰です。特Ａ級（Ａ級との併願を含む）の試験地は**東京と大阪**になります。あらかじめご了承願います。

UNA-JAPAN
公益財団法人　日本国際連合協会
http://www.unaj.or.jp/

I. Fill in each of the following blanks with the most appropriate of the four alternatives according to the knowledge and information gained from *New Today's Guide to the United Nations*.

1. Basic Facts about the United Nations

Other than the six principal organs, there are _________ related organizations and specialized agencies which operate in areas as diverse as health, setting standards for radiation protection, international postal regulation and meteorology.

A. 23 B. 27
C. 32 D. 35

2. Security Council

The Security Council may investigate any dispute that could endanger international peace and security, and may recommend _________ for adjusting such disputes or terms for their settlement.

A. orderliness B. reasoning
C. impasses D. methods

3. Human Rights Council

The _________ Procedure, formerly known as the 1503 procedure, has also been established by the Council to address consistent patterns of gross and reliably attested violations of all human rights and all fundamental freedoms occurring in any part of the world and under any circumstances.

A. Inspection B. Complaint
C. Parallel D. Arbitral

4. International Labour Organization (ILO)

The main purposes of the ILO are to contribute to the establishment of lasting peace by promoting _________; to improve, through international action, labor conditions and living standards; and to promote economic and social stability.

A. mutual cooperation B. social justice
C. human rights D. economic equality

5. United Nations Educational, Scientific and Cultural Organization (UNESCO)

The purpose of UNESCO is to contribute to peace and security in the world by promoting collaboration among nations through education, science, culture and _________ in order to further universal respect for justice.

A. communication B. sport
C. media D. information

6. **International Fund for Agricultural Development (IFAD)**

The International Fund for Agricultural Development (IFAD) was established on 30 November _________ to provide additional resources for agricultural and rural development in the poorest rural areas, particularly in the least developed countries.

A. 1957 B. 1967
C. 1977 D. 1987

7. **Peacekeeping and Peacebuilding**

Many postwar internal conflicts occurred in states lacking in governance, often referred to as "_________ states". After the end of the hostilities, therefore, it was necessary to help such a state build or rebuild its state functions.

A. lost B. abandoned
C. ruined D. failed

8. **Peaceful settlement of disputes**

In short, the peaceful settlement of international disputes is a legal obligation of the United Nations Member States. Furthermore, the Charter's _________ (1) stipulates methods of peaceful settlement.

A. Article 2 B. Article 14
C. Article 23 D. Article 33

9. **Environmental Issues**

In 1985, the _________ Protocol on Substances that Deplete the Ozone Layer was adopted. The United Nations Conference on the Environment and Development (Earth Summit) was held in Rio de Janeiro in 1992.

A. Montreal B. Cartagena
C. Geneva D. Madrid

10. **Japan and the United Nations**

From the late 1960s through the early 1970s when a proposal made by then Secretary-General _________ to establish a United Nations University (UNU) was deliberated in the UN, major powers like the U.S., the U.K., France, and the Soviet Union were all reluctant to approve the idea because they saw no urgent need in it. Japan was the only major UN member that welcomed the Secretary-General's proposal.

A. U Thant B. Dag Hammarskjöld
C. Javier Pérez de Cuéllar D. Kurt Waldheim

II. Choose from among the four alternatives the one that most closely corresponds to the meaning contained in the following passage.

(1) Modern liberalism carries with it two legacies. The first of these legacies is the pacification of foreign relations among liberal states. Beginning in the eighteenth century and slowly growing since then, a zone of peace, which Kant called the "pacific federation" or "pacific union," began to be established among liberal societies. Most are in Europe and North America, but they can be found on every continent. Here, the predictions of liberal pacifists are borne out: liberal states do exercise peaceful restraint and a separate peace exists among them. This separate peace provides a political foundation for the United States' crucial alliances with the liberal powers (NATO, the alliances with Japan, Australia and New Zealand). This liberal alliance engendered the unbalanced, preponderance of resources that the "West" enjoyed during the Cold War. This foundation appears to be impervious to economic competition and personal quarrels with liberal allies. It also offers the promise of a continuing peace among liberal states. And, **as the number of liberal states increases, it announces the possibility of global peace this side of the grave.**

(2) Of course, the outbreak of war, in any given year, between any two given states, is a low probability event. But the occurrence of a war between any two adjacent states, considered over a long period of time, would be more probable. The apparent absence of war between liberal states, whether adjacent or not, for almost two hundred years may therefore have significance. Similar claims cannot be made for feudal, "fascist," communist, authoritarian or totalitarian forms of rule; nor for pluralistic, or merely similar societies. More significant perhaps, is that when states are forced to decide on which side of an impending world war they will fight, liberal states wind up all on the same side, despite the complexity of the paths that take them there. These characteristics do not prove that the peace among liberals is statistically significant, nor that liberalism is the peace's sole valid explanation. **(　A　)**

(3) Liberalism also carries with it a second legacy – international "imprudence." Peaceful restraint only seems to work in the liberals' relations with other liberals. Liberal states have fought numerous wars with non-liberal states. Many of these wars have been defensive, and thus prudent by necessity. Liberal states (1) ＿＿＿＿＿ by non-liberal states that do not exercise any special restraint in their dealings with liberal states. **(　B　)** Authoritarian rulers both stimulate and respond to an international political environment in which conflicts of prestige, of interest, and of pure fear of what other states might do, all lead states toward war. War and conquest (2) ＿＿＿＿＿ the careers of many authoritarian rulers and ruling parties – from Louis XIV and Napoleon Bonaparte to Benito Mussolini's fascists, Adolf Hitler's Nazis, and Joseph Stalin's communists.

(4) But we cannot simply blame warfare on the authoritarians or totalitarians, as many of

our more enthusiastic politicians would have us do. Most wars arise out of calculations and miscalculations of interest, misunderstandings, and mutual suspicions, such as those that characterized the origins of World War One. But aggression by the liberal state has also characterized a large number of wars. Both France and Britain fought expansionist colonial wars throughout the nineteenth century. The United States fought a similar war with Mexico in 1846-48, waged a war of annihilation against the American Indians, and intervened militarily against sovereign states many times before and after World War Two. Liberal states invade weak non-liberal states and display striking distrust in dealings with powerful non-liberal states. **(C)**

(5) Kant's theory of liberal internationalism helps us understand these two legacies. The importance of Immanuel Kant as a theorist of international ethics has been well appreciated. But Kant also has an important analytical theory of international politics. Perpetual Peace, written in 1795, helps us understand the interactive nature of international relations. Methodologically, he tries to teach us that we cannot study either the systemic relations of states or the varieties of state behavior in isolation from each other. Substantively, he anticipates for us the ever-widening pacification of a liberal pacific union, explains that pacification, and at the same time suggests why liberal states are not pacific in their relations with non-liberal states. Kant argues that perpetual peace will be guaranteed by the ever-widening acceptance of "definitive articles" of peace. When all nations have accepted the definitive articles in a metaphorical "treaty" of perpetual peace he asks them to sign, perpetual peace will have been established.

(6) First, republican governments, he argues, tame the aggressive interests of absolutist monarchies and ingrain the habit of respect for individual rights. ① Wars then appear as direct charges on the people's welfare that he and the other liberals thought them to be. ② Yet these domestic republican restraints do not end war. If they did, liberal states would not be warlike, which is far from the case. **(D)** They do introduce republican caution, Kant's "hesitation," in place of monarchical caprice. Liberal wars are only fought for popular, liberal purposes. ③ The historical liberal legacy is laden with popular wars fought to promote freedom, protect private property or support liberal allies against non-liberal enemies. ④ But how do alliances remove the occasion of wars among liberal states and wars between liberal and non-liberal states?

(7) Second, complementing the constitutional guarantee of caution, international law adds a guarantee of respect. The separation of nations is reinforced by the development of separate languages and religions. These further guarantee a world of separate states—an essential condition needed to avoid a "global, soul-less despotism." Yet, at the same time, they also morally integrate liberal states. Kant says, "as culture grows and men gradually move towards greater agreement over their principles, they lead to mutual understanding and peace." As republics emerge (the first source) and as culture progresses, the established practice of recognized legal rights resting on an

understanding of the legitimate rights of all citizens and of all republics comes into play; and this, now that caution characterizes policy, sets up the institutional and moral foundations for the liberal peace.

11. Which is correct according to the information explicitly stated in Paragraph 1?

A. An agreement established among liberal states in the eighteenth century fueled tensions among the West during the Cold War.

B. A liberal peace between states in Europe and North America exists which differs to those in Japan, Australia and New Zealand.

C. Despite the political foundation underlying the United States and Europe alliance, competition and disagreement remains.

D. In spite of economic rivalry among liberal states they remain peaceful in their relations with one another.

12. In the context of Paragraph 1, what does "as the number of liberal states increases, it announces the possibility of global peace this side of the grave" mean?

A. While a rise in the number of liberal states might bring peace, this will not be achievable in our generation.

B. The increasing number of liberal states suggests that widespread peace within our lifetime is feasible.

C. As the number of liberal states rise, they offer either global peace or the threat of conflict and suffering.

D. The prospect of global peace in the near future is beyond the scope of liberal states, however many exist.

13. According to the information explicitly stated in Paragraph 2, we can conclude that __________.

A. a war between neighboring liberal states is a statistically improbable event

B. the long absence of conflict between liberal allies explains the peace they enjoy

C. alliances among authoritarian forms of rule are more resistant to collapse

D. liberal states are more likely to form alliances during an impending world war

14. **In the context of the information presented in Paragraph 3, which of the following sets (A to D) best fits the blanks (1) and (2) in the paragraph?**

A. (1) seem to be intimidated (2) do not necessarily reflect

B. (1) experience hostilities and invasion (2) infrequently portray

C. (1) have been attacked and threatened (2) have thus characterized

D. (1) can thereby be overwhelmed (2) are a clear depiction of

15. **Which of the following is NOT correct according to the information presented in Paragraph 4?**

A. The origins of World War One can be characterized by, inter alia, miscalculations of interest among states.

B. Liberal states can be just as responsible for causing wars as authoritarian and totalitarian ones.

C. Liberal states such as France, Britain and the United States exhibit expansionist colonial tendencies which lead to war.

D. Liberal states go to war with weaker non-liberal states and have a salient mistrust of more powerful ones.

16. **Which of the following most accurately describes Kant's Perpetual Peace (1795) according to the information explicitly stated in Paragraph 5?**

A. It suggested we should study the interactive nature of liberal states and their behaviour in relation to each other.

B. It anticipated that a liberal pacific union would expand and suggested that liberal states would exercise peaceful restraint with non-liberal ones.

C. It posited that "definitive articles" of peace are a prerequisite for a lasting peace to be established among all nations.

D. It asked all states to accept a metaphorical perpetual peace by signing a formal treaty with one another.

17. **In Paragraph 6, which of the underlined sections, ① to ④ , should be omitted because it is either unnecessary or inappropriate there?**

A. ① B. ② C. ③ D. ④

18. **Which part of the essay, indicated by the capital letters in parentheses, is MOST appropriate for the following sentence?**

But they do suggest that we consider the possibility that liberals have indeed established a separate peace – but only among themselves.

A. (A) B. (B) C. (C) D. (D)

19. Which of the following ideas is explicitly stated in the essay?

A. Avoiding a challenge to another liberal state's law or even enhancing each other's law by means of alliance is the consequence of interdependence.

B. Linguistic and religious diversity reinforces a world system of distinct nation states which has the positive effect of preventing a "global, soul-less despotism".

C. Liberal states do not need to assume either that international laws control government policy or that, conversely, governments are unable to shape those laws.

D. As mutual culture progresses, the recognition of diversity and the experience of cooperation among states helps foster behavior which is mutually beneficial.

20. If we divide paragraphs (1) to (7) into four main topics, which set, A, B, C, or D, is the most representative?

	Topic 1	Topic 2	Topic 3	Topic 4
A.	(1)	(2) (3)	(4) (5) (6)	(7)
B.	(1)	(2) (3)	(4) (5)	(6) (7)
C.	(1) (2)	(3) (4)	(5) (6)	(7)
D.	(1) (2)	(3)	(4)	(5) (6) (7)

Ⅲ. Choose from among the underlined phrases the one that is grammatically or idiomatically incorrect.

21. State Senate Majority Leader Andrea Stewart-Cousins is now **(A)** calling on the resignation of New York Gov. Andrew Cuomo -- a sign of **(B)** escalating pressure from members of his own party **(C)** to step aside amid allegations of sexual harassment and inappropriate conduct. The Democratic governor said Sunday he **(D)** has no plans to step down.

22. The Biden administration has **(A)** notified facilities caring for migrant children that they **(B)** can open back up to pre-Covid-19 levels, acknowledging "extraordinary circumstances" due to a rising number of **(C)** minors cross the US-Mexico border. The increase in arrivals of unaccompanied children has **(D)** put additional strain on the immigration system.

23. Cuba may be **(A)** on verge of a coronavirus vaccine **(B)** breakthrough and not a moment too soon, as deaths and cases spike on the communist-run island. Starting in March, **(C)** two of the island's four homegrown vaccine candidates will begin **(D)** their third and final trials, the Cuban government has announced.

24. A long-forgotten painting by Amrita Sher-Gil, **(A)** one of India's most important modern artists, **(B)** are going under the hammer for the first time. The rediscovered portrait **(C)** is expected to fetch up to $2.8 million at a rare auction appearance for **(D)** the painter's work, little of which remains in private hands.

25. Scientists have unearthed fossils **(A)** of what may be the oldest-known member of the dinosaur group known as **(B)** titanosaurs that includes the largest land animals in Earth's history. The dinosaur's **(C)** incomplete skeletal remains were discovered in Argentina's Patagonian wilderness. Researchers said on Monday **(D)** the fossils representing a dinosaur species named Ninjatitan zapatai that lived 140 million years ago during the Cretaceous Period.

26. **(A)** Indian police have detained more than 150 Rohingya refugees found living in the northern territory of Jammu **(B)** and Kashmir illegally. Authorities have begun deporting them to Myanmar, resulting in dozens of Rohingya, **(C)** a Muslim minority population, are now located in **(D)** a makeshift holding center at Jammu's Hira Nagar jail.

27. Solar energy **(A)** is poised for what could be its biggest transformation **(B)** in over half a century. Materials called perovskites are being **(C)** used to create the next generation of solar panels, which could eventually perform twice **(D)** as efficient as current models, and flexible enough to wrap around entire buildings.

28. The Manhattan district attorney's office subpoenaed **(A)** documents from an investment company that loaned the Trump Organization millions of dollars for its Chicago skyscraper **(B)** in a sign that the investigation into the former **(C)** president's finances continues to expand. The investment company **(D)** has not been accused for wrongdoing.

29. **(A)** A homeless man risked his life to save cats and dogs **(B)** trapped at an Atlanta animal shelter after it caught a fire, the facility's founder said. Keith Walker, 53, **(C)** rushed into the W-Underdogs shelter on December 18 after fire engulfed **(D)** its kitchen. He was able to rescue all the animals -- six dogs and 10 cats.

30. **(A)** A fireball that lit up the sky over Northern Europe on February 28 was an extremely **(B)** rare type of meteorite. Fragments of the space rock could provide answers to questions about the early history of the solar system and life on Earth. According to scientists, **(C)** nearly all of meteorites that we find come to us from asteroids, **(D)** the leftover building blocks of the solar system.

IV. Choose the answer that uses the most logically and grammatically appropriate form of each underlined infinitive, in whichever manner (transitive, intransitive, participle, or otherwise) it is used, in the context of the following article.

Having grown up a Jewish child in Nazi-occupied Europe, Irene Butter said on Wednesday during a UN commemorative event online, that the United States had seen for itself "echoes of the Holocaust" on 6 January during what she described as an 'attempted coup' at the Capitol, in Washington DC. Some of the rioters that day, "**(31)** **to wear** Nazi symbols and used Nazi slogans", she attested.

Born in Berlin in 1930, she was only three years old when Hitler came to power and the persecution of the Jews in Germany began.

Speaking at a virtual ceremony marking the International Day of Commemoration in memory of the victims of the Holocaust, Dr. Butter said the events that unfolded with the **(32)** **to storm** of the Capitol, showed that "democracy is vulnerable, and we cannot take anything for granted".

"As we remember those who died in the Holocaust and honour the survivors, our best tribute is the creation of a world of equality, justice and dignity for all."

"It is up to us, to the people, to preserve and protect our democratic institutions and our Constitution", she stated, which is why she believes that everyone in the US **(33)** **to need** to be educated about what took place during the Holocaust, from those who survived it.

"We have that responsibility to be active citizens, to confront hatred, and to confront the violations of our democracy and in that way, it can be preserved and protected", she said.

Dr. Butter told of how her family **(34)** **to flee** to Amsterdam to escape the Nazis, but just two years later, the Nazis invaded the Netherlands, and the "persecution of the Jews escalated".

"We were deported to two concentration camps", she said. "First a German concentration camp in Holland, and then to Bergen-Belsen in Germany because my father had managed to apply for Ecuadorian passports thinking that that might save our lives".

After one grueling year in Bergen-Belsen, their Ecuadorian passports enabled them to be included in a Nazi-administered prisoner-exchange programme.

"But then, sadly my father died on the train to Switzerland and when we arrived in Switzerland, my mother and my brother were hospitalized immediately", she recalled.

Separated from her family, the then 14-year-old was **(35)** **to send** to a refugee camp in Algiers for almost a year, before arriving in the US in 1945.

"I was separated from my mother and my brother for eighteen months before we were reunited in New York to start a new life", she said. "I've **(36)** **to live** in the United States ever since and was lucky to take advantage of so many opportunities."

Dr. Butter acknowledged that it took 40 years before she was able to follow the guidance of Elie Wiesel, who considered that providing testimony and bearing witnesses was the "duty" of all survivors.

Since the late 1980s, she has been teaching students about the Holocaust and the lessons she learned during those traumatic years, affirming the need never to become numb to what is happening in the here and now.

"We have to continue and be awake and act," she said. "It's very easy to get **(37) to immerse** in the day-to-day, but there are a lot of things that are happening around us and it's really important to speak up".

According to Israeli Professor, Yehuda Bauer, the Holocaust was an "unprecedented genocide…because of its global form".

"Jews were intended to be annihilated all over the world", not only in Europe, he said.

The professor warned that it was "a precedent" that can be repeated, "so, when we **(38) to deal** with mass atrocity hate crimes today, with genocides today, we need to start from the Holocaust…not just for remembering but acting in accordance with the history that we are witnesses of".

"We have to remember it, and we have to act in accordance with the lessons that we have learned from it", stressed Professor Bauer.

Ari Folman who also spoke during the day of online commemoration, is the son of Holocaust survivors who met and married in the Lodz ghetto.

His award-winning animated documentary *Waltz with Bashir*, recounts the story at the Łódź ghetto in September 1942, where for three days, 15,000 Jewish children were deported to concentration camps — never to return.

Mr. Folman quoted the very last sentence of the film in which an elderly Holocaust survivor from Łódź says: "Once we are all gone from this world, all the Holocaust survivors, the point of view that would be **(39) to take**, looking back at the events, will be so far away - it will be like looking from a satellite on Jewish history in World War Two".

He said that that was the reason why he was **(40) to dedicate** eight years of his life to "finding new dimensions, new ways of storytelling in regards of the Holocaust".

He said that for him, it was comics and animation that can be used for educational purposes, "all over the world, to keep the story alive."

31. **to wear**

A. wear B. wears C. wore D. wearing

32. **to storm**

A. storm B. storming C. stormed D. storms

33. **to need**

A. need B. needing C. needs D. to need

34. **to flee**

A. fled B. flee C. flees D. fleeing

35. **to send**

A. send B. sends C. sending D. sent

36. **to live**

A. live B. lived C. lives D. living

37. **to immerse**

A. immerse B. immersed

C. immersing D. immerses

38. **to deal**

A. deal B. dealing C. deals D. dealt

39. **to take**

A. take B. taken C. took D. takes

40. **to dedicate**

A. dedicated B. dedicate

C. dedicates D. dedicating

V. Choose from among the four alternatives the one that most closely corresponds to the meaning contained in the following passage.

When the American colonies began their resistance to English tyranny, the women—all this inherited tendency to freedom **(41) <u>surging</u>** in their veins—were as active, earnest, determined, and self-sacrificing as the men, and although, as Mrs. Ellet in her "Women of the Revolution" remarks, "political history says but little, and that vaguely and incidentally, of the women who bore their part in the revolution," yet that little shows woman to have been endowed with as **(42) <u>lofty</u>** a patriotism as man, and to have as fully understood the principles upon which the struggle was based.

Among the women who manifested deep political insight were Mercy Otis Warren, and Abigail Smith Adams. Mrs. Warren was a sister of James Otis, whose fiery words did so much to arouse and intensify the feelings of the colonists against British aggression. This brother and sister were united to the end of their lives in a friendship rendered firm and enduring by the similarity of their intellects and political views. **(43) <u>The home of Mrs. Warren was the resort of patriotic spirits and the headquarters of the rebellion.</u>** She herself wrote, "By the Plymouth fireside were many political plans organized, discussed, and digested." Her correspondence with eminent men of the Revolution was extensive and belongs to the history of the country. She was the first one who based the struggle upon "inherent rights," a phrase afterward made the corner-stone of political authority.

Mrs. Warren asserted that "'inherent rights' belonged to all mankind, and had been conferred on all by the God of nations." She **(44) <u>numbered</u>** Jefferson among her correspondents, and the Declaration of Independence shows the influence of her mind. Among others who sought her counsel upon political matters were Samuel and John Adams, Dickinson, that pure patriot of Pennsylvania, Jefferson, Gerry, and Knox. She was the first person who counseled separation and pressed those views upon John Adams, when he sought her advice before the opening of the first Congress. At that time even Washington had no thought of the final independence of the colonies, emphatically denying such intention or desire on their part, and John Adams was **(45) <u>shunned</u>** in the streets of Philadelphia for having dared to hint such a possibility. Mrs. Warren sustained his sinking courage and urged him to bolder steps. Her advice was not only sought in every emergency, but political parties found their arguments in her conversation.

Abigail Smith Adams, the wife of John Adams, was an American woman whose political insight was worthy of remark. She early protested against the formation of a new government in which woman should be unrecognized, demanding for her a voice and representation. She was the first American woman who threatened rebellion unless the rights of her sex were secured. In March, 1776, she wrote to her husband, then in the Continental Congress, "I long to hear you have declared an independency, and, by the way, in the new code of laws which I suppose it will be necessary for you to make, I desire you would remember the ladies, and be more generous and favorable to them than your ancestors. Do not put such unlimited power into the hands of husbands. Remember, all men would be tyrants if they could. If particular care and attention are not paid to the ladies, we are determined to **(46) foment** a rebellion, and will not hold ourselves bound to obey any laws in which we have no voice or representation." Again and again did Mrs. Adams urge the establishment of an independency and the limitation of man's power over woman.

(47) Nor was she less mindful of equal advantages of education. "If you complain of education in sons, what shall I say in regard to daughters, who every day experience the want of it?" She expressed a strong wish that the new Constitution might be distinguished for its encouragement of learning and virtue. Although the first **(48) plot** of ground in the United States for a public school had been given by a woman (Bridget Graffort), in 1700, her sex were denied admission. Mrs. Adams, as well as her friend Mrs. Warren, had in their own persons felt the deprivations of early educational advantages.

The boasted public school system of Massachusetts, created for boys only, opened at last its doors to girls, merely to secure its share of public money. The women of the South, too, early demanded political equality. The counties of Mecklenberg and Rowan, North Carolina, were famous for the patriotism of their women. Mecklenberg claims to have issued the first declaration of independence, and, at the centennial celebration of this event in May, 1875, proudly accepted for itself the derisive name given this region by Tarleton's officers, **(49)** "**The Hornet's Nest of America**." This name—first bestowed by British officers upon Mrs. Brevard's mansion, then Tarleton's headquarters, where that lady's fiery patriotism and stinging wit **(50) discomfited** this General in many a sally—was at last held to include the whole county.

41. Here the word "surging" means

A. seeping B. leaking
C. swelling D. curdling

42. Here the word "lofty" means

A. exalted B. widespread
C. divine D. hawkish

43. This sentence functions in the passage to illustrate

A. the key role Mrs. Warren played in calming revolutionary sentiment.
B. Mrs. Warren's complex identity as a homemaker and a revolutionary.
C. Mrs. Warren's love and devotion to her brother.
D. the key role Mrs. Warren played in the revolution.

44. **Here the word "numbered" means**

A. estimated
B. needed
C. trusted
D. included

45. **Here the word "shunned" means**

A. silenced
B. attacked
C. avoided
D. arrested

46. **Here the word "foment" means**

A. spur
B. commandeer
C. thwart
D. rescind

47. **This sentence functions in the passage to**

A. explain the reasons for a point made in the previous paragraph.
B. dispute a point made in the previous paragraph.
C. introduce a new point related to the one made in the preceding paragraph.
D. draw a conclusion based on information previously introduced.

48. **Here the word "plot" can best be replaced by**

A. parcel
B. storyline
C. plan
D. point

49. **The author of this passage would most likely regard "The Hornet's Nest of America" as**

A. a sexist term that should be avoided.
B. illustrative of women's contributions to the revolution.
C. illustrative of men's violent tendencies.
D. a male-created stereotype of how women should behave.

50. **Here the word "discomfited" can best be replaced by**

A. disqualified
B. disconcerted
C. disenfranchised
D. dismembered

VI. Choose from among the four alternatives the one that best completes the following sentences.

51. **For many people who work as tour guides, showing people around a new city involves a little bit of getting off the ________. But when there is no trail at all, you just have to ________ one yourself. That has been the story of Fatima, the only woman working as a tour guide in Afghanistan.**

A. garden path - thrash
B. beaten track - blaze
C. warpath - whip
D. fast track - forge

52. **After almost a full year of ________ with the effects of the Covid-19 pandemic, including nearly nine months of virtual school, 11-year-old London Loree simply has had enough. Her focus is waning. School, something she loves, has become a________.**

A. grappling - drag
B. tussling - downer
C. endeavoring - yawn
D. scuffling - clog

53. **Swiss voters have approved a ________ on full facial coverings including niqab and burqa in nearly all public places in a closely ________ referendum on Sunday.**

A. boycott - disputed
B. embargo - rebutted
C. ban - contested
D. prohibition - contented

54. **Wealthy people don't just have bigger bank balances and more ________ lifestyles than the rest of us. They also tend to have bigger carbon ________. The more stuff you own, and the more you travel, the more fossil fuels are burned, and the more greenhouse gases are emitted into the atmosphere.**

A. lavish - footprints
B. luxurious - imprints
C. lush - trails
D. opulent- stamps

55. **With a history spanning millennia across the Middle East, North Africa, and South Asia, henna is ________ tradition and cultural rituals. The natural dye is typically used to create temporary, intricate body art for religious festivals and celebrations, such as weddings. Now, a Dubai-based designer is on a mission to give the ancient practice a modern ________.**

A. riddled with - changeover
B. drenched in - crossover
C. permeated with - takeover
D. steeped in - makeover

56. **Troops in Myanmar have occupied hospitals and university campuses, and _________ nighttime raids ahead of a nationwide strike to protest against the military coup. It's the latest move by the military junta, which seized power on February 1, to _________ its control of the country.**

A. stepped up - condense B. marked up - fortify
C. fired up - solidify D. ramped up - consolidate

57. **A new investigation will look at events in the Palestinian territories from June 13, 2014 onwards, and is _________ to focus on the Gaza war fought between Israel and Hamas in the summer of 2014, actions by the Israeli army during _________ along the Gaza fence in 2018, as well as Israel's settlement activities in the West Bank.**

A. expected - hostilities B. assumed - contention
C. supposed - animosities D. predicted - antagonism

58. **After weeks of declines in COVID cases, numbers have _________ at very high levels -- with the US averaging roughly 60,000 new cases daily in the past week. Multiple governors have eased Covid-19 safety measures despite health officials' warnings as spring break events _________ across the country, threatening the potential for further spread of the virus.**

A. buttressed - set forth B. equilibrated - usher in
C. fastened - lift off D. plateaued - kick off

59. **India _________ strict new rules on Thursday for Facebook (FB), Twitter (TWTR) and other social media platforms weeks after the country's government attempted to pressure Twitter to take down accounts it _________ incendiary.**

A. delivered - sensed B. issued - deemed
C. dispensed - appraised D. released - surmised

60. **At least 31 people died in multiple accidental explosions at a military base in the port city of Bata, in Equatorial Guinea. More than 400 were injured and many missing under the _________, the Central African country's health ministry had said after the huge _________ on Sunday. The explosion is believed to be accidental, caused by the improper storage of explosives.**

A. ruins- eruptions B. rubble - blasts
C. debris - charges D. wreckage - bursts

Ⅶ. Choose from among the four alternatives the one that best explains each of the underlined words.

The rule-of-law sector includes the courts, ministry of justice, correctional system, legal statutes, and other institutions that ensure, in Aristotle's words, "a government of laws, not men." Rule of law refers to an ideal that ensures fairness, justice, and equality before the law. Rule of law also implies preventing official **(61) arbitrariness**. Almost by definition, rule of law will have broken down in any postconflict society, which is often characterized by nonfunctioning courts, substandard prisons, inadequate salaries for judges and other personnel, insufficient operating budgets, and poor training.

Protecting private property and enforcing contracts are critical to the operation of a market economy. Security requires a functioning justice system that is able to prosecute criminals and determine innocence or guilt on the basis of objective rules of evidence. Failure to establish a **(62) viable** justice system has plagued many efforts to reconstruct police and security forces. The rule of law improves human rights conditions by ensuring due process, equality before the law, and judicial checks on executive power. Without the rule of law, arrests and detentions are arbitrary, there is no effective mechanism for preventing torture or **(63) extrajudicial** execution, individuals or groups may be free to take the law into their own hands, and abuses may go unpunished. There are a number of key challenges to establishing the rule of law once major conflict has ended.

Preconflict Legal Planning. There is often a **(64) paucity** of information on the status of a postconflict society's justice system. Personnel working for NGOs who have spent significant time in the country may provide useful advice. What are the characteristics of the legal system? How effective has it been? What are the key challenges? How should the international community prioritize and sequence efforts to rebuild rule of law?

Establishing Applicable Law. In many postconflict settings, such as Afghanistan and Somalia, village councils and tribal elders have played the primary role in resolving disputes and **(65) meting out** justice—especially in rural areas. The formal justice system may be weak, lack legitimacy, or serve only a small portion of the population. Customary law is used widely in many parts of the world. It often survives conflicts more intact than the formal courts. Customary law may play a complementary role in providing justice and a nonviolent means for resolving disputes during the postconflict phase.

Recruiting, Vetting, and Training Judges and Lawyers. A frequent difficulty in recruiting, **(66) vetting**, and appointing legal personnel is identifying candidates who have the necessary professional experience and are politically acceptable to the general public. Ethnic, tribal, or religious cleavages may create a significant challenge to choosing judges because communities may not give their consent to the process unless they have adequate representation.

Improving the Corrections System. In postconflict settings, pretrial detention facilities and prisons are often in poor condition. Compounding this problem, donor states may be reluctant to become involved in rebuilding a system with a reputation for significant human rights violations. Following the overthrow of the Taliban regime, prison staff struggled to hold thousands of people, many for long periods, in poor conditions. These conditions **(67) violated** international standards relating to the treatment of detainees.

Establishing a Rule-of-Law Culture. Many justice systems are characterized by the absence of judicial independence, political elites who use the judiciary to serve their own interests, and **(68) entrenched** corruption. The executive and judicial branches often compete for management of the judicial system, with the ministry of justice and the supreme court vying for control. Training judges and other legal personnel, providing technical assistance, and helping rebuild infrastructure are unlikely on their own to fix a system **(69) debilitated** by corruption and political interference.

Supporting Transitional Justice. Virtually all conflicts involve human rights abuses. In many cases, these abuses are widespread and systematic. Transitional justice incorporates a range of approaches that societies undertake to deal with legacies of abuse as they move from a period of violent conflict or oppression toward peace and respect for individual and collective rights. In making such a transition, societies may have to confront the painful legacy of the past to achieve a sense of justice for all citizens, establish or renew civic trust, reconcile people and communities, and prevent future abuses. However, war crime trials, truth commissions, and other types of transitional justice can also trigger nationalist **(70) backlashes** and revive tensions.

61. **arbitrariness**

A. impishness B. immutability
C. incontinence D. irregularity

62. **viable**

A. amiable B. credible
C. feasible D. protractible

63. **extrajudicial**

A. beyond usual legal interpretations
B. bound by legal conventions
C. legally exempted of due process
D. outside of normal legal proceedings

64. **paucity**

A. amplitude B. dearth
C. copiousness D. surfeit

65. **meting out**

A. administering
B. bestowing
C. disseminating
D. pledging

66. **vetting**

A. approving
B. examining
C. ruminating
D. surveilling

67. **violated**

A. affronted
B. befouled
C. contravened
D. defiled

68. **entrenched**

A. concomitant
B. ephemeral
C. ingrained
D. transient

69. **debilitated**

A. enfeebled
B. impotent
C. inured
D. prostrated

70. **backlashes**

A. counterreactions
B. convictions
C. redundancies
D. revulsions

Ⅷ. Fill in each of the following blanks with the most appropriate of the four alternatives as required by the context.

When it comes to the state, the French attitude has long been "We can't live with it, we can't live without it." But that old **(71)** ________ has taken on a new and unsettling meaning of late. President Emmanuel Macron came to power three years ago in part on the promise of creating a more agile and responsive state. The pledge of renewal was both paradoxical and credible, coming from a graduate of the elite École Nationale d'Administration (ENA) who was reputed to be a brilliant technocrat but whose campaign had released a biography titled, quite simply, *Révolution.*

Three years later, the revolution has yet to happen. Instead, the man who **(72)** ________ himself as a revolutionary found himself in the role of a reactionary. Sparked by a gasoline tax hike, the protest movement now known as the *gilets jaunes* ("yellow vests") exploded in 2019, fueled in part by the perception that the president was supremely indifferent to ordinary people's financial and material struggles. Macron cut taxes and toured the country so that he could "**(73)** ________." By the end of 2019, the rip tide of protests had reduced to a ripple. But the arrival of a new coronavirus in early 2020 gave Macron's government little respite and less time to reinitiate its bureaucratic revolution. **(74)** ________, the COVID-19 pandemic has forced Macron to fall back on *l'état providence* that he had promised to fell.

Throughout the pandemic, the **(75)** ________ technocratic expertise of the French government has repeatedly fallen short. Eight ministers in Macron's government, including Édouard Philippe, who was prime minister when the virus first attacked, were *énarques*—the **(76)** ________ given to graduates of the ENA. But their efforts to manage the pandemic more often resembled *l'anarchie* than *l'énarchie.*

The first hurdle the government failed to clear came in early spring with the supply and distribution of masks. France faced an acute shortage. A subsequent parliamentary inquiry revealed that in 2018, the Ministry of National Health had learned that 600 million masks in its strategic stockpile did not meet the necessary standards. It began to destroy them, and the minister of national health ordered just 100 million replacements. Remarkably, Philippe, whom Macron gently **(77)** ________ last summer, revealed during the same inquiry that he had "never heard anyone speak about masks" between 2017 and early 2020. Imagine his shock, then, upon learning that the nation's medical personnel needed 40 million masks a week, not the five million the actual stockpile could supply. The only **(78)** ________ left to the tens of millions of French citizens who were not first responders was *le système D*—the French phrase for muddling through on one's own.

Macron's government was determined to do better with the vaccines, the first of which arrived from Pfizer in early winter. In late November, the National Authority for Health (Haute Autorité de Santé, or HAS), which oversees the implementation of all health-related policies, issued a plan detailing the stages of vaccination for the general public as well as the residents and staffs of the nation's 15,000 nursing homes. But the officials who devised the program failed to account for drastically variable local capacities to store the vaccine and to administer it. Criticism of such omissions spanned the political **(79)** _________. The Gaullist president of Normandy's regional council declared, "We would have had a process that worked. But, **(80)** _________, they look at us and ask themselves, 'Who are these rubes?'" The socialist mayor of Nancy insisted, "Only we have the capacity to organize a massive vaccination campaign."

71. A. walnut B. chestnut
C. pecan D. acorn

72. A. marketed B. fashioned
C. served D. labeled

73. A. keep his hand on the wheel B. put his ear to the ground
C. take his life in his hands D. have his nose to the grindstone

74. A. Moreover B. Indeed
C. Instead D. Nevertheless

75. A. vaunted B. daunted
C. jaunted D. taunted

76. A. dirge B. tirade
C. moniker D. nostrum

77. A. hit below the belt B. showed the door
C. gave the axe D. caught off guard

78. A. devolution B. conundrum
C. affront D. recourse

79. A. spectrum B. animosity
C. impasse D. oblivion

80. A. instead B. meanwhile
C. indeed D. otherwise

IX. Write a short essay in English of 200-250 words as your answer to the following question:

How are the mottos "build back better" and "no country left behind" being applied in United Nations' COVID-19 pandemic recovery efforts?

マークシート記入例

東京の本会場で特A級を受験する、国連 太郎さん、受験番号が「東京01-10001」、生年月日が「1980年10月24日」の場合の記入例です。

【受験番号/氏名】
それぞれ受験票の記載通りに記入してください。

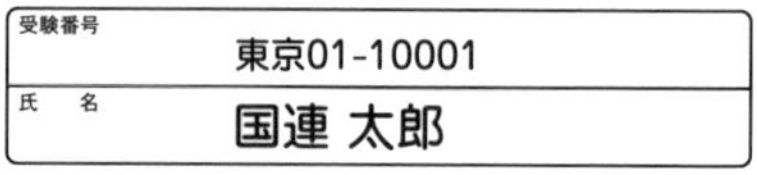

【受験地区】
下段の都道府県部分を塗りつぶしてください。

【会場番号】
都道府県部分に続く2桁の数字を塗りつぶしてください。

【受験番号】
ハイフン（－）以降の5桁の数字を塗りつぶしてください。

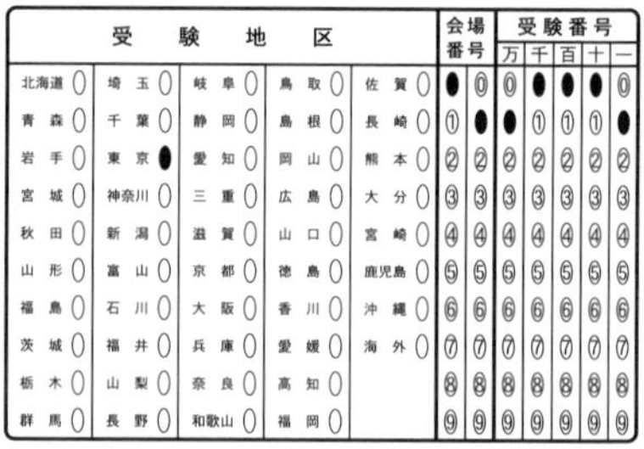

【受験級】
「特A」と記入し、下段の特A級部分を塗りつぶしてください。

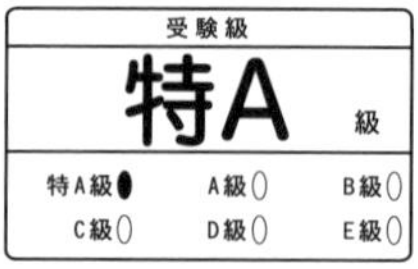

【生年月日】
4桁の西暦・月・日を塗りつぶしてください。
10未満の月・日の十の位は、「0」を塗りつぶしてください。

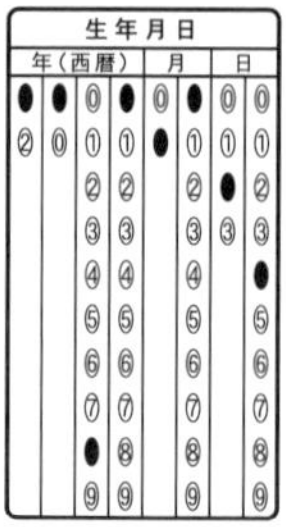

※HB以上の鉛筆を用いてマークをしてください。

※他の地区から会場を変更して受験する場合でも、受験票に記載されている受験地区・会場番号をマークしてください。

2021年 第1回試験

解答・解説

2021年　国連英検特A級第1回試験
解答・解説

＊〔　〕内は訳出上の補足や説明

I 『新 わかりやすい国連の活動と世界』に基づき，
空所を埋めるのに最も適切なものを4つの選択肢の中から1つ選びなさい。

1. 解答：A

訳例　主要6機関のほかに国連の関連機関・専門機関が23あり，保健衛生，放射線防護の規準設置，国際郵便規則や気象観測など様々な分野で活動している（『新 わかりやすい国連の活動と世界』p.42。以下，書名略）。

2. 解答：D

訳例　安全保障理事会は，国際の平和および安全を危うくするおそれのある紛争に対して調査を行い，その調整方法，あるいは解決の条件を勧告する（同p.55）。

3. 解答：B

訳例　不服審査手続は，1503手続として知られていたものを引き継いで人権理事会により設けられ，世界のあらゆる場所，状況下で起きたすべての人権とすべての基本的自由についての侵害で重大かつ信頼できる証拠のある一貫した形態を示すものに対処する（同p.59）。

4. 解答：B

訳例　ILOの主要目的は，社会正義を向上させることで永久平和の樹立に貢献し，国際的行動を通じて労働条件と生活水準を改善し，経済的かつ社会的安定を促進することである（同p.76）。

5. 解答：A

訳例　ユネスコの目的は，正義に対する世界の人々の敬意をさらに深いものとするために，教育，科学，文化，通信を通じて諸国間の協力を促進し，世界の平和と安全に貢献することである（同p.78）。

6. 解答：C

訳例 国際農業開発基金（IFAD）は，特に開発の遅れている開発途上国など最も貧しい地域の農業開発に援助資金を供給するため，1977年11月30日に設立された（同 p.84）。

7. 解答：D

訳例 冷戦後の国内紛争の多くは，「破綻国家」とも呼ばれる，統治能力を欠いた国家で多発した。そのため，紛争後，国家としての機能を構築または再建させる必要があった（同 p.105）。

8. 解答：D

訳例 これは，国際紛争の平和的解決が国連加盟国にとって法的な義務であることを意味している。さらに国連憲章第33条1項は紛争の平和的解決について規定している（同 p.110）。

9. 解答：A

訳例 1985年，オゾン層保護のためのモントリオール議定書が採択された。1992年には，環境と開発に関する国連会議（地球サミット）がリオデジャネイロにおいて開催された（同 p.140）。

10. 解答：A

訳例 1960年代末から1970年代初頭に亘って，ウ・タント国連事務総長（当時）の発案で国際連合大学（略称，国連大学）の設置が国連のなかで審議されていた際，米英仏ソなどの大国は同大学を不要不急のものと見なし，その設立を渋っていた。それに対して，日本は主要加盟国中でほぼ唯一，事務総長の提案に賛意を表しただけでなく，その設置費用をねん出するために多額な自発拠出を行った（同 p.169）。

II 以下の文章の中に含まれる意味に文脈上最も近いものを4つの選択肢の中から1つ選びなさい。

11. 解答：D

解説 パラグラフ (1) 頭から6～7行に，liberal states do exercise peaceful restraint and a separate peace exists among them，またパラグラフ末から4～3行に，This foundation appears to be impervious to economic competition and personal quarrels with liberal allies と述

べられている。これを簡潔にまとめているのはDである。

12.　解答：B

解説　問題の箇所は，「自由主義国家の数が増えるにつれて，地球規模での平和が現世において可能だと告知する」の意。これと同じ趣旨を述べているBを選ぶ。

13.　解答：D

解説　パラグラフ（2）末から5～3行にwhen states are forced to decide on which side of an impending world war they will fight, liberal states wind up all on the same sideとある。Dはこれを簡潔に言い換えたもの。

14.　解答：C

解説　空所（1）の前は，自由主義国と非自由主義国の間でこれまで起きた戦争について述べており，特に直前のセンテンスはその大半が自衛戦争であったことを強調している。（1）に続くのはこれを敷衍《ふえん》する部分と考えられるので，時制と内容から「非自由主義国家によって攻撃され，脅かされてきた」の意味となるCを選ぶ。空所（2）は，その内容に対して後続センテンスが過去の戦争や征服の例示となっていることに注目すると，やはりCが適切。

15.　解答：C

解説　Aはパラグラフ（4）頭から2～4行に，Bはパラグラフ頭から4～5行に，Dはパラグラフ末尾のセンテンスの内容に対応するが，C.「フランス，イギリス，米国などの自由主義国家は，戦争につながるような拡張主義的植民地化の傾向を示している」という内容はパラグラフのどこにも書かれていない。

16.　解答：C

解説　パラグラフ（5）末から5行より次のように書かれている。Kant argues that perpetual peace will be guaranteed by the ever-widening acceptance of “definitive articles” of peace. これに対応するのはCで

ある。Aはパラグラフ頭から4行目以降に対応するようであるが，その箇所ではAのようにliberal statesのみを取り上げているわけではない。Bはパラグラフ末より6～5行のat the same time［Kant］suggests why liberal states are not pacific in their relations with non-liberal statesと矛盾する。Dはパラグラフ末から3～2行目以下にWhen all nations have accepted the definitive articles in a metaphorical “treaty” of perpetual peaceとある内容と矛盾する。

17. 解答：D

解説 パラグラフ（6）頭のセンテンスは，共和政政府が個人の権利尊重を定着させる旨を述べている。それを受けて，下線部①～③は自由主義国家と戦争の関わりについて展開するが，④はそこに唐突に同盟関係を持ち出しており，また次のパラグラフにも内容的につながらない。

18. 解答：A

解説 挿入文は「ただ，それは，自由主義国家が単独講和を確立している可能性が考えられるということを示唆するものである――ただし〔それは〕自由主義国家間だけ〔の単独講和〕であるが」の意。自由主義国家間の単独講和について述べる箇所を探すと，Aがそれに当たる。パラグラフ（1）に始まる単独講和（近代自由主義の第1の遺産）に関する所論をまとめるセンテンスとなっている。

19. 解答：B

解説 パラグラフ(7)の2～4行に次のように述べられている：The separation of nations is reinforced by the development of separate languages and religions. These further guarantee a world of separate states—an essential condition needed to avoid a “global, soul-less despotism.” Bはこれに対応する。A（各国法律間の関係）は問題文中に言及なし。Cの国際法についての内容は，パラグラフ（7）頭のセンテンスと対応しない。Dが取り上げる文化の発展については，パラグラフ（7）頭から5行より下に述べられているが，Dが示す相互利益には言及がない。

20. 解答：D

解説 パラグラフ構成を概観すると，パラグラフ（1）(2)「近代自由主義の遺産①：自由主義国家間の外交関係が平和に」，パラグラフ（3)「遺産②：自由主義国家間の平和的自制」，パラグラフ（4)「自由主義国の戦争遂行理由」，パラグラフ（5）（6）（7)「カントの国際政治分析論」。したがってトピック別に分類するとDになる。

訳例 (1)　近代自由主義（リベラリズム）は２つの遺産を抱えている。この２つの遺産の第一は，自由主義国家間の国際関係に平和をもたらしたことである。18世紀から始まり，以来ゆっくり拡大してきた平和地帯（カントはこれを「平和連盟」または「平和連合」〔foedus pacificum〕と呼んだ）が，複数の自由主義社会の間で確立されはじめた。〔こうした社会は〕大半は欧州と北米にあるが，すべての大陸に見られるものである。ここにおいて，自由主義的平和主義者の予言〔の正しさ〕が証明された。すなわち，自由主義国家は平和的自制を行い，相互に単独講和が成立しているのである。この単独講和は，米国が自由主義の大きな勢力（NATO，日本，オーストラリア，ニュージーランドとの同盟）との間に結んでいる重要な同盟関係に対して政治的な基盤を与えるものである。この自由主義〔国家間〕の同盟は，冷戦期に「西側」が享受していた，資源に関する不均衡な優越を生み出した。この基盤は，自由主義の同盟国との経済競争や個人的な争いには影響されないように見える。それはまた，自由主義国家間の継続的平和を約束している。そして，**自由主義国家の数が増えるにつれて，世界平和が現世において実現できる可能性を告知している。**

(2)　もちろん，いずれかの年にいずれか２国間に戦争が勃発することは，可能性としては低いが，しかし，隣り合う２国間に戦争が起きる確率は，長期的に考えれば高くなる。隣国どうしかどうかはさておき，自由主義国家間にこれまでほぼ200年にわたって確かに戦争がないということは，それゆえ意味のあることかもしれない。同様の主張は，封建的な統治形態や「ファシズム」的，共産主義的，権威主義的あるいは全体主義的な統治形態についてはなしえないし，多元的国家や単に類似しているだけの社会についても同様である。おそらくそれよりも重要なのは，世界大戦が勃発しそうになって各国家がいずれの陣営に付くか決めるよう迫られたとき，自由主義国家は〔結論〕に至る道筋は複雑であって，結局すべて同じ側に付くということだろう。こうした特徴は，自由主義国家間の平和が統計的に有意であることを証明するものではないし，また，自由主義というものが，平和〔が保たれている理由について〕の唯一妥当な説明となることを示すものでもない。(A)〔ただ，それは，自由主義国家が単独講和を確立している可能性が考えられるということを示唆するものである――ただし〔それは〕自由主義国家間だけ〔の単独講和〕であるが。〕

(3)　自由主義はまた，別の遺産をも抱えている。国際的な「軽率さ」である。〔すなわち〕平和的な自制というものが，自由主義国家が他の自由主義国家に対して持つ関係においてのみ働くように思われる〔ことである〕。自由主義国家は，非自由主義国家との間で数多くの戦争を行ってきた。これらの戦争の多くは防衛的なものであり，したがって必要に迫られて慎重に行われたものであった。自由主義国家は，自由主義国家との関係において特段の自制心を持たない非自由主義国家によって攻撃され，脅かされてきた。(B) 権威主義的な統治者は，威信や利害の対立，他国のありうべき行動に対する単なる恐怖を相互に抱くことなど，すべてが諸国家を戦争に向かわせるような国際的な政治環境を助長し，それに対応していく。それゆえ，戦争と征服は多くの権威主義的統治者や政権党が取る行動を特徴づけるものとなってきた。ルイ 14 世やナポレオン・ボナパルトをはじめ，ベニート・ムッソリーニのファシスト党，アドルフ・ヒトラーのナチ党，ヨシフ・スターリン率いる共産党に至るまで。

(4)　しかし，戦争を単に権威主義者や全体主義者のせいにすることはできない。より熱心な政治家の多くは我々をそのように仕向けようとするのだが……。戦争というものは，利害関係についての計算や誤算，あるいは誤解や相互不信などから生じる場合がほとんどであって，第 1 次世界大戦の原因にも同様の要素が含まれていた。しかし，自由主義国家による，侵略を要因とする戦争もまた，数多く行われてきている。フランスとイギリスはいずれも 19 世紀を通じて，拡張主義的な植民地戦争を遂行したし，米国は，1846 年から 48 年にかけてメキシコとの間で同様の戦争を行ったほか，アメリカン・インディアンに対しては殲滅《せんめつ》戦をしかけ，また第 2 次世界大戦の前後には主権国家に対して何度も軍事介入を行っている。自由主義国家は，弱い非自由主義国家に対しては侵略を行い，強力な非自由主義国家との関係においては著しい不信を示す。(C)

(5)　カントの自由主義的国際主義理論は，この 2 つの遺産を理解する上で有用である。イマヌエル・カントが国際倫理の理論家として重要であることは十分に認識されてきたが，カントにはまた，国際政治を分析した重要な理論がある。『永遠の平和のために』(1795 年)〔である。この書は〕国際関係が持つ相互作用的な性質を理解する助けとなるもので，方法論の面から言えば，国家どうしの組織的関係と国家行動の多様なあり方〔の 2 つ〕は，いずれも一方を他方から切り離してそれだけで考えることができない，ということを示そうとしている。また実質的な内容においては，自由主義的な平和連合の絶えざる和平拡大を予想するとともに，その和平〔のプロセス〕を説明し，そして同時に，自由主義国家が非自由主義国家との関係において平和的でない理由を示している。永遠の平和は，平和の〔ための〕「確定条項」の受け入れが絶えず拡大することによって保障されるとカントは言う。カントは各国に対し，隠喩的な永遠平和の「条約」に署名するよう求めたが，この条約に含まれる確定条項をすべての国が受け入れた時点で，永遠の平和が確立されたことになるのである。

(6)　まず，共和政の政府は，絶対君主国の攻撃的利害〔追求〕を抑制し，個人の権利尊重という習慣を根付かせると，カントは主張する。①戦争はその場合，カントや他の自由主義者が考えていたような，国民の福祉に対する直接の侵害となって現れる。②だが，このような国内的に共和政がもたらす抑制は，戦争をなくすものではない。もしそうであれば，自由主義国家は好戦的ではなくなるはずだが，実際には決してそうではない。(D)自由主義国家は君主の気まぐれに代えて，共和政特有の慎重さ，カントのいわゆる「ためらい」を導き入れるのである。〔すなわち〕自由主義〔国家〕の戦争は，民衆の目的のため，自由主義的な目的のためにのみ遂行される。③自由主義の歴史遺産の中には，自由の促進や私有財産の保護，それに，非自由主義の敵に対する自由主義同盟国の支援を目的として行われた大衆戦争が数多く見られる。④〔削除対象〕しかし，同盟関係は，自由主義国家間の戦争や自由主義国家と非自由主義国家間の戦争の契機をどのように除去するのだろうか。

(7)　第二に，憲法の規定が保障する慎重さを補うものとして，国際法による尊重の保障がある。諸国家の分立は，それぞれ異なる言語や宗教の発展によって強化される。これら〔別々の言語や宗教〕は，分立した国家から成る世界をいっそう保障する。それは，「グローバルな，魂が込められていない専制政治」を避けるために必要な本質的条件なのである。しかし同時に，それら〔条件〕によって自由主義国家は道徳的に統合されていく。カントは言う，「しかし，文化が進み，また人間が原理に関してより大きな合意にしだいに近づいてゆくにつれて，ある平和状態における〔相互〕承認へと導くのである*」。共和国が出現し（最初の源泉），文化が進むにつれて，すべての市民とすべての共和国の正当な権利についての理解に基づく，認められた法的権利の定着した慣行が効果を現しはじめる。そしてこのことが――今や慎重さが政策の特徴となったのだから――自由主義的な平和のための制度的および道徳的な基盤を築くのである。

＊訳注：「ある平和状態」以下はドイツ語原文より訳出

Ⅲ 文法的，語法的にふさわしくないものを下線の中から 1 つ選びなさい。

21. 解答：A

解説 calling on → calling for。文脈から「要求する」の意と考えられるから call for が正しい。

訳例 米ニューヨーク州のアンドリュー・クオモ知事に対して，民主党のアンドレア・スチュワートカズンズ同州上院院内総務がついに辞職を要求する〔姿勢を見せ〕はじめた。〔クオモ知事をめぐっては〕セクハラや不適切行為の疑惑が〔浮上しており，その中で〕同知事所属の〔民主〕党議員からも〔辞任〕要求が高まってきた表れ。知事は日曜日，退陣する考えはないと述べた。

22. 解答：C

解説 cross → crossing。cross 以下は minors を修飾する形容詞句であるべき。

訳例 バイデン政権は，移住者の子供の世話をする各施設に対して，コロナ禍以前の水準まで再開を認めると通知した。米メキシコ国境を越境する未成年者が増加している「異常事態」を認めたもので，同伴者なしで入国する子供の増加が移住〔者受け入れ〕制度のさらなる逼迫《ひっぱく》を招いている。

23. 解答：A

解説 on verge of → on the verge of。成句。

訳例 共産党が支配する島国キューバが，まもなくコロナウィルス・ワクチンで大躍進を遂げるかもしれない。死者や感染者が急増していることから，あまり早い〔成果〕とは言えない〔ものの〕国産ワクチン候補 4 種類のうち 2 種類を対象に 3 月から第Ⅲ相と最終の治験が実施される。同政府が発表した。

24. 解答：B

解説 are → is。主語は A long-forgotten painting ... である。

訳例 インド現代美術の第一人者として知られるアムリタ・シェールギルの作品で，長年の間忘れられていた絵画が，初めてオークションにかけられることになった。再発見された肖像画の落札額は最高 280 万ドルとなる見通し。個人所蔵がごく少数しか残っていないシェールギル作品を対象とする希少なオークション〔となる〕。

25. 解答：D

解説 representing → represent。直前の the fossils は上行にある動詞過去形

saidの目的節（that節）内の主語。

訳例　地球史上最大の陸生動物を含む恐竜，ティタノサウルス類の仲間で，これまで知られているものとして最古となる可能性がある化石が，科学者〔グループ〕による発掘〔調査〕で見つかった。〔この〕化石は恐竜の不完全な骨格で，アルゼンチンのパタゴニア平原で発見された。研究者らは月曜日，この化石について発表を行い，1億4,000万年前の白亜紀に生息していたニンジャティタン・ザパタイという恐竜種のもの〔と述べた〕。

26.　解答：C

解説　are now → now being。下線部（C）に先立つresulting in以下で前置詞inの目的語となる部分がdozens of Rohingya ... are now located in ...のように節（主語＋定動詞）の形になっていることが間違い。主語付きの動名詞句とすれば文法的に正しくなる。

訳例　インド警察は，北部のジャンムー・カシミール地方に不法に居住していたロヒンギャ難民150人以上を拘束した。当局はこの難民のミャンマーへの送還を開始したが，そのためイスラム教少数民族ロヒンギャの数十人が現在，ジャンムーにあるヒラ・ナガル刑務所内の仮設収容所に収容される結果となった。

27.　解答：D

解説　efficient → efficiently。twice as ... as以下は直前の動詞performを修飾する副詞句なので，as ... asの間には副詞が必要。

訳例　太陽エネルギーは今，半世紀以上の〔歴史の〕中で最大となりうる変革期を迎えようとしている。ペロブスカイトと呼ばれる材料を使って次世代ソーラーパネルを〔開発〕する動きが進んでおり，いずれは運転効率が現在のパネルの2倍，しかも建物全体を包み込めるほど柔軟〔なパネル〕となる可能性が出てきた。

28.　解答：D

解説　accused for → accused of。accuseは，accuseする理由を示す語句を導く前置詞ofと共起する。

訳例　マンハッタン地方検事局は，トランプ・オーガニゼーションがシカゴに超高層ビルを建設する〔資金として〕数百万ドルを同社に貸し付けた投資会社から文書を召喚した。前大統領の資金調達に関する捜査が引き続き進展していることを示す〔動き〕だ。ただ，同投資会社は不正行為の告発を受けていない。

29. 解答：B

解説 caught a fire → caught fire。fireがこの場合不可算だからという説明は可能だが，成句として覚えるのがよい。

訳例 アトランタの動物保護施設が火事になり，閉じ込められた犬猫をホームレスの男性が命がけで救出した。施設の創設者が明らかにした。〔男性は〕キース・ウォーカーさん（53）。12月18日，保護施設Wアンダードッグズで厨房が炎に包まれると〔施設へ〕突入。見事すべての動物を救出した。犬6匹と猫10匹〔が命拾いした〕。

30. 解答：C

解説 nearly all of meteorites → nearly all meteorites。allの後にofが決まって必要なのは，人称代名詞の所有格（my, hisなど）や目的格（you, themなど）が続く場合。単なる名詞の複数形や形容詞＋名詞複数形の前ではallのみ。

訳例 2月28日，北欧の〔夜〕空を照らした火球は，きわめて希少な種類の隕石である〔ことが分かっ〕た。隕石の破片から，太陽系の初期の歴史や地球上の生命の謎が解ける可能性がある。科学者の説明によると，地球上で見つかるほとんどの隕石は，太陽系の「建築資材」の余り物とされる小惑星に由来するという。

IV 以下の文章の下線を引いた動詞（原形）について，文脈に沿って論理的，文法的に最も適切な変化形（他動詞，自動詞，分詞など）を４つの選択肢の中から１つ選びなさい。

31. 解答：C

解説 下線部前のthat dayは上行の6 Januaryを指す。下線部の動詞の主語はSome of the riotersであるから，これを過去形に置くのが正しい。

32. 解答：B

解説 下線部stormはこの場合「襲撃する」の意味。前後the ... ofと囲まれているから動名詞とするのが適切。

33. 解答：C

解説 下線部needは前のeveryone in the USを主語とする定動詞。したがって正しい形は三人称単数現在形となる。

34. 解答：A

解説 下線部前の how her family 以下は，その前の定動詞 told of の目的語となる名詞節で，flee は節中の定動詞。名詞節の内容が過去の出来事なので，過去形とする。

35. 解答：D

解説 下線部前の was と組み合わされた受動態。過去分詞の形を選ぶ。

36. 解答：B

解説 下線部前の I've から続く現在完了形。

37. 解答：B

解説 前後の文意は「日々の生活に埋没してしまう」なので，受け身形にするのが正しい。

38. 解答：A

解説 下線部前の主語 we に続く定動詞とする。時制は同じ行に today とあるので現在形が適切。

39. 解答：B

解説 上の行の Once we are all gone ... 副詞節に続く主節の主語が the point of view ...。下線部前の that would be ... はその主語を修飾する関係詞節。be 動詞に着目して受け身形とする。

40. 解答：D

解説 下線部前の was と現在進行形となる。ここで能動の意味となっていることは，「dedicate O to 名詞」のつながりに注意して判断する。

訳例　ナチス占領下のヨーロッパで，ユダヤ人の子供として育ったアイリーン・バター氏が水曜日，〔国際ホロコースト記念日に関する〕国連の記念式典にオンラインで参加し，1 月 6 日のワシントン D.C. の連邦議事堂での出来事を「クーデター未遂事件」だとして，〔そこで〕米国が目の当たりにしたものこそ「ホロコーストの残響」なのだと述べた。この日の暴徒の中には，「ナチのシンボルを身につけ，ナチのスローガンを用いた者もいた」と同氏は証言した。

1930年にベルリンで生まれたバター氏は，ドイツでヒトラーが政権を取り，ユダヤ人迫害が始まったときはまだ3歳だった。

「ホロコースト犠牲者追悼国際記念日」に関するオンライン式典で発言したバター博士は，米連邦議事堂襲撃事件について，民主政が脆弱《ぜいじゃく》なものであり，何事も当り前と思ってはいけない，ということを示していると述べた。

「ホロコーストで命を落とされた方々を偲《しの》び，生存者の方々に敬意を表するに当たり，私たち〔にできる〕最高の贈り物は，すべての人にとって平等と正義と尊厳ある世界を作り出すことです」。

同氏は「民主的な制度や憲法を守り抜く責任は，私たち国民にあります」と述べた。だからこそ，米国に暮らす人はみな，ホロコーストで何が起きたのかをその生存者から学ぶ必要があると考えている〔と〕。

「私たちには，アクティブシチズンである責任，そして憎しみに立ち向かい，私たちの民主政を侵害する行為に立ち向かう責任があります。民主政はそうした行動によって守り抜くことができるのです」。

また，自らの家族については，ナチスから逃れようとアムステルダムへ逃げたが，そのわずか2年後にナチスがオランダに侵攻してきて，「ユダヤ人に対する迫害がエスカレートした」と語った。

「私たちは2カ所の強制収容所に送られました。最初はオランダにあったドイツの強制収容所，そして次はドイツのベルゲン・ベルゼンです。これは父がエクアドルのパスポートをどうにか申請できたためでした。父はそれで私たちの命が助かるかもしれないと考えたのです」。

ベルゲン・ベルゼンで過酷な1年を過ごすと，エクアドルのパスポートがあったおかげで，ナチが運営する捕虜交換制度の対象となった。

同氏は次のように回想した。「しかしその後，あいにく父はスイスに向かう列車の中で亡くなりました。そしてスイスに着いたかと思ったら，すぐに母と兄〔弟〕が入院してしまいました」。

家族と離れ離れになった当時14歳〔のバター氏〕は，アルジェの難民キャンプへ送られて1年近く〔収容された〕後，1945年に米国にたどり着いた。

「母，兄〔弟〕と1年半も離れ離れになりましたが，ニューヨークで再会を果たし，新しい生活を始めました。それからずっと米国暮らしですが，多くの機会に恵まれたことは幸運でした」。

証拠を提出し，証言をすることがすべての生存者の「責務」であると考えたエリ・ヴィーゼルの教えに従うことができるまでには，40年の歳月が必要だった――バター博士はそう吐露した。

〔そして〕1980年代後半から同氏は学生たちにホロコーストや自分がその悲惨な時代に学んだことを教えており，いまここで起きていることに決して無感覚になってはいけないと訴え続けている。

同氏は次のように述べた。「私たちはずっと目覚めた状態を保ち，行動しなければなりません。日々の生活に埋没してしまうのはいとも簡単なことですが，私たちの周りでは多くの出来事が起きていますし，声を上げることが非常に大事なのです」。

イスラエルの大学教授，イェフダ・バウアー氏によると，ホロコーストは「グローバルな形態〔で行われた〕ことから，〔……中略……〕前例のない集団虐殺」となった。

「ユダヤ人抹殺の計画は全世界を対象とするものであり」，ヨーロッパだけではなかった，と同教授は述べた。

バウアー教授は，ホロコーストは繰り返されるおそれがある「前例」であると警告し，「このことから現在，大量残虐行為となるヘイトクライムや集団虐殺に対処する際には，ホロコーストから始める必要があります……単に忘れないだけでなく，私たちが証言者となった歴史〔事実〕に従って行動する必要があります」と述べた。

「私たちはホロコーストを忘れてはならないし，そこから学んだ教訓に従って行動しなければなりません」とバウアー教授は力説した。

また，オンライン記念式典当日に講演を行ったアリ・フォルマン氏は，〔ポーランド〕ウッチ・ゲットーで出会って結婚した〔2人の〕ホロコースト生存者の2世に当たる。

数々の賞を受賞したドキュメンタリーアニメーション〔映画〕『戦場でワルツを』には，1942年9月のウッチ・ゲットーでの出来事が詳しく描かれている。3日間にわたってユダヤ人の子供1万5,000人が強制収容所に送られ，戻ってこなかった〔と言われるものだ〕。

フォルマン氏は，映画の末尾でウッチのホロコースト生存者の老人が語る言葉を紹介した。「私たちがすべて，つまり，すべてのホロコースト生存者がこの世からいなくなれば，出来事を振り返る視点はたいへん遠いものになるでしょう。第2次世界大戦におけるユダヤ人の歴史を人工衛星から見ているような〔捉え方〕になってしまうでしょう」。

フォルマン氏は，そのことこそ同氏が「ホロコーストに関して新しい次元や新しい物語の方法を見いだすこと」に人生の8年もの時間を捧げた理由だと語った。

同氏はまた，それは同氏にとって「世界中で物語を語り継ぐために」教育目的で使える漫画・アニメーション作品なのだと述べた。

V 以下の文章の中に含まれる語句の意味として文脈上最も近いものを4つの選択肢の中から1つ選びなさい。

41. 解答：C

解説 下線部 surging < surge は make someone have a strong feeling の意。最も近いのは，C. swelling < swell「(感情が）高まる」。

42. 解答：A

解説 下線部の意味は showing high moral standards。最も近いのは A.「高貴な」。

43. 解答：D

解説 下線部は「ウォレン夫人の家は，愛国心溢《あふ》れる人々の憩いの場であり，反乱軍の本部でもあった」。これは文脈上 D.「革命においてウォレン夫人が果たした役割」を例示するもの。

44. 解答：D

解説 下線部 numbered < number は include as a member of a group の意。

45. 解答：C

解説 下線部 shunned < shun は deliberately avoid, ignore, or reject の意。

46. 解答：A

解説 下線部の意味は cause ... to develop（革命，反乱，不和などを）であるから，これに最も近いのは A.「促進する」。

47. 解答：C

解説 下線部は「アダムズ夫人は教育の有益さが平等である点についても同様に留意していた」という意味。また，前の段落は女性参政権についてのアダムズ夫人の主張を紹介している。したがって，下線部の文脈上の役割は，「前パラグラフの論点に関する新たな論点を導入する」ことと言える。

48. 解答：A

解説 下線部から続く a plot of ground は，a small piece of land の意味。A. parcel も a parcel of land で同様の意味に用いる。

49. 解答：B

解説 下線部は，もともとイギリス将校がブレヴァード夫人の邸宅に付けた呼び名であり，下線部に続いて独立戦争におけるブレヴァード夫人の活躍ぶりが言及されていることに着目する。

50. 解答：B

解説 下線部 discomfited < discomfit は，make someone feel slightly uncomfortable or embarrassed の意味。これに最も近いのは disconcert > B. disconcerted「狼狽《ろうばい》させた」。

訳例　アメリカ植民地がイギリスの専制政治に対して抵抗を始めるや，女性たちは――その血管には自由を求めるこの生来の性向が脈々と流れていた――男性に劣らず活発にして熱心，固く覚悟を決め，自己犠牲の気概に溢れていた。そして，エレット夫人が『〔アメリカ〕独立戦争の女たち』において述べているように，「政治史は，この革命の一翼を担った女たちのことをほとんど語っていない。しかも曖昧に，事のついでという形でしか語っていない」のであるが，そのわずかな記述からも，女性が男性と同じく崇高な愛国心を授けられていたこと，そして闘争の基礎となった諸原則を同じく十全に理解していたことが分かるのである。

深い政治的洞察力を発揮した女性の中には，マーシー・オーティス・ウォレンやアビゲイル・スミス・アダムズなどがいた。ウォレン夫人はジェームズ・オーティスの妹であるが，後者の烈火のごとき言葉は，英国の侵略に対する入植者たちの感情を喚起し，激昂《げっこう》させる上で大いに役立った。この兄妹は終生，友情で結ばれていた。それは知性〔のあり方〕と政治的見解の類似によって固められ，永続するものとなった。ウォレン夫人の家は，愛国心溢れる人々の憩いの場であり，反乱軍の本部でもあった。夫人自身，「プリマスの炉辺では，多くの政治計画が策定・議論され，理解を得た」と書いている。夫人が文通していた独立戦争の名士は広い範囲に及び，米国史に刻まれている。夫人は，この闘争を「生得権」に基づけた最初の人物であるが，この語は後に政治的権威の礎石となるに至った。

ウォレン夫人は，「『生得権』は全人類に属し，諸国の神によってすべての人に与えられた」と主張した。ジェファーソンも夫人の文通相手の 1 人であり，

『独立宣言』には夫人の思想からの影響が見られる。政治問題について夫人の助言を求めたそのほかの人々としては，サミュエルおよびジョン・アダムズ，ディキンソン＝かの純粋なペンシルベニアの愛国者，ゲリー，ノックスがあった。夫人は，初めての議会〔第1次大陸会議〕の開会に先立ってジョン・アダムズが助言を求めてきたとき，分離独立を進言し，その考え方を採るよう迫った最初の人物であった。当時はワシントンでさえ植民地の最終的な独立については考えておらず，植民地にそうした意図や願望はないと断言していたし，ジョン・アダムズに至っては，その可能性をあえて示唆したことからフィラデルフィアの街で人に避けられるようになった。ウォレン夫人は，勇気を失いかけていたアダムズを支え，より大胆な行動に出るよう促した。夫人の助言は，緊急事態が起きるといつも求められた。のみならず，政党も夫人の会話の中に自分たちが主張〔すべき内容〕を見いだした。

ジョン・アダムズの妻であるアビゲイル・スミス・アダムズは，注目すべき優れた政治的洞察力を備えた米人女性であって，女性〔の参加〕を認めないものとするような新政府が作られることに早くから抗議し，女性に対して発言権と代表権を与えるよう求めた。自らの性の権利が確保されなければ反乱を起こすと脅迫発言を行った初めての米人女性である。1776年3月，当時大陸会議に参加していた夫に宛てて次のような手紙を書いている。「あなたが独立を宣言したという知らせが来るのを今か今かと待っています。ところで，思うに今後あなたは新しい法典を制定することが必要となるでしょう。その法典では，女性のことを忘れずに，女性に対してご先祖様方よりも寛大で，有利な〔ものにして〕もらいたいと思います。夫にそのような無限の権限を与えないでください。男性はみな，できることなら暴君になりたりたがるものだということを忘れずに。もし女性に特別な配慮がなされないのであれば，私たちは反乱を起こす覚悟です。私たちに発言権や代表権がない法律には従う義務はありません」。アダムズ夫人は，独立国家の樹立と男性の女性に対する権限を制限するよう繰り返し訴えた。

また，教育がもたらす有利さを〔男女で〕平等〔にすべきであるという〕点についても同様に留意していた。「親が男子の教育に不満を漏らすなら，女子については私はどう言えばよいのでしょう？　女子は毎日，教育の不十分さを味わっているのですから」。そして，新憲法が学びと美徳の奨励という点で傑出したものとなってほしいとの強い願いを夫人は表明した。米国で初めて公立学校用地を提供したのは女性（ブリジット・グラフォート）だ（1700年）というのに，女子は入学を認められていなかった。アダムズ夫人も，その友人であるウォレン夫人も，自分が早期教育の利益を奪われていることを身をもって感じていたのだ。

マサチューセッツ自慢の公立学校制度は，男子校として設けられたものであったが，ついに女子にも門戸を開いた。それは単に公金の受給確保という目的のためであった。南部の女性たちも，早くから政治的な平等を求めていた。ノースカロライナのメクレンバーグ郡とローワン郡は，女性が強い愛国心を持つことで知られていた。メクレンバーグ郡は〔米国で〕初めて独立宣言を発表したと主張している。実際，1875年5月に行われた独立100周年記念式典では，〔独立戦争で戦ったイギリス軍人〕タールトン率いる将校たちからこの地域に与えられた「アメリカのスズメバチの巣」という蔑称を誇らしく受け入れたのである。この名前は，もともとイギリスの将校らがブレヴァード夫人の邸宅（当時タールトン将軍の司令部となっていた）に付けたものであるが，その司令部で将軍は数多くの出撃の際，夫人の燃えるような愛国心と鋭いウィットによって狼狽させられたのであった。その名前がついに郡全体を指すものとなったのである。

VI

以下の文章に最も適切に当てはまる単語のペアを4つの選択肢の中から1つ選びなさい。

51. 解答：B

解説　第1空所はin or into an isolated placeを意味するoff the beaten trackを知っていればBが選べる（beatenはこの場合「踏みならされた，人通りが多い」の意）。第2空所のB. blazeはblaze a track/trailで，「（焼き払って）道を切り開く」の意。

訳例　ツアーガイドとして働く多くの人々にとって，新しい街を案内するのは通常のコースを少しばかり外れる仕事になる。しかし，道がまったくない場合は，自分で道を切り開くしかない。アフガニスタンで唯一の女性旅行ガイド，ファティマさんの物語はその〔一例〕だ。

52. 解答：A

解説　第1空所はA，B，Dの原形が「格闘する」の意味で候補となるが，この文脈で「問題などを解決しようとして取り組む」意味ではa successful struggleの含意が強いgrappleが最も自然。第2空所もA. dragは口語でsomething obnoxiously tiresomeの意味があり，文意に合う。

訳例　9カ月近くオンラインスクールに通うなど，ほぼ丸1年にわたってコロナ禍の影響〔による問題〕と闘ってきた11歳のロンドン・ロリー。とにかくもうたくさんだ〔という気持ちになってきた〕。集中力も落ちてきている。学校は大好きなのに，〔いまは〕面倒くさくなってきた。

53. 解答：C

解説 第 1 空所は文意から「禁止」の意味なので，C と D が候補となる。第 2 空所は C. contested が文意に合う。

訳例 スイスの有権者は，接戦となった日曜日の国民投票で，ブルカやニカブなど顔全体を覆う服装をほとんどの公共の場で禁じる〔法案〕を支持した。

54. 解答：A

解説 第 2 空所は carbon footprints が「CO2 排出量」を意味する決まった言い方。第 1 空所も sumptuously rich or luxurious を意味する A. lavish は文意に合う。

訳例 富裕層は，他の人に比べて預金が多く，贅沢《ぜいたく》なライフスタイルを送っているだけではなく，二酸化炭素の排出量も多い傾向がある。持ち物が多く，移動が多いほど，燃焼される化石燃料が増え，大気中に放出される温室効果ガスが多くなる〔からだ〕。

55. 解答：D

解説 第 1 空所は steeped in tradition が慣用的な表現となっていることから D を選ぶ。第 2 空所についても，D. makeover を挿入すれば，そこまでが「ドバイ在住のデザイナーがこの古い慣習を現代的に作り直す仕事を進めている」の意味となり，文脈に合う。

訳例 中東や北アフリカ，南アジアで数千年間の歴史を持つ天然染料のヘナは，伝統や文化的儀式と深く結びついている。一般的には，宗教的な祭りや結婚式などのお祝いに，その場かぎりの精緻な身体装飾を施す目的で使われるが，現在，ドバイ在住のデザイナーがこの古い芸術を現代的にアレンジする仕事を進めている。

56. 解答：D

解説 第 1 空所は「強化する」を意味する A，D が候補となる。C. fired up は「スタートさせる」の意味があるが，目的語にはエンジンなどの機械装置を取る。第 2 空所は文意から D. consolidate = strengthen the position of power が適している。

訳例 ミャンマーの軍隊は，病院や大学キャンパスを占拠するとともに，軍事クーデターに抗議して行われる全国ストライキを前に，夜間襲撃作戦を強化した。2 月 1 日に権力を掌握した軍事政権が，国の支配権を強固なものとするために打った新たな一手。

57. 解答：A

解説 第1空所は「予測される」の意。B，C は別の意味になる。D. predicted < predict は確実性が expected より弱い。本文は空所後に「新たな調査」の具体的な内容を挙げているので，かなり確実な根拠にもとづく記述と見るのが妥当。第2空所の A. hostilities は複数形で「戦闘」を意味する。

訳例 新たな調査では2014年6月13日以降のパレスチナ自治区の状況を対象に，2014年夏に発生したイスラエルとハマスとのガザ戦争や，2018年のガザ地区〔国境〕フェンス沿いで起きた戦闘中のイスラエル軍の行動，それにイスラエルによるヨルダン川西岸への入植活動を重点とするものとみられる。

58. 解答：D

解説 第1空所は前後から「横ばいとなる」の意を読み取り，D を選ぶ。第2空所も D. kick off は「始まる」の意で文脈に合う。

訳例 コロナウィルスによる感染者数は，数週間にわたって減少したが，その後は非常に高い水準で横ばいを続けている。米国では過去1週間の新規感染者の日平均が約6万人に達した。春休みのイベントが全国で始まる中，保健当局の警告にもかかわらず，複数の州知事が感染対策を緩和。ウィルスがさらに広がる恐れが出てきた。

59. 解答：B

解説 第1空所は「発表する，発布する」の意で A，B，D が可能。第2空所は「(扇動的) と見なす」の意味で B. deemed が適切。D. surmised < surmise は guess that something is true, using the information available の意。

訳例 インドは木曜日，フェイスブックやツイッターなどのソーシャルメディアに対する新たな厳しい規制を発表した。同国政府は数週間前にも，ツイッターに対し，扇動的と判断したアカウントを削除するよう圧力をかけようとした〔経緯がある〕。

60. 解答：B

解説 第1空所は A，B，C，D とも候補となる。第2空所は爆発により生じる爆風を意味する B. blasts が適切。C. charges ＜ charge = a headlong rush forward, as in an attack, D. bursts ＜ burst は（加圧した気体などを詰めた容器などの）「破裂」というニュアンスでの爆発の意。

訳例　中央アフリカの国，赤道ギニアの港湾都市バタにある軍事基地で，複数の爆発が発生し，少なくとも 31 人が死亡した。400 人以上が負傷したほか，多数がガレキに埋まって行方不明となっている。日曜日に起きた大規模爆発の後，ギニア保健省が明らかにした。爆発は，火薬の保管が不適切だったことによる偶発的な事故と考えられる。

Ⅶ

下線部の単語や句の意味を最もよく表しているものを
４つの選択肢の中から１つ選びなさい。

61.　解答：D

解説　下線部「恣意，専断」の意味に最も近いのは，D. irregularity ＜ irregular = contrary to the usually accepted legal rules である。

62.　解答：C

解説　下線部は capable of working successfully の意。よって，C.「実行可能な」が最も近い。

63.　解答：D

解説　下線部は文字どおり「裁判外の」の意味。よって最も近いのは D.「通常の法的手続きの外で行われる」。

64.　解答：B

解説　下線部は smallness of quantity の意。B. dearth = a scarcity or lack が同義。

65.　解答：A

解説　下 線 部 meting out ＜ mete out は dispense or allot (justice or a punishment) の意。よって最も近いのは A. administering ＜ administer = deal out or inflict (a punishment) となる。

66. 解答：B

解説 下線部vetting＜vetはcheck someone thoroughly, especially in order to ensure that they are suitable for a particular jobの意。これに近いのはB. examining＜examine「審査する」。

67. 解答：C

解説 下線部violated＜violateはfail to comply withの意。最も近いのはC. contravened＜contravene「違反する」。

68. 解答：C

解説 下線部はfirmly established and difficult to changeの意。同義語はC. ingrained「(習慣などが) 染みついた」。

69. 解答：A

解説 下線部debilitated＜debilitateはmake (something) less effective or powerfulの意。したがって最も近いのはA. enfeebled＜enfeeble「弱める」。

70. 解答：A

解説 下線部backlashes＜backlashは，a strong negative reaction by a large number of people to recent eventsの意。よって最も適切なのはA. counterreactions＜counterreaction「反動」。

訳例　法の支配部門には，裁判所，法務省，更生制度，法令その他の機関や制度が含まれる。これらは，アリストテレスの言葉を借りれば「人治ではなく法治」を確固たらしめるものである。法の支配とは，法の下で公正，正義，平等を確保するという理念をいうが，また，官吏の恣意を防ぐことをも含意する。紛争後社会においては，法の支配はほぼ定義からして崩壊しており，機能しない裁判所や，施設として標準に満たない刑務所，裁判官やその他の職員に対する不十分な給与，不十分な運営予算，貧弱な訓練などが特徴となっている場合が多い。

私有財産を守り，契約を履行することは，市場経済の運営にとって不可欠である。治安維持のためには，犯罪者を訴追し，証拠という客観的なルールに基づいて罪の有無を判断できるような，機能する司法制度が要求される。実施可能な司法制度確立に失敗したことから，警察や治安部隊復活の取り組みに支障が出てしまった例は多い。法の支配は，適正手続き，法の下の平等，および行政権に対する司法の抑止機能を確保することにより，人権状況を改善する。法の支配がなければ，逮捕や拘禁は恣意的なものとなり，拷問や超法規的処刑を防ぐ有効なメカニズムもなくなる。そして個人や集団が自由に法を私物化したり，虐待を行っても罰を免れたりできるようになる恐れがある。大規模な紛争が終結した後に法の支配を確立するに当たっては，重要な課題がいくつかある。

紛争前の法制計画　紛争後の社会の司法制度の状態については，情報が不足していることが多いが，その国に長期間滞在経験のあるNGO職員から有益なアドバイスが得られる可能性がある。その法制度の特徴は何か？　有効性はどうだったか？　主な課題は何か？　国際社会は，法の支配を再び確立する努力についてどのような優先順位づけや順序づけを行うべきか？

適用法の制定　アフガニスタンやソマリアなどの紛争後の状況では，村の評議会や部族の長老らが紛争を解決したり，裁きを行う上で主要な役割を果たしたりしてきた。このことは特に地方に顕著に見られる。正式な司法制度が脆《ぜい》弱《じゃく》であったり，正当性を欠いていたり，人口のごく一部だけを対象としている場合もある。慣習法は，広く世界の多くの地域で行われているが，正式な法廷よりも紛争で失われにくい〔ことから〕，紛争後の段階において裁きを行い，紛争を非暴力で解決する手段を提供する上で補完的な役割を果たすことがある。

裁判官と弁護士の採用，審査，訓練　法律専門家の募集，審査，任命でしばしば問題となるのは，必要な専門的経験を持ち，一般市民に政治的に受け入れられる候補者を特定することである。裁判官の選任に当たっては，民族間，部族間，宗教間の分断が大きな問題となる場合がある。というのも，各コミュニティーは自らを代表する適切な人物がいないかぎり，選任の過程に同意しないおそれがあるからである。

更生制度の改善　紛争後の状況においては，未決拘禁施設や刑務所が劣悪な状態となっている場合が多い。この問題をさらに悪化させるのが，重大な人権侵害で悪評のある制度を復活させる作業への関与を資金供与国が渋る場合があることである。タリバン政権の崩壊後，刑務所の職員は，何千人もの受刑者の拘禁を続けようと必死に努力した。多くは長期にわたって，劣悪な条件の下で収容されることとなった。その状態は，被拘禁者の処遇に関する国際基準に違反していた。

法の支配の文化の確立　多くの司法制度は，司法の独立性の欠如，司法を利用して自らの利益を追求する政界のエリート，汚職の蔓延《まんえん》などの特徴〔的な問題〕を抱えている。また，行政府と司法府は司法制度の管理について競合することが多く，司法省と最高裁判所が主導権を争い合う状況となる。裁判官やその他の法律専門家の養成や技術支援，インフラ再建の援助を行っても，それだけでは汚職や政治的干渉で弱体化した制度は修復される可能性は低いのである。

移行期正義に対する支援紛争というものは事実上すべて人権侵害を伴うものであり，多くの場合，侵害は広く組織的に行われている。移行期正義とは，社会が暴力紛争や抑圧の時代から，平和で個人および集団の権利が尊重〔される時代〕へと移行する際に，虐待の残滓《ざんし》に対処すべく行うさまざまなアプローチから成るものである。このような移行を行う際，社会は，全市民に対して正義が行われるという感覚の醸成，市民の信頼の確立または刷新，個人間やコミュニティー間の和解，将来の虐待防止のために，過去の痛ましい遺産に向き合わなければならない場合がある。しかし，戦争犯罪法廷や真実委員会といったタイプの移行期正義は，ナショナリストの反発を招き，緊張を再燃させる恐れがある。

VIII 文脈上，空所を埋めるのに最もふさわしいものを 4つの選択肢の中から1つ選びなさい。

71.　解答：B

解説 old chestnut = a joke or subject that has become tedious by frequent repetition.

72.　解答：B

解説 前のパラグラフに，選挙戦で「Révolution（革命）」という書名の自叙伝を出版したことが紹介されていることに着目すると，D. labeled < label = assign to a category, especially inaccurately or restrictivelyよりは，B. fashioned < fashion = make into a particular characterの方が適切。

73.　解答：B

解説 下線部で終わるセンテンスは，「マクロンは減税を行い，＿＿＿ ように全国を回った」の意。よって下線部には「現状を把握する」などを意味する語句が予測できる（正解Bは成句）。

74.　解答：C

解説 下線部前は，コロナ禍で「革命」再開の時間が削られたことを，下線部の後は，マクロンが結局は福祉国家に頼ったことを述べている。よって下線部には「(革命) どころか (後退した)」という意味の語が適切。

75. 解答：A

解説 「フランスが ______ するテクノクラートの専門知識」という文脈にふさわしいのは，A. vaunted < vaunt「自慢する」。

76. 解答：C

解説 前後の énarques，ENA (国立行政学院) に注目すると，前者は後者卒業生の C.「通称」と推定できる。

77. 解答：B

解説 パラグラフの下線部に先立つ部分に，コロナ禍以前に Ministry of National Health (連帯保健省) がマスク備蓄管理を怠ったことが述べられているので，その長が後に解任されたことが推測される。

78. 解答：D

解説 前後は「(マスクが仕事で支給される以外の) フランス市民に残された唯一の ______ は自助」の意。よって，下線部には D.「頼みとするもの」が最適。

79. 解答：A

解説 下線部で終わるセンテンスは，「こうした不備に対する批判は，政治的な ______ にわたって広がった」。文意から最適なものは A. spectrum = a range of related qualities, ideas, or phenomena.

80. 解答：A

解説 下線部前後は，「〔高等保健局がきちんとしていれば〕我々は有効に機能するプロセスを持てていただろう。しかし，______ あの人たちは我々を見て不審に思っている」という文脈。この場合「それどころか反対に」というニュアンスとなる A. instead が最適。

訳例　昔から国家に対して，「あってもなくても生きられない」という態度を取ってきたフランス人。だが近ごろは，この陳腐な決まり文句が人を不安にさせる新たな意味を持つようになった。エマニュエル・マクロン大統領は３年前に政権の座についた際，公約のひとつとして，機敏で対応力に優れた国家を作るという〔政策を掲げていた〕。この改革の公約は逆説的であると同時に信頼に値するものであった。名門校の国立行政学院（ENA）を卒業し，優秀なテクノクラートとして高い評価を受けながら，選挙戦〔の一環として〕「Révolution（革命）」という簡潔な書名を付けた自叙伝を発表した〔マクロン〕の約束だったのだから。

３年を経たいま，革命は未発のままだ。それどころか，革命家を自任していた〔マクロン〕が反動的な役割を演ずることとなってしまった。ガソリン増税に端を発し，現在「ジレ・ジョーヌ（黄色いベスト）」と呼ばれる抗議運動は2019年に爆発的に広まったが，その背景のひとつには，大統領が庶民の経済的・物質的な苦しみに極度に無関心だという〔人々の〕思いがあった。マクロンは減税を行い，「実際の状況を把握する」ために全国を回った。2019年末には抗議のうねりは収まり，さざ波〔のよう〕になった。しかし，2020年初めに新型コロナウィルスが〔フランスにも〕到達したことで，マクロン政権はほとんど息つくひまもなくなり，官僚革命を再開する時間的余裕はなおさら少なくなった。それどころか，コロナウィルスの大流行によってマクロン大統領は，さきに自ら打ち壊すと約束していた「福祉国家」に頼らざるを得なくなったのである。

フランス政府が誇るテクノクラートの専門知識は，コロナ禍の間ずっと失態を繰り返した。マクロン政権では，コロナウィルス第１波の際に首相を務めていたエドゥアール・フィリップをはじめとする８人の閣僚がエナルク（ENA卒業生の通称）であったが，コロナ禍への対応はしばしば，エナルシー（ENA卒高級官僚による支配体制）というよりもアナルシー（無政府状態）に近いものとなった。

政府がクリアできなかった最初のハードルは，春先，マスクの供給と配布を行う際に立ち現れ，フランスは深刻なマスク不足に陥った。その後の議会調査で明らかになったところによると，連帯保健省は2018年，戦略備蓄中のマスク６億枚が必要な基準を満たしていないことを把握していた。同省はその廃棄を開始したが，連帯保健相が発注した補充マスクはわずか１億枚であった。驚くべきことに，昨年の夏にマクロン大統領からそっと辞任を求められたフィリップ氏は，上述の調査の中で，2017年から2020年の初めにかけて「マスクの話は誰からも聞いたことがない」と暴露した。フランスの医療従事者が１週間に必要とするマスクの数が，実際の備蓄から供給可能な500万枚ではなく，4,000万枚であることを知ったときの同氏のショックは想像に難くない。救急隊・消防隊・警察など以外の何千万人ものフランス市民に残された唯一の手段は，「ル・スィステーム・デー」であった（フランス語で「自分で何とかする」

の意）。

マクロン政権はワクチンによって対応を改善していく決意を固めた。そして，ファイザー社からの初回納入分が初冬に到着。11 月下旬には，保健関連政策の実行を統括する高等保健局（HAS）が，一般市民および全国 1 万 5,000 カ所の老人ホーム入居者と職員を対象に，ワクチン接種の段取りを詳細に示した計画を発表した。しかし，この計画を策定した同局職員らは，ワクチンを保管したり投与したりする能力が地域によって大きく異なることを考慮していなかった。こうした不備に対する批判は，政治的に異なる立場を越えて広がった。ド・ゴール主義者〔として知られる〕ノルマンディー地域圏議会議長は，「我々は〔HAS がきちんとしていれば〕有効に機能するプロセスを持てていただろう。それなのに，あの人たちは我々を見て，『この田舎者たちは何者だ』と不思議がっている」と力説した。また，ナンシー市の社会主義を奉じる市長は，「大規模な予防接種キャンペーンを計画実施する能力を持つのは当市だけだ」と断言した。

IX

以下の質問に対し，200 ～ 250 語の短いエッセイを英語で書きなさい。

質問文：コロナ禍からの復興に向けた国連の取り組みにおいて，「よりよい復興」と「一国も取り残さない」というモットーはどのように生かされているか？

解答例 I will discuss the UN mottos for sustainable COVID-19 pandemic recovery as a formula to balance challenges and opportunities.

Challenges, the first half of the equation, are global action wake-up calls. Threats to physical health impact mental health—suicides and domestic violence increase. Urgent treatment, including quarantine measures to stop infection transmission, have severe results: overburdening health systems; unemployment; suspending educational, cultural, and consumer activities; disrupting manufacturing supply chains, production, and distribution; crippling in-person service industries; bankrupting businesses. The economic consequences—global GDP decline and increased poverty—must be urgently addressed; moreover, recovery depends on turning system challenges into opportunities to create a more sustainably balanced world.

The second half of the calculation, opportunity, takes many forms. Severe decreases in human activity, due to Covid-19 lockdowns, may let oceans improve somewhat and also reduce greenhouse gas emissions by 6 percent—it's not the 7.6 percent yearly decrease needed to limit global warming to 1.5°C annually, but helps us imagine the goal of "decoupling" economic activity from old patterns of environmental destruction. Truly, the best opportunities will come from using Covid-19 recovery as a "reset button" that makes SDG action into everyday life.

Political will and public demand, demonstrated in the COVAX immunization initiative, and understanding inequality creates global threats, are positive signs reset is wanted. Overwhelmingly, new patterns for sustainable Covid-19 recovery must—as Secretary-General António Guterres said in the December 2020 UN General Assembly special session—resolve "pre-existing conditions" and "long-standing fragilities" to improve all systems for all nations.

解説　解答例はまず，与えられたテーマを「課題」と「機会」を両辺とする「公式」の形に組み替えて提示している。

第２パラグラフは，上の「課題」を多面的に展開し，必要な対策や考え方を示している。

第３パラグラフは，公式第２項の「機会」に関して，コロナ禍に伴う経済活動の縮小を，CO2 排出削減に生かせる文字通りの「機会」として考察する。

第４パラグラフは上記の両辺に関する所論を総合する形で，世界の持続可能な発展に対して，すべての国の利益となるまったく新しいパターンを提案している。

このように，エッセイ問題では，自分が知る事実や情報を整理して論理的に順序立てて配置し，問いに対する批判的思考や建設的な提案を展開することが重要である。

訳例　コロナ禍からの持続可能な復興を目指す国連のモットーを対象に，これを課題と機会との間のバランスを見いだす公式として考えてみたい。

公式の前半に当たる「課題」とは，グローバルな行動を促すモーニングコールである。身体の健康に対する脅威は心の健康に影響を及ぼす――そして自殺や家庭内暴力が増加していく。感染拡大を防ぐ検疫対策などの緊急措置は，結果として医療システムの逼迫《ひっぱく》や失業，教育・文化・消費活動の中止，製造業のサプライチェーンや生産・流通の混乱，対人サービス業の不振，企業の倒産など，深刻な事態を招く。世界的なGDPの減少と貧困の拡大という経済への影響については，早急に対処しなければならない。さらに，復興〔の成否〕は，システムの課題を転換して，より持続的にバランスの取れた世界を作る機会とすること〔ができるかどうか〕にかかっている。

式の後半に当たる「機会」はさまざまな形を取る。コロナ禍に伴うロックダウンにより人間活動が著しく低下した場合，海〔の状態〕はいくぶんか改善され，温室ガスの排出量も〔年間〕6%削減できる可能性がある——世界的な気温上昇を1.5℃に抑えるのに必要な年間削減率7.6%には及ばないが，経済活動を環境破壊という古いパターンから「切り離す」というゴール〔がどういうことなのか〕を想像するのに役立つ。コロナ禍からの復興を，SDGsの行動を日常生活に取り入れるための「リセットボタン」として利用することから，間違いなく最高の機会がもたらされるだろう。

コロナウィルス・ワクチン接種の取り組みで示された政治的意思と社会の要求，そしてまた，不平等によって世界規模での脅威が生まれるとの認識〔の広がり〕は，リセットが必要とされていることを示す明るい兆候だ。コロナ禍からの持続可能な復興のための新しいパターンは——2020年12月に開かれた国連総会の特別会合でアントニオ・グテーレス事務総長が述べたように——「既存の条件」と「長期にわたって続く脆弱性」に圧倒的な力で解決することで，すべての国のためにあらゆるシステムを改善する必要がある。

2021年特A級第1回試験　正解一覧

Ⅰ

1. A　2. D　3. B　4. B　5. A　6. C　7. D　8. D　9. A　10. A

Ⅱ

11. D　12. B　13. D　14. C　15. C　16. C　17. D　18. A　19. B　20. D

Ⅲ

21. A　22. C　23. A　24. B　25. D　26. C　27. D　28. D　29. B　30. C

Ⅳ

31. C　32. B　33. C　34. A　35. D　36. B　37. B　38. A　39. B　40. D

Ⅴ

41. C　42. A　43. D　44. D　45. C　46. A　47. C　48. A　49. B　50. B

Ⅵ

51. B　52. A　53. C　54. A　55. D　56. D　57. A　58. D　59. B　60. B

Ⅶ

61. D　62. C　63. D　64. B　65. A　66. B　67. C　68. C　69. A　70. A

Ⅷ

71. B　72. B　73. B　74. C　75. A　76. C　77. B　78. D　79. A　80. A

2021年

第2回試験

問題

UNA-JAPAN

特Ａ級第１次試験問題用紙

特Ａ級

外務省後援

２０２１年度第２回国際連合公用語

英語検定試験（120分）

受験上の注意

1．問題用紙は試験開始の合図があるまで開いてはいけません。その間に、この**受験上の注意を熟読しておいてください。**

2．**受験番号と氏名を解答用紙（マークシートと作文用紙）**に記入してください。

3．解答用紙の配布は１人１部のみです。複数の配布は致しません。

4．試験開始前は、答案への解答記入は禁止です。

5．マークシートの記入は、１～100までの記入箇所がありますが、この級では１～80までを使います。

6．マークシートの記入は、必ずＨＢ以上の濃い鉛筆を使って該当箇所を黒く塗りつぶしてください。書き間違いの場合は「アト」が残らないように消してください。マークシートは絶対に折ったり曲げたりしないでください。

7．受験級、受験地区、会場番号、受験番号のマークシートへの記入は監督者の指示に従い、間違いなく記入してください。**（裏表紙の「マークシート記入例」参照）**

8．作文は、⑴読みやすい文字をペン、ボールペンまたはＨＢ以上の濃い鉛筆で書いてください。⑵使用語数の200～250語を目安にしてください。

9．試験問題についての質問は、印刷が不鮮明な場合を除き、一切受けつけません。

10．中途退室の際は、マークシートと作文用紙を持って監督者に渡し、他の受験者の迷惑にならないように静かに退室してください。中途退室後の再入室はできません。

11．試験中は他の受験者の妨げとなる行動は慎んでください。また携帯電話等の電源はお切りください。

12．マークシートと作文用紙は監督者に提出し、問題用紙はご自由にお持ち帰りください。

＊試験問題の複製や転載、インターネットへのアップロード等、いかなる媒体への転用を禁止します。

試験結果について

1．第１次試験の結果は2021年11月24日㈬頃に受験申込書に記載された住所に郵送で通知します。

2．その間に住所変更をされた方は、郵便局へ住所変更の届け出を忘れずに行ってください。

3．発表前の試験結果のお問合せには応じられません。

第２次試験について

1．第１次試験合格者には、試験結果発表と同時に試験日時、会場を指定して通知します。

2．第２次試験は2021年12月12日㈰です。特Ａ級（Ａ級との併願を含む）の試験地は**東京と大阪**になります。あらかじめご了承願います。

UNA-JAPAN

公益財団法人 日本国際連合協会

http://www.unaj.or.jp/

I. Fill in each of the following blanks with the most appropriate of the four alternatives according to the knowledge and information gained from *New Today's Guide to the United Nations*.

1. Address to the General Assembly by Secretary-General António Guterres

I will focus today on ________ threats and tests that stand in our way. For each, the dangers are all too clear. Yet for each, if we act as truly united nations, we can find answers

A. four B. five C. six D. seven

2. Membership

If the Council recommends admission of the new Member, the application is passed to the General Assembly, which must accept it by a ________ majority.

A. one-third B. two-thirds
C. quarter D. three-fifths

3. Economic and Social Council

The Economic and Social Council generally holds one substantive session each year. This annual session used to alternate between New York and Geneva, but now is held only in New York every year, with the exception of ________.

A. the High-Level Political Forum
B. the Development Cooperation Forum
C. the Humanitarian Affairs Segment
D. the Management Segment

4. The United Nations System

The first group of specialized agencies includes international organizations that were established earlier than the United Nations itself, such as ________ and the Universal Postal Union (UPU), both of which were founded in the 19th century.

A. the International Telecommunication Union (ITU)
B. the International Monetary Fund (IMF)
C. the International Finance Corporation (IFC)
D. the International Labour Organization (ILO)

5. **<u>United Nations Industrial Development Organization (UNIDO)</u>**

The UNIDO renewed its mandate at the 15th session of the General Conference of the UNIDO held in ________ in Lima, Peru and reaffirmed the UNIDO's mission to promote and accelerate inclusive and sustainable industrial development in member States.

A. 2012 B. 2013 C. 2014 D. 2015

6. **<u>Doctrinal changes, failures, and present situation of PKO</u>**

The then Secretary-General ________ published the report titled "An Agenda for Peace" in 1992. This report emphasized that the United Nations could play a positive role following the "cycle" of conflict.

A. Kofi Annan B. Javier Pérez de Cuéllar
C. Boutros Boutros-Ghali D. Kurt Waldheim

7. **<u>Disarmament</u>**

The Treaty on the Prohibition of Nuclear Weapons (TPNW) was adopted by 122 votes to 1, with one Member abstaining, in ________.

A. October 2016 B. December 2016
C. July 2017 D. September 2017

8. **<u>From the Millennium Development Goals (MDGs) to the Sustainable Development Goals (SDGs)</u>**

In 2015, the General Assembly adopted the new Sustainable Development Goals (SDGs) to be achieved by 2030. The SDGs include 17 goals, ________ for measuring progress in achieving the targets.

A. 128 targets and 196 indicators B. 169 targets and 230 indicators
C. 180 targets and 213 indicators D. 197 targets and 242 indicators

9. **<u>Environmental Issues</u>**

Concern about the deterioration of the environment through air and water pollution, erosion, waste, noise, biocides and other agents prompted the United Nations to hold the Conference on the Human Environment in ________ in 1972

A. Helsinki B. Stockholm
C. Vienna D. Rome

10. **<u>The End of the Cold War and the Revival of UN Diplomacy</u>**

Seeking a more influential status in the UN, since 2004, Japan aligned with Germany, ________ and India to ask for the expansion of the permanent membership of the Council.

A. Canada　　B. Italy

C. Spain　　D. Brazil

II. Choose from among the four alternatives the one that most closely corresponds to the meaning contained in the following passage.

(1) Documented evidence of large-scale human rights abuses in China's northwestern Xinjiang region has painted a clear picture that Beijing is perpetrating mass atrocities against Uyghurs and other Turkic Muslim ethnic groups. But even in the face of transparent evidence, the strategies the international community and the United States typically deploy to prevent atrocities have failed to stop the problem. The United States and like-minded countries have an obligation to act to end the ongoing atrocities and to protect the Uyghur people. While many important steps have been taken, none have had a noticeable impact on Beijing. It's time for the international community to take stock of the atrocity prevention toolkit, to consider why it has failed the Uyghurs, and to discuss how these failures can inform updates or adaptations to respond to the Xinjiang crisis.

(2) Since 2018, human rights researchers have documented solid evidence of an intensified campaign to assimilate the Uyghur people that hinges on several key pillars: a mass detention and forced labor program, a sophisticated mass surveillance system, restrictions on cultural and religious practice, and population control measures. More than 1.3 million people—(1) ________________, though researchers allege more—have been arbitrarily detained in political "re-education" camps in the Xinjiang Uyghur Autonomous Region (XUAR), where they have faced political indoctrination, forced labor, separation from their families, and, in some cases, torture. Once released, they remain under a surveillance system so strict rights groups allege it has turned Xinjiang into an "open-air prison." (2) ________________ the use of forced sterilization and mandatory birth control to slash Uyghur birth rates, as well as strict controls on Islamic practice, and a campaign to destroy mosques and cultural heritage sites.

(3) The international community has a toolkit, evolved from years of practice responding to conflict scenarios, of bilateral and multilateral interventions designed to mitigate atrocity risk. **(A)** Formal and informal early warning mechanisms are typically used to signal rising atrocity risk, but do not exist in any robust form in Xinjiang. Security and operational constraints on civil society and the diplomatic community have prevented the flow of information from XUAR. **(B)** The diaspora community and researchers outside the country have worked to fill this gap, providing information on individual Uyghur victims and using satellite data to document detention centers. Leaked government documents have exposed the clear intent of the Chinese government to pursue repressive policies. **(C)** Regardless, the slow flow of information constrained the ability of diplomats to engage before the atrocities began.

(4) Globally, recent atrocities have occurred during situations of armed conflict or severe political instability, where diplomatic intervention can be used to deter action or

provide support and legitimacy to one of the opposing parties in a conflict. **(D)** In Xinjiang, however, the conflict scenario is markedly different: It is not between two conventional warring parties but between the state and civilians, and the political situation remains stable under Beijing's control. Low-level, sporadic clashes between civilians and police have broken out, but Beijing's strict security apparatus has, so far, kept a lid on potential escalations. **This context** narrows the kind of opportunities for diplomatic intervention that tend to be readily available during more conventional violent conflicts. Moreover, China has resisted diplomatic pressure to change these policies, framing their handling of the Uyghur population in Xinjiang as a matter of internal sovereignty, blocking diplomatic interference from outside.

(5) The atrocity prevention toolkit's financial mechanisms have also proved insufficient for deterring or halting atrocities in XUAR. As the world's second-largest economy, China does not depend on foreign assistance, and is therefore unlikely to ____________________. Party leaders most responsible for the ongoing atrocities maintain few assets outside of China, limiting the effectiveness of individual sanctions. More comprehensive or multinational sanctions or import restrictions on Chinese goods could have an impact but present the political challenge of building a coalition capable of challenging China's political and economic power.

(6) At the U.N., China's role makes concerted action to halt the atrocities difficult if not unlikely. Beijing's permanent seat on the Security Council provides the opportunity to veto resolutions calling for the end of the violence or for concrete U.N. action to halt it. Further, China has built up a constituency of supportive states that would likely oppose a General Assembly resolution. The closest the U.N. has come to date to directly addressing the atrocities in Xinjiang was in an exchange of letters at the Human Rights Council. In the summer of 2019 a group of 22 states, including the United States, submitted a letter to the Human Rights Council calling upon China to halt its policies of mass detention. This letter was followed days later by one signed by 37 states in defense of China's human rights policies. The situation was repeated again in October of this year.

(7) It's time to recognize that the existing atrocity prevention toolkit was developed based on conflict contexts that bear little resemblance to the current situation in Xinjiang. Like-minded international actors should reassess the toolkit to consider necessary adaptations to halt ongoing atrocities and to protect the Uyghurs. Washington should play a key role in leading this conversation, and the incoming administration has an important opportunity to do so. The current administration has already taken decisive steps to deter China's forced labor program in Xinjiang and elevate attention to the Uyghur crisis within the U.S. government, including by imposing sanctions on key Chinese officials and government entities. ①Other actions have included banning cotton imports from a government-affiliated producer in Xinjiang, seizing other goods believed to be made with forced labor, and removing a Uyghur-linked group from

a list of foreign terrorist organizations. ②The second bill would put the burden on importers to prove that goods coming from the XUAR or using workers from XUAR are not made with forced labor. ③These efforts can be strengthened and expanded upon to improve their effectiveness. ④Indeed, several promising U.S. efforts to halt the violence remain pending and may support consideration of the adaptation of the atrocity prevention toolkit.

11. Which is correct according to the information explicitly stated in Paragraph 1?

A. Human rights abuses against Uyghurs and other ethnic groups in the Xinjiang region have been documented though to date the evidence is somewhat inconclusive.

B. The international community has developed many important strategies to prevent atrocities in Xinjiang and have an impact on Beijing.

C. The international community must update its atrocity prevention methods and consider how to respond to the crisis occurring in Xinjiang.

D. The United States and its allies must consider whether they have an obligation to stop the ongoing atrocities and to protect the Uyghur people.

12. In the context of the information presented in Paragraph 2, which of the following sets (A to D) best fits the blanks (1) and (2) in the paragraph?

A. (1) a figure Beijing has put forward (2) The U.N. has failed to mandate

B. (1) by China's own admission (2) Rights groups have also documented

C. (1) consistent with Western think tanks (2) China has also adequately addressed

D. (1) not by any means a conservative estimate (2) NGOs have vehemently rejected

13. Which part of the essay, indicated by the capital letters in parentheses, is MOST appropriate for the following sentence?

To date, however, the international community has failed to address the situation in Xinjiang in any meaningful way.

A. (A) B. (B) C. (C) D. (D)

14. Which of the following (A to D) is the underlined phrase "This context" in Paragraph 4 NOT referring to?

A. Beijing's strict security apparatus
B. conflict between the state and civilians
C. sporadic clashes between civilians and police
D. two conventional warring parties

15. In the context of Paragraph 5, which of the following (A to D) best fits the blank?

A. accommodate practices that conflict with its economic norms
B. neglect the rights of ethnic minorities within this region
C. pursue any campaigns to undermine its sovereignty
D. respond to the stick or carrot measures such mechanisms offer

16. Which of the following is NOT correct according to the information presented in Paragraph 6?

A. China is able to use its position in the U.N. to block attempts aimed at ending the atrocities in Xinjiang.
B. The exchange of letters at the Human Rights Council suggests an effective resolution to the atrocities in Xinjiang.
C. There are numerous states who are willing to oppose any moves towards ending China's policies in Xinjiang.
D. When China has been called upon to halt its policies of mass detention, it has responded with letters signed by allies defending its policies.

17. Which of the following most accurately represents the author's view according to the information explicitly stated in Paragraph 7?

A. A call by U.N. experts for greater scrutiny on Beijing's human rights track record would enable independent investigators to enter the region.
B. Beijing favors dialogue among states rather than accountability in the application of human rights standards.
C. International effort to reassess the atrocity toolkit should be led by the U.S., which is already acting to deter atrocities in Xinjiang.
D. Policymakers should consider international fact-finding missions that can be pursued even without access to investigations within China's borders.

18. **In Paragraph 7, which of the underlined sections, ① to ④, should be omitted because it is either unnecessary or inappropriate there?**

A. ①　　B. ②　　C. ③　　D. ④

19. **Which of the following ideas is <u>explicitly stated</u> in the essay?**

A. China considers external involvement in its handling of the Uyghurs as interference in its sovereignty and has resisted diplomatic pressure to change its policies.

B. China framed its policies in Xinjiang as an attempt to prevent terrorism and extremism, playing on these global threats to build support for their efforts.

C. China has control over its population through extensive surveillance, economic strength, and an ability to manipulate domestic and international media.

D. China's actions could be labelled as genocide, which would be the strongest message to date that the atrocities must end and would provide critical support to the Uyghurs.

20. **If we divide paragraphs (1) to (7) into four main topics, which set, A, B, C, or D, is the most representative?**

	Topic 1	Topic 2	Topic 3	Topic 4
A.	(1)	(2)	(3) (4) (5) (6)	(7)
B.	(1) (2)	(3) (4) (5)	(6)	(7)
C.	(1) (2)	(3) (4)	(5)	(6) (7)
D.	(1) (2) (3)	(4)	(5) (6)	(7)

Ⅲ. Choose from among the underlined phrases the one that is grammatically or idiomatically incorrect.

21. More than **(A)** five dozen of countries are urging "all parties" to safeguard **(B)** the departure of foreign nationals and Afghans **(C)** who wish to leave the country, according to a joint statement released by the US State Department on Sunday. "Afghans and international citizens who wish to leave **(D)** must be allowed to do so," the statement says.

22. **(A)** China's biggest tech companies lost more than $50 billion in market value Tuesday **(B)** after the government proposed sweeping new rules to further curb anti-competitive behavior among big internet firms. **(C)** The latest effort to clamp down on the sector comes from the State Administration for Market Regulation (SAMR), which **(D)** has been spearheaded the government's antitrust campaign against Big Tech.

23. New Zealand's first community Covid-19 **(A)** case in six months is the Delta variant, and genome sequencing shows **(B)** that it's linked to the growing outbreak in neighboring Australia. On Wednesday, New Zealand authorities announced they **(C)** had confirmed other six positive cases all linked to the **(D)** first case. One of the new cases worked at a hospital in Auckland.

24. Around 1.2 million people, including 540,000 **(A)** children, have been impacted by the 7.2-magnitude **(B)** earthquake which struck southwestern Haiti on Saturday morning, according to UNICEF. The quake left **(C)** at least 1,941 people died and more than 6,900 injured; that toll is **(D)** expected to rise in the coming days.

25. **(A)** It's been a month since England dropped most of its coronavirus restrictions, a move that was welcomed by much of the country's hard-pressed business sector but **(B)** criticized by thousands of scientists as a "dangerous and unethical experiment." **(C)** A month on, it has become clear that while vaccination works, **(D)** the reopening has come at cost.

26. The National Gallery of Australia announced Thursday that **(A)** it will return more than a dozen "culturally significant" artworks to India due to **(B)** the items' having allegedly links to looting and trafficking networks. Thirteen **(C)** of the works had been purchased directly from a disgraced New York art dealer, **(D)** who stands accused of smuggling thousands of antiquities from across Asia.

27. The last surviving leader of Cambodia's Khmer Rouge regime on Thursday **(A)** denied involving in genocide and being responsible **(B)** for crimes against humanity, in one of his final appearances **(C)** before an international tribunal. Khmer Rouge-era President Khieu Samphan, 90, was speaking **(D)** during his appeal of a 2018 guilty verdict.

28. Ebrahim Raisi **(A)** was inaugurated for Iran's next president on Thursday, **(B)** signaling the start of a new harder-line era that could herald major shifts in the Islamic Republic's policies at home and abroad. After eight years of Hassan Rouhani's **(C)** moderate administration, Iran now turns to Raisi, an ultra-conservative judiciary chief whose views **(D)** are fully in line with the thinking of the country's powerful clergy.

29. Zambia's President- elect Hakainde Hichilema **(A)** will have his work cut out as he takes office next Tuesday. The 59-year-old business tycoon **(B)** now faces the task of trying to revive Zambia's fortunes. The economy, which had suffered a brutal pandemic-fuelled slowdown, **(C)** have been buoyed only slightly by more favourable copper prices - now **(D)** hovering around decade highs, driven partly by the boom in electric cars.

30. A BBC journalist working in Moscow said Saturday that she felt **(A)** shocked she was being expelled from Russia, **(B)** in what for her employer described as a "direct assault on media freedom." The BBC's Moscow correspondent said **(C)** her forced departure comes amid "a massive **(D)** deterioration in relations between Russia and the UK and, more broadly, Russia and the West."

IV. Choose the answer that uses the most logically and grammatically appropriate form of each underlined infinitive, in whichever manner (transitive, intransitive, participle, or otherwise) it is used, in the context of the following article.

The private sector in Thailand has a key role to play in the country's transition to a net zero carbon economy. "Social responsibility and sustainable profit" can go hand in hand according to the chief of Thailand's government pension fund. The UN, and some of the biggest players in the Thai economy, are working together to support efforts by the country's finance and banking institutions to speed up the South East Asian country's transition to a net zero carbon economy.

It is increasingly recognized that the finance and banking sectors can have a huge influence on the economy, through the way that they decide to invest in, and fund, businesses, and in Thailand, the UN is helping the government to raise awareness of the importance of sustainable finance.

Ahead of a UN-backed event aimed at encouraging Thai finance leaders **(31)** **to adopt** sustainable business practices, Eric Usher, the head of the UN Environment Programme Finance Initiative, spoke with Srikanya Yathip, Secretary General of the Thai Government Pension Fund (GPF) and Kattiya Indaravijaya, CEO of Kasikornbank for UN News.

Eric Usher: When the UN Environment Programme Finance Initiative began in 1992, as one of the first partnerships with the global financial sector based on sustainable finance, it's fair to say that it was a niche topic. After all, financial institutions don't cut down trees, so what do they have to do with the environment?

Since then, it has been **(32)** **to understand** that lending has a real impact: banks can **(33)** **to choose** whether or not to finance clients who cut down trees, so the actions and policies of banks have a big impact on the environment. Why is sustainable finance a relevant topic for your organizations?

Srikanya Yathip: Because we believe that our investment decisions can have a transformational effect. If we can rebuild our world sustainably, there will no longer be a need to protect the environment or society.

As a pension fund and institutional investor, we are privileged to be able to decide what and where we invest, and we make sure to align our corporate behaviour with the wider objectives of society, as well as look for long-term financial returns. For us, it's about doing well by doing good: Social responsibility and sustainable profit can go hand in hand.

And, taking the current situation into consideration, with the extreme pressures we are all facing from COVID-19, if we want to protect our bottom line, we have to protect others.

Kattiya Indaravijaya: We need to care about all stakeholders: customers, employees, suppliers and community. Sometimes that **(34)** **to mean** a trade-off between short-term pain and long-term gain.

In the banking industry you **(35)** **to need** two kinds of licence. The first is a banking licence, that allows you to operate. The second is a social licence that we need to earn from the community. If the community cannot survive, neither can we.

A recent survey **(36) <u>to find</u>** that 74 per cent of those **(37) <u>to survey</u>** do not want to support products that are not environmentally friendly. This shows that society is moving towards sustainable development. If we want to stay relevant, we can't ignore this trend.

Eric Usher: There are two camps today when it comes to sustainable development. One camp says that recovering from the crisis is the priority, and sustainability should be put on hold. The other camp says that now is the opportunity to invest sustainably, respond to the climate crisis and shift to a net-zero carbon economy. What is your view?

Srikanya Yathip: In Thailand the government is currently **(38) <u>to produce</u>** a national masterplan, with a goal of achieving net zero. From what I understand, the government will present this masterplan at COP26. I've seen some drafts of the plan, and it would affect many businesses. The proposed changes include a move to more low carbon power generation, support for the electric vehicle industry, and for the circular economy [which refers to a systemic approach to economic development designed to benefit businesses, society, and the environment—a circular economy is regenerative by design and aims to gradually decouple growth from the consumption of finite resources].

Kattiya Indaravijaya: Moving to net zero is very important, and we've seen nations and organizations committing to reaching the goal within the next 30 years. That means that everyone knows that it's important, but it will take time and a lot of effort to get there.

Kasikornbank is willing to participate in net zero and sustainable growth, by **(39) <u>to help</u>** our customers to do business in a more sustainable way. We have the policies in place, and the intention to make it happen. We have already **(40) <u>to achieve</u>** some of our targets, but we need to speed up and do more as an industry: responsible lending practices must be part of business operations; financial institutions need to work more closely together; and businesses, regulators and consumers need to be engaged on sustainability issues.

Srikanya Yathip: I agree. As a corporate citizen, we have a responsibility to society. Collective efforts speak louder: alone we can do little, together we can do so much, and the sky's the limit.

31. **to adopt**

A. adopt	B. adopted
C. adopting	D. to adopt

32. **to understand**

A. understand　B. understood
C. understanding　D. to understand

33. **to choose**

A. choose　B. chose
C. choosing　D. to choose

34. **to mean**

A. mean　B. meaning
C. means　D. to mean

35. **to need**

A. need　B. needing
C. needs　D. to need

36. **to find**

A. find　B. found
C. finding　D. to find

37. **to survey**

A. survey　B. surveyed
C. surveying　D. surveys

38. **to produce**

A. produce　B. produced
C. produces　D. producing

39. **to help**

A. help　B. helped
C. helping　D. to help

40. **to achieve**

A. achieve　B. achieved
C. achieves　D. achieving

V. Choose from among the four alternatives the one that most closely corresponds to the meaning contained in the following passage.

Patriotism as a religion is unsatisfactory because of its lack of universality. The good at which it aims is a good for one's own nation only, not for all humankind. The desires which it inspires in an Englishman are not the same as the desires which it inspires in a German. A world full of patriots may be a world full of **(41) strife**. The more intensely a nation believes in its patriotism, the more fanatically indifferent it will become to the damage suffered by other nations. When once men have learnt to subordinate their own good to the good of a larger whole, there can be no valid reason for stopping short of the human race. It is **(42) the admixture of national pride** that makes it so easy in practice for men's impulses towards sacrifice to stop short at the frontiers of their own country. We cannot avoid having more love for our own country than for other countries, and there is no reason why we should wish to avoid it, any more than we should wish to love all individual men and women equally. But any adequate religion will lead us to **(43) temper** inequality of affection by love of justice, and to universalize our aims by realizing the common needs of man.

In practice, patriotism has many other enemies to contend with. **(44) Cosmopolitanism cannot fail to grow as people acquire more knowledge of foreign countries through education and travel.** Socialism, syndicalism, and anti-capitalist movements generally, are against patriotism in their tendency, since they make men aware that the present State is largely concerned in defending the privileges of the rich, and that many of the conflicts between States have their origin in the financial interests of a few **(45) plutocrats**. This kind of opposition is perhaps temporary, a mere incident in the struggle of labor to acquire power. Australia, where labor feels its triumph secure, is full of patriotism and militarism, based upon determination to prevent foreign labor from sharing the benefits of a privileged position. It is not unlikely that England might develop a similar nationalism if it became a socialist State. But it is probable that such nationalism would be purely defensive. Schemes of foreign aggression, entailing great loss of life and wealth in the nation which adopts them, would hardly be initiated except by those whose instincts of **(46) dominion** have been sharpened through the power derived from private property and the institutions of the capitalist State.

The evil **(47) wrought** in the modern world by the excessive power of the State is very great, and very little recognized. The chief harm caused by the State is promotion of efficiency in war. If all States increase their strength, the balance of power is unchanged, and no one State has a better chance of victory than before. And when the means of offense exist, even though their original purpose may have been defensive, the temptation to use them is likely, sooner or later, to prove overwhelming. In this way the very measures which promoted security within the borders of the State promote insecurity elsewhere. It is of the essence of the State to suppress violence within and to facilitate it without. The State makes an entirely artificial division of humankind and of our duties toward them: towards one group we are bound by the law, towards the other **(48) only by the prudence of highwaymen**.

The State is rendered evil by its exclusions, and by the fact that, whenever it embarks upon aggressive war, it becomes a combination of men for murder and robbery. The present system is irrational, since external and internal anarchy must be both right or both wrong. It is supported because, so long as others adopt it, it is thought the only road to safety, and because it secures the pleasures of triumph, which cannot be obtained in a good community. **(49) If these pleasures were no longer sought, or no longer possible to obtain, the problem of securing safety from invasion would not be difficult**.

The first step towards remedying this state of things is a genuine interest in foreign affairs on the part of the ordinary citizen, and an insistence that national pride shall not be allowed to jeopardize his other interests. During war, when he is roused, he is willing to sacrifice everything to pride; but in quiet times he will be far more ready than men in authority to realize that foreign affairs, like private concerns, ought to be settled **(50) amicably** according to principles, not brutally by force or the threat of force.

41. Here the word "strife" means

A. unfair treatment
B. economic instability
C. bitter disagreement
D. immense disappointment

42. The author of this passage would most likely regard "the admixture of national pride" as

A. essential for social cohesion.
B. a potential threat to international security.
C. beneficial in some countries but not others.
D. an increasingly popular alternative to religion.

43. Here the word "temper" means

A. eradicate
B. counterbalance
C. aggravate
D. evade

44. This sentence functions in the passage to

A. exemplify an alternative to nationalism.
B. illustrate the benefits of urban living.
C. explain the importance of social cohesion.
D. demonstrate the vulnerability of liberal societies.

45. **Here the word "plutocrats" means**

A. scaremongers
B. imposters
C. despots
D. magnates

46. **Here the word "dominion" means**

A. control
B. violence
C. adversity
D. apathy

47. **Here the word "wrought" means**

A. put out
B. covered up
C. passed over
D. brought about

48. **Here the phrase "only by the prudence of highwaymen" suggests behavior that is**

A. valiant
B. nefarious
C. quaint
D. virtuous

49. **This sentence functions in the passage to**

A. acknowledge an alternative viewpoint of the benefits of the state.
B. provide an example of the pleasures of triumph.
C. conclude an argument about the irrationality of the state.
D. transition to a new point about the importance of national pride.

50. **Here the word "amicably" means**

A. genially
B. decisively
C. skeptically
D. viciously

VI. Choose from among the four alternatives the one that best completes the following sentences.

51. **In 2016, Hanson Robotics took the world by storm with Sophia, who was famously given Saudi Arabian citizenship. Now, the Hong Kong-based robotics firm has _________ its latest invention: Grace, a humanoid robot it hopes will _________ healthcare.**

A. divulged – contaminate B. trumpeted – convert
C. unveiled – revolutionize D. dispersed – revamp

52. **A US man is fighting to send a message about his battle with Covid-19 in a Virginia hospital. He really regrets not getting vaccinated. And while he hopes he's turned a corner, for a very scary _________, he thought he needed to make arrangements in case he died. The father of several children has been recording a video diary of _________ from his room, documenting a startling roller coaster of declines and improvement.**

A. stint – forms B. spell – types
C. span – kinds D. stretch – sorts

53. **Zambians started voting on Thursday in a showdown between President Edgar Lungu and main opposition rival Hakainde Hichilema that looks too tight to call and comes amid mounting debt and a _________ economy. Polling opened at 6 a.m. with long queues seen at voting booths in the capital Lusaka, which could _________ a huge turnout.**

A. dwindling – flag B. flagging – point to
C. spoiling – signal D. disintegrating – look to

54. **Naomi Osaka has _________ to donate her earnings from next week's tennis competition to support earthquake relief efforts in Haiti, the Caribbean nation her father hails from. She made the announcement in response to the quake that struck the impoverished country on Saturday. "Really hurts to see all the devastation that's going on in Haiti, and I feel like we really can't _________," Osaka said on Twitter.**

A. pledged – catch a break B. vouched – strike it lucky
C. vowed – push our luck D. sworn – call it quits

55. **Coronavirus deaths in Africa rose rapidly over the past month, as _________ surged by 80 percent within the last four weeks, the World Health Organization has said. The pandemic's worsening death toll and rapid infection rate are being driven by the highly _________ Delta variant, which is considered to be more deadly than the original strain of coronavirus.**

A. casualties – ambulatory
B. fatalities – transmissible
C. mortalities – contactable
D. lethalities – respiratory

56. **More than 5 million residents in Japan have been ordered to evacuate their homes due to the threat of flooding and landslides, as torrential rains _________ the country's southwestern tip. The strongest evacuation warning, Level 5, was _________ on Saturday to more than a million people across the prefectures of Saga, Nagasaki, Fukuoka, and Hiroshima, according to public broadcaster NHK.**

A. liquify – disclosed
B. berate – publicized
C. entrench – declared
D. batter – issued

57. **Team Ireland athlete Patrick Flanagan said he was "_________" when he found out that his wheelchair had been broken on his journey to Tokyo to compete in the 2020 Paralympic Games. "The wheels have been damaged so much that they no longer spin, along with a lot of other _________ and scraps," he posted on Twitter.**

A. gutted – dents
B. pumped – nicks
C. tanked – dimples
D. shattered – gulfs

58. **On Wednesday night, Lebanon's Central Bank issued an announcement that seemed to finally sound the death _________ on the country's floundering economy. Fuel subsidies, long seen as a _________ for the country's growing legions of impoverished people, were halted.**

A. gong – watchdog
B. knell – lifeboat
C. siren – watermark
D. bell – blackball

59. **Mexico _________ a lawsuit Wednesday against eleven gun manufacturers over firearms that flow from the United States across the border and into criminal hands in Mexico. "This flood is not a natural phenomenon or an inevitable consequence of the gun business or of U.S. gun laws. It is the foreseeable result of the Defendants' deliberate actions and business practices," the _________ reads.**

A. enacted – gripe
B. deposited – accusation
C. alleged – grievance
D. filed – complaint

60. **Civil Human Rights Front (CHRF), the pro-democracy group that organized some of Hong Kong's biggest protests, announced Sunday that it was _________ — the latest of a string of civic organizations that have dissolved in the _________ of a sweeping national security law.**

A. disbursing - event
B. dismembering - offspring
C. disbanding - wake
D. disenfranchising - fallout

Ⅶ. Choose from among the four alternatives the one that best explains each of the underlined words.

In recent academic scholarship it has become commonplace to see international politics described as "socially constructed." Drawing on a variety of social theories—critical theory, postmodernism, feminist theory, historical institutionalism, sociological institutionalism, symbolic interactionism, structuration theory, and the like—students of international politics have increasingly accepted two basic **(61) principles** of "constructivism": (1) that the structures of human association are determined primarily by shared ideas rather than material forces, and (2) that the identities and interests of purposive actors are constructed by these shared ideas rather than given by nature. The first represents an "idealist" approach to social life, and in its emphasis on the sharing of ideas it is also "social" in a way that the opposing "materialist" view's emphasis on biology, technology, or the environment, is not. The second is a "holist" or "structuralist" approach because of its emphasis on the emergent powers of social structures, which opposes the "individualist" view that social structures are **(62) reducible** to individuals. Constructivism could therefore be seen as a kind of "structural idealism."

As the list above suggests there are many forms of constructivism. In this book I defend one form and use it to theorize about the international system. The version of constructivism that I defend is a moderate one that draws especially on structurationist and symbolic interactionist sociology. As such it concedes important points to materialist and individualist perspectives and endorses a scientific approach to social inquiry. For these reasons it may be rejected by more **(63) radical** constructivists for not going far enough; indeed it is a thin constructivism. It goes much farther than most mainstream International Relations (IR) scholars today, however, who sometimes dismiss any talk of social construction as "postmodernism." Between these extremes I hope to find a philosophically principled middle way. I then show that this makes a difference for thinking about international politics.

The international system is a hard case for constructivism on both the social and construction counts. On the social side, while norms and law govern most domestic politics, self-interest and **(64) coercion** seem to rule international politics. International law and institutions exist, but the ability of this superstructure to counter the material base of power and interest seems limited. This suggests that the international system is not a very "social" place, and so provides intuitive support for materialism in that domain. On the construction side, while the dependence of individuals on society makes the claim that their identities are constructed by society relatively uncontroversial, the primary actors in international politics, states, are much more autonomous from the social system in which they are embedded. Their foreign policy behavior is often determined primarily by domestic politics, the **(65) analogue** to individual personality, rather than by the international system (society). Some states, like Albania or Burma, have interacted so little with others that they have been called “autistic.” This suggests that the international system does not do much “constructing” of states, and so provides **(66) intuitive** support for individualism in that domain (assuming states are “individuals”). The underlying problem here is that the social structure of the international system is not very thick or dense, which seems to reduce substantially the scope for constructivist arguments.

Mainstream IR scholarship today largely accepts these individualist and materialist conclusions about the states system. It is dominated by *Theory of International Politics,* Kenneth Waltz’s powerful statement of “Neorealism,” which combines a micro-economic approach to the international system (individualism) with the Classical Realist emphasis on power and interest (materialism). Waltz’s book helped generate a partially competing theory, “Neoliberalism,” stated most systematically by Robert Keohane in *After Hegemony,* which accepted much of Neorealism’s individualism but argued that international institutions could **(67) dampen**, if not entirely displace, the effects of power and interest. The fact that Neorealists and Neoliberals agree on so much has contributed to progress in their conversation, but has also substantially narrowed it. At times the debate seems to **(68) come down to** no more than a discussion about the frequency with which states pursue relative rather than absolute gains.

Despite the intuitive **(69) plausibility** and dominance of materialist and individualist approaches to international politics, there is a long and varied tradition of what, from the standpoint of social theory, might be considered constructivist thinking on the subject. A constructivist worldview underlies the classical international theories of Grotius, Kant, and Hegel, and was briefly dominant in IR between the world wars, in the form of what IR scholars now, often **(70) disparagingly**, call “Idealism.”

61. **principles**

A. creeds B. edicts
C. pronouncements D. tenets

62. **reducible**

A. scalable B. dismissible
C. attributable D. suppressible

63. **radical**

A. conformist B. illiberal
C. progressive D. reactionary

64. **coercion**

A. craving B. compulsion
C. constriction D. curtailment

65. **analogue**

A. appendage
B. counterpart
C. opposite
D. replica

66. **intuitive**

A. inactive
B. ineffectual
C. instinctive
D. instructive

67. **dampen**

A. irrigate
B. muffle
C. quench
D. diminish

68. **come down to**

A. add up to
B. build up to
C. end up to
D. sum up to

69. **plausibility**

A. credibility
B. fallaciousness
C. posterity
D. speciousness

70. **disparagingly**

A. incongruously
B. paradoxically
C. reprovingly
D. uncannily

Ⅷ. Fill in each of the following blanks with the most appropriate of the four alternatives as required by the context.

When the Taliban ruled Afghanistan from 1996 to 2001, they were international **(71)** __________. Their hospitality to global jihadists, oppression of women, medieval brutality and cultural vandalism alienated most of the world. Only three governments recognised their self-proclaimed Emirate—those of Pakistan, Saudi Arabia and the United Arab Emirates—and those were quick to turn against them after the September 11th attacks orchestrated by al-Qaeda from Afghanistan.

Twenty years on, the Taliban seem intent on ensuring that their second regime will be on a sounder diplomatic footing. Having largely avoided bloodshed in their takeover of Kabul, they are presenting themselves as a moderate, stabilising force. Unlikely allies in this effort are some supporters of a rival militant group, Islamic State, who have decried the Taliban as an "apostate militia" and even, absurdly, an American **(72)** __________. The West will take some convincing of the Taliban's apostasy, but their humiliation of America has predisposed some big countries in their favour, including China, Iran and Russia. Even these countries, however, are extremely wary of the Taliban. The victors in Kabul are a long way from achieving widespread international acceptance.

As Western governments scrambled to extricate their citizens and some local staff from the country, China and Russia have kept their embassies in Kabul open, under Taliban protection, and indicated they are ready to deal with the new regime. On August 17th the Russian ambassador, Dmitry Zhirnov, was the first foreign official to sit down with Taliban leaders in Kabul. Russia has its own memories of humiliation and failure in Afghanistan. And the chaotic scenes of the past few days at least have the merit, viewed from Moscow, of making the Soviet Union's withdrawal from the country in 1989 look less calamitous **(73)** __________. The Afghan government it left behind survived for three years, rather than collapsing instantly. Its fall (leading to a period of turmoil and, ultimately, to the Taliban's taking power) was **(74)** __________ by the collapse of the Soviet Union in 1991 and the withdrawal of its financial support. The Russian government has long had contacts with the Taliban, despite listing them as a terrorist group, and prepared for their possible triumph. In July Russia played host in Moscow to a Taliban delegation.

In what seems in **(75)** __________ to have been part of a concerted diplomatic push ahead of taking power, that same month a Taliban delegation, led by Mullah Abdul Ghani Baradar, the group's de facto leader, was also in Beijing, where it was accorded a well-publicised meeting with China's foreign minister, Wang Yi. The official Chinese press has relished America's embarrassment, celebrating what one commentator called the end of the "second period of US strategic **(76)** __________" (the first having ended, in this view, with the withdrawal from Saigon in 1975).

Iran, too, has enjoyed the Great Satan's **(77)** __________, and this week has maintained a diplomatic presence both in Kabul and in Herat, close to its border. Its long-standing hostility to the Taliban has moderated in recent years, with its leaders holding meetings with them. This week Iran's new president, Ebrahim Raisi, celebrated America's withdrawal and "military defeat" as "an opportunity to restore life, security and lasting peace to the country".

It is not just America's foes and rivals that have kept their doors open to the Taliban. **(78)** _________ , one has long invited them in, to make themselves at home. Pakistan has for decades balanced its close ties with America with **(79)** _________ support for the Taliban. Osama bin Laden went into hiding in Pakistan after he was forced to flee Taliban protection. And the group's leading council is still known as the "Quetta shura", after the city in the Pakistani province of Balochistan where it was based. This reflects an obsession held by Pakistan's army and security services with the necessity of a friendly Afghanistan to provide "strategic depth" should relations with India deteriorate disastrously. The prime minister, Imran Khan, did not hide his glee at events in Afghanistan, congratulating its people on having "broken the shackles of slavery".

(80) _________ , Turkey's foreign minister, Mevlut Cavusoglu, has said he "views positively" the messages the Taliban have been sending, and that Turkey is in dialogue with all sides. Even India, which has opposed the Taliban as strongly as Pakistan has backed them, is reported to have opened discreet talks with the group.

71. A. revenants B. echelons
C. pariahs D. ripostes

72. A. master B. gang
C. agent D. leader

73. A. by comparison B. on average
C. at bottom D. in particular

74. A. aggrandized B. stymied
C. vitiated D. precipitated

75. A. retrospect B. general
C. order D. consequence

76. A. conundrum B. profligacy
C. predicament D. hedonism

77. A. discomfiture B. chagrin
C. juncture D. subterfuge

78. A. Moreover B. Instead
C. Indeed D. Thus

79. A. tacit B. clandestine
C. contingency D. tepid

80. A. More ruefully B. More demurely
C. Less plaintively D. Less effusively

IX. Write a short essay in English of 200-250 words as your answer to the following question:

Why and how must the working lives of women be improved for the world to recover from the COVID-19 pandemic?

マークシート記入例

東京の本会場で特A級を受験する、国連 太郎さん、受験番号が「東京01-10001」、生年月日が「1980年10月24日」の場合の記入例です。

【受験番号/氏名】
それぞれ受験票の記載通りに記入してください。

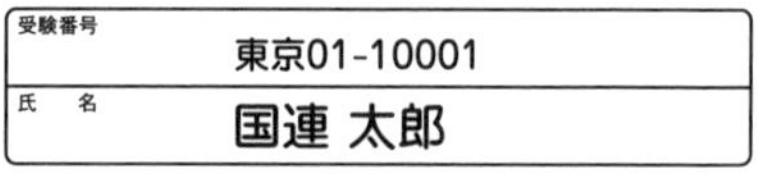

【受験地区】
下段の都道府県部分を塗りつぶしてください。

【会場番号】
都道府県部分に続く2桁の数字を塗りつぶしてください。

【受験番号】
ハイフン（－）以降の5桁の数字を塗りつぶしてください。

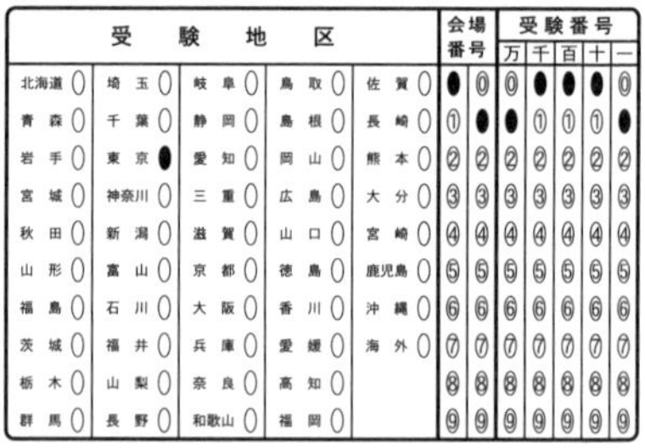

【受験級】
「特A」と記入し、下段の特A級部分を塗りつぶしてください。

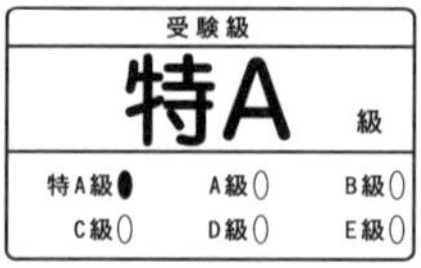

【生年月日】
4桁の西暦・月・日を塗りつぶしてください。
10未満の月・日の十の位は、「0」を塗りつぶしてください。

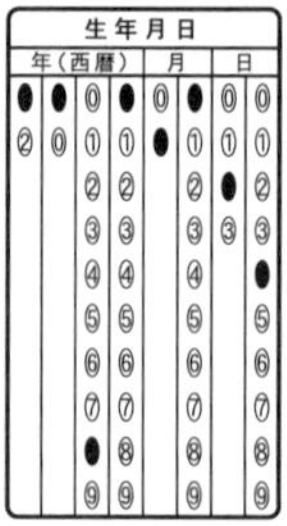

※HB以上の鉛筆を用いてマークをしてください。

※他の地区から会場を変更して受験する場合でも、受験票に記載されている受験地区・会場番号をマークしてください。

2021年
第2回試験

解答・解説

2021年　国連英検特A級第2回試験
解答・解説

＊〔　〕内は訳出上の補足や説明

I 『新 わかりやすい国連の活動と世界』に基づき，
空所を埋めるのに最も適切なものを4つの選択肢の中から1つ選びなさい。

1.　解答：D

訳例　私は今日，私たちの前途に立ちはだかる7つの脅威と試練を中心にお話ししたいと思います。誰の目にも，その危険はあまりにも明らかです。しかし，私たちが本当の意味で国々の連合として機能すれば，それぞれに対する答えを見つけることができます（(『新 わかりやすい国連の活動と世界』p.24。以下，書名略)。

2.　解答：B

訳例　安全保障理事会が新規加盟の勧告を行い，総会の3分の2以上の多数により加盟が決定される（同 p.45)。

3.　解答：C

訳例　経済社会理事会は通常毎年1回，通常会期をニューヨークとジュネーブにおいて交互に開催していたが，現在は，人道支援部門を除き，毎年ニューヨークで開催している（同 p.57)。

4.　解答：A

訳例　専門機関には，①国際電気通信連合（ITU）や万国郵便連合（UPU）のように，19世紀に設立され，国際連盟や国連よりも古い歴史を持つもの〔中略〕がある（同 p.72)。

5.　解答：B

訳例　2013年，ペルーのリマにおいて開催されたUNIDOの総会15会期で職務を新たにしたUNIDOは，加盟国の包摂的で持続可能な産業開発を促進し加速すること〔……中略……〕とした（同 p.85)。

6. 解答：C

訳例 〔そのような中で〕出されたのが，当時の国連事務総長であったブトロス・ブトロス＝ガーリによる1992年の報告書『平和への課題』である。その報告書では，〔……中略……〕紛争のサイクルに合わせて，国連が積極的な役割を演じられることが強調された（同p.106）。

7. 解答：C

訳例 核兵器禁止条約（TPNW）は2017年7月，122カ国の賛成，1カ国の反対，1カ国の棄権で採択された（同p.116）。

8. 解答：B

訳例 2015年，総会では2030年までに達成すべき新たな目標として，持続可能な開発目標（SDGs）を設定した。SDGsにおいては，17の目標，169のターゲット，ターゲットの実現達成度を測るために230の指標が定められた（同p.139）。

9. 解答：B

訳例 大気や水の汚染，土壌浸食，ごみ，騒音，生命破壊剤や他の薬品などによる環境の悪化に対する懸念から，国連は，1972年に国連人間環境会議をストックホルムにおいて開催した（同p.140）。

10. 解答：D

訳例 とりわけ，2004年以降，日本はドイツ，ブラジル，インドとともに安全保障理事会常任理事国の議席の拡大を要請し，国連におけるより強い発言権の獲得に努めている（同p.168）。

II 以下の文章の中に含まれる意味に文脈上最も近いものを4つの選択肢の中から1つ選びなさい。

11. 解答：C

解説 パラグラフ（1）最後のセンテンスに，It’s time for the international community to take stock of the atrocity prevention toolkit, ... and to discuss how ... to respond to the Xinjiang crisis. とある。これを簡潔にまとめているのはCである。

12. 解答：B

解説　パラグラフ（2）全体が2018年以降，人権研究者や人権団体が報告している具体的な事実を列挙していることに着目する。空所（1）は，直前から続くダッシュ内で空所の後にthough researchers allege moreとあるので，ダッシュ内はダッシュ前の1.3 million peopleという数字に関して，対照的な立場が併記されていると推測される。空所（2）は，続く部分が人権侵害の事実を挙げていることから主語が推測できる。

13. 解答：A

解説　挿入文は「しかし，これまでのところ国際社会は，新疆《しんきょう》ウイグル自治区の状況に何ら意味ある形で対処できていない」と逆接の意味を表しているので，先立つセンテンスとしては，「同様の状況に対応するような方策はある」という類の内容を述べたものが予想される。

14. 解答：D

解説　下線部の前を見ると，Aはパラグラフ（4）の下線部This contextの前の行に，BとCは下線部の上3行目と上2行目にそれぞれ対応するが，D.「2者の従来型戦争当事者」についてはパラグラフのどこにも書かれていない。

15. 解答：C

解説　空所の前に「世界第2位の経済大国である中国は，外国からの援助に依存していない。したがって」とあるので，中国が資金的に自立した状態にあることの帰結として適切なものを選ぶ。

16. 解答：B

解説　Aはパラグラフ（6）の頭から4行halt it.までに，Cは同じ4行の次のセンテンスに，Dはパラグラフ頭より7行のIn the summer of 2019に始まりパラグラフ末までの2センテンスに，それぞれ対応するが，Bは上のDに対応する部分の内容と矛盾する。

17. 解答：C

解説　Cの内容がパラグラフ（7）の最後のセンテンス④に対応する。そのほかは，A が独立系調査団の新疆入りについて，B が中国政府の対話希望について，D が現地入りなしで行える事実調査について，それぞれ述べているが，いずれもパラグラフ（7）には言及がない。

18. 解答：B

解説 下線部①の直前に，中国が新疆で行っている強制労働を阻止するため米国が講じている措置が列挙され，①はその一部となっている。それに続く②も強制労働を阻止するための方策を挙げてはいるが，文頭の The second bill が唐突で，しかも the first bill に当たると思われる内容がそれまでの部分に見当たらない。③は①が挙げる複数の措置を These efforts で受けて「効果を高めるため強化や拡大が可能」としており，④は③の「強化や拡大」のために今後いくつかの取り組みが行われると述べているので，③と④は①から自然な論理でつながると見てよい。

19. 解答：A

解説 パラグラフ (4) 末より3行以降に次のように述べられている：Moreover, China has resisted diplomatic pressure to change these policies, framing their handling of the Uyghur population in Xinjiang as a matter of internal sovereignty, blocking diplomatic interference from outside. A はこれに対応する。B に言われるテロリズムの関連では，問題文には米国がウイグル関連組織に対するテロ組織指定を解除したことだけが述べられる一方，過激主義については言及がない。C が述べる中国の国民全体に対する統制は問題文のテーマから外れている。D に見える genocide の語は問題文中に使われていない。

20. 解答：A

解説 パラグラフ構成を概観すると，パラグラフ（1）「導入と論旨提示」，パラグラフ（2）「新疆危機について詳しく紹介」，パラグラフ（3）～（6）「ツールキットが失敗に終わった事例」(3＝早期警告メカニズム，4＝外交介入，5＝資金メカニズム，6＝国連決議)，パラグラフ（7）「結論と今後の方向性」。したがってトピック別に分類すると A になる。

訳例 (1) 中国北西部新疆ウイグル自治区における大規模な人権侵害を示す証拠文

書により，中国政府がウイグル人や他のトルコ系イスラム民族に対して大規模な残虐行為を行っていることが明らかになった。しかし，残虐行為を防ぐために国際社会と米国が通常展開している戦略は，明白な証拠を前にしても問題を解決しえないでいる。米国や米国と考えを同じくする国々は，現在進行中の残虐行為を終わらせ，ウイグル人を守るために行動する義務がある。〔これまで〕多くの重要な措置が実施されてきたが，いずれも中国政府にこれと言った影響は及ぼしていない。国際社会は，残虐行為防止用「ツールキット」を見直し，なぜそれがウイグル人に対して無効だったのかを検討し，新疆の危機に対応する「更新」や「アダプテーション」の上でこうした失敗がどう生かせるのかを議論する時期に来ているのである。

(2)　2018 年以降，ウイグル人同化運動の激化を示す確固たる証拠が人権の研究者らによって報告されてきた。この運動は，大量拘留・強制労働プログラム，高度な集団監視システム，文化的・宗教的行為の制限，人口抑制策など，いくつかの重要な柱から成る〔とされる〕。新疆ウイグル自治区の政治的「再教育」キャンプに恣意的に拘留され，政治的洗脳，強制労働，家族からの引き離し，場合によっては拷問を受けた人は 130 万人以上にのぼる（中国側が認めた数字。研究者はもっと多いと主張）。こうした人々は解放されても厳しい監視体制の下に置かれる。人権団体によれば，監視はきわめて厳重で，新疆は「野外刑務所」となってしまっているという。また，ウイグル人の出生率を下げるために，強制的な不妊手術や強制避妊が行われていることや，イスラム教の宗教行為に対する厳しい規制や，モスクや文化遺産を破壊する運動が行われていることも，人権団体によって報告されている。

(3)　国際社会は，紛争シナリオに対応する長年の実践から進化してきた，残虐行為のリスクを緩和するための二国間および多国間の介入策ツールキットを有している (A)〔が，これまでのところ国際社会は新疆ウイグル自治区の状況に何ら意味ある形で対処できていない。〕残虐行為のリスクが高まった場合に通知する目的では，一般に公式・非公式の早期警告メカニズムが用いられるが，新疆には〔そうしたものは〕強固な形では存在しない。市民社会と外交官らに対して課せられる安全保障上および運用上の制約から，新疆ウイグル自治区からは情報の流れが妨げられてきた。(B) 国外の離散ウイグル人や研究者らは，このギャップを埋めるべく，個々のウイグル人犠牲者に関する情報提供や，衛星データ活用による収容所の状況把握を行ってきた。また，リークされた政府文書によって，中国政府が抑圧的な政策を進める明確な意図〔を持っていること〕が暴露された。(C) にもかかわらず，情報の流れが遅いために，外交官が残虐行為の発生前に関与する能力が抑えられてしまった。

(4)　世界的に見れば，最近の残虐行為は武力紛争や深刻な政情不安の状況がある中で発生しており，外交介入は行動を抑止したり，紛争当事者の一方に支持や正当性を与えたりするために利用されることがある。(D) しかし新疆ウイグル自治区では，紛争のシナリオが顕著に異なっている。すなわち，従来の戦争当事者間ではなく，国家と民間人の対立であり，政治状況も中国政府の支配の下で安定が続いている。民間人と警察との軽微で散発的な衝突は発生してきているが，それがエスカレートする可能性は，中国政府の厳格な治安体制によって今のところ抑えられている。このような状況下では，従来に近い形の暴力紛争の中ではどちらかといえば容易に行えるタイプの外交介入の機会が狭められてしまう。さらに中国は，新疆ウイグル自治区におけるウイグル人の処遇を国内の主権問題であるとして，こうした政策の変更を求める外交圧力に抵抗し，外部からの外交介入を阻止してきた。

(5)　残虐行為防止ツールキットをめぐっては，その資金メカニズムについても，新疆ウイグル自治区における残虐行為の抑止や停止には不十分であることが判明している。世界第2位の経済大国である中国は，外国からの援助に依存していないため，この資金メカニズムによって実施しうる「アメとムチ」的な措置〔を受けても〕行動を変える可能性は低い。現在も続く残虐行為に最も責任のある党幹部は中国国外にほとんど資産を持たないから，個人に対する制裁の効果は限られたものとなる。より包括的な，あるいは多国間の制裁や中国製品の輸入制限は打撃となるだろうが，それには中国の政治・経済力に対抗しうる連合体を構築する政治課題が伴う。

(6)　国連では，中国が担う役割から，残虐行為を停止させるための協調行動が，不可能ではないにせよ，困難となっている。〔すなわち〕中国政府は安全保障理事会の常任理事国であるため，暴力の終結を求める決議案や，暴力をやめさせるために国連の具体的な行動を求める決議案に対して拒否権を行使できるのである。さらに中国は，自国を支持する国々のグループをすでに形成しているため，総会決議〔案が提出されても〕これらの国々が反対する可能性が高い。これまで国連が新疆における残虐行為に直接対処する状況に最も近かったのは，人権理事会における書簡の応酬においてであった。2019年夏，米国を含む22カ国のグループが，大量拘束政策の停止を中国に求める書簡を人権理事会に提出したが，その数日後には，中国の人権政策を擁護する37カ国が署名した書簡が提出された〔という出来事である〕。この事態は今年〔2020年〕の10月にも再び起きた。

(7)　既存の残虐行為防止ツールキットは，新疆ウイグル自治区の現在の状況とは似ても似つかない紛争状況に基づいて開発されたものであり，そのことをそろそろ認識すべき時である。考えを同じくする国際的行為主体は，このツールキットに対して評価をやり直し，現在進行中の残虐行為の終結とウイグル人保護のために必要な変更を検討すべきである。米国政府はこの対話をリードする重要な役割を果たすべきであり，次期政権にはその大きなチャンスがある。現政権はすでに，中国による新疆ウイグル自治区での強制労働を抑止し，中国要人や政府機関に制裁を科すなど，米国政府内でウイグル危機への関心を高めるための決定的な措置を講じている。①これまで行われたその他の措置としては，新疆ウイグル自治区の政府系生産者からの綿花の輸入禁止，強制労働で作られたと考えられる商品の押収，ウイグル関連団体の外国テロ組織リストからの削除などが挙げられる。②〔削除対象〕第２号議案では，新疆ウイグル自治区からの出荷された商品や新疆ウイグル自治区出身の労働者を使用した商品が強制労働で作られたものでないことを証明する責任を輸入業者に負わせるものであった。③これらの取り組みは，強化・拡大を図ることで効果を高めることができる。④実際，暴力停止に向けた米国によるいくつかの有望な取り組みが保留となっているが，これらは残虐行為防止ツールキットの変更検討を下支えするものとなるかもしれない。

III

文法的，語法的にふさわしくないものを下線の中から１つ選びなさい。

21. 解答：A

解説 five dozen of → five dozen。現在では five dozens of countries よりも five dozen countries のように形容詞として用いるのが普通。

訳例　米国務省が日曜日に発表した共同声明によると，〔アフガニスタンからの〕退去を希望する外国人とアフガニスタン人について，60 以上の国が「すべての当事者」に対し，出発時の安全を確保するよう求めている。声明は，「退去を希望するアフガニスタン人と各国市民は，退去を認められなければならない」としている。

22. 解答：D

解説 has been → has。spearhead は他動詞で lead (a movement) の意。

訳例　中国の最大手技術系企業各社は火曜日，時価総額〔の合計〕が 500 億ドル以上も下落する〔事態となった〕。大手インターネット企業の反競争的行為をいちだんと抑制すべく，政府が抜本的な新ルールを提案したため。同業界を取り締まるこの新たな措置は，大手技術系企業に対する政府の反トラストキャンペーンの先頭に立つ国家市場監督管理総局が実施するもの。

23. 解答：C

解説 other six → another six または six other, six more。additional の意味では複数名詞に対して another を上のように使える。

訳例 ニュージーランドで6カ月ぶりに発生したコロナウィルスの市中感染はデルタ株によるもので，ゲノム解析の結果，隣国オーストラリアで起きている感染拡大との関連が明らかになった。ニュージーランド当局は水曜日，いずれも上の感染者に関連する6例の陽性を確認したと発表した。この新たな陽性者の1人はオークランドの病院に勤務していた〔という〕。

24. 解答：C

解説 died → dead。(C) の前の left に注目して leave＋O＋C の文型を見抜く。

訳例 ハイチ南西部を土曜朝に襲ったマグニチュード 7.2 の地震で，子供 54 万人を含む約 120 万人が被害を受けた。ユニセフが発表した。このうち死者は少なくとも 1,941 人，負傷者は 6,900 人以上となっており，その数は数日後にはさらに増えるものとみられる。

25. 解答：D

解説 at cost → at a cost。come at a cost で「代償が伴う」の意の成句的表現。

訳例 イギリスがコロナウィルス感染対策をほぼ全面解除してから 1 カ月。解除は，経営難に苦しむ国内企業部門の大半からは歓迎される一方，科学者数千人から「危険で倫理に反する実験」として批判された。1 カ月を経過した今，ワクチン接種には効果があるものの，経済再開には代償が伴うことが明らかとなった。

26. 解答：B

解説 having allegedly → allegedly having。副詞は通常，動詞と目的語の間に置くことはない。

訳例 オーストラリア国立美術館は木曜日，〔所蔵する〕「文化的に重要な」美術品十数点について，略奪や密売のネットワークとの関連が指摘されていることを理由に，インドに返還すると発表した。このうち 13 点は，アジア全域から何千点もの古美術品を密輸した罪で起訴され，信用を失墜したニューヨークの美術商から直接購入されたものだった。

27. 解答：A

解説 involving → being involved または involvement。involve を使って「～に関与する」の意味を表すには受け身の形にすることが必要。

訳例　カンボジアのクメールルージュ政権指導者で，存命する最後の 1 人が木曜日，最終盤を迎えた国際法廷に出廷し，大量虐殺への関与と人道に対する罪に対する責任を否定した。クメールルージュ時代に大統領を務めたキュー・サムファン〔被告〕(90) が 2018 年の有罪判決に対する控訴審で述べたもの。

28. 解答：A

解説 inaugurated for → inaugurated as。「就任する」の意味の be inaugurated と共起する前置詞を正確に押さえること。

訳例　イスラム共和国，イランで木曜日，エブラヒム・ライシ氏が次期大統領に就任した。国内・対外政策に大きな転換をもたらす可能性がある，〔保守〕強硬派の新たな時代が到来した。ハッサン・ロウハニ氏率いる 8 年間の穏健な政権に続いて，イランは今，超保守的な司法府長官〔を務めた〕ライシを〔指導者に〕選んだ。同氏の思想は，同国の有力な聖職者の考え方と完全に一致している。

29. 解答：C

解説 have been buoyed → has been buoyed。この箇所を含むセンテンスの主語は The economy である。

訳例　ザンビアのハカインデ・ヒチレマ次期大統領は，来週火曜日の就任時から大変な仕事を抱えることになるだろう。ヒチレマ氏 (59) は財界の実力者であるが，いまやザンビアの運勢を好転させる課題を引き受けることとなった。コロナ禍に伴う過酷な景気後退に見舞われた経済は，電気自動車のブームもあって銅価格が好転し，現在は 10 年来の高値圏にあることから，ほんのわずかだが浮揚している。

30. 解答：B

解説 in what for → in what。what が導く関係節の構造はセンテンス Her employer described something as a ... の something を前に繰り出して what に代えたもの。

訳例　モスクワで活動する BBC の記者が土曜日，自らがロシアから追放されることになり，ショックを受けていると語った。記者の雇用主〔BBC〕はこの事態を「メディアの自由に対する直接的な攻撃」としている。〔記者は〕BBC のモスクワ特派員。今回の追放について，「ロシアとイギリスの関係，そしてより広くは，ロシアと欧米諸国との関係の大幅な悪化」に伴うものとしている。

IV

下線を引いた動詞（原形）の最も適切な変化形（他動詞、自動詞、分詞など）を示している１語動詞または語句を４つの選択肢の中から１つ選びなさい。

31. 解答：D

解説 下線部前の aimed at に続く部分は，encouraging が導く動名詞句。その中で「encourage＋O＋to 不定詞」の文型が使われている。

32. 解答：B

解説 前パラグラフで国連環境計画・金融イニシアチブ発足当時の状況が説明されており，それを受けてパラグラフ頭からは金融に対する考え方が当時から変化したことが述べられている。これに着目すると，下線部前の it が形式主語で，下線部後の that 節の内容を指す文型となっていることが分かる。

33. 解答：A

解説 下線部前に助動詞 can があるので，下線部動詞は原形とする。

34. 解答：C

解説 下線部前の that が主語。

35. 解答：A

解説 下線部前の you が主語。

36. 解答：B

解説 下線部前の A recent study が主語，その後ろに that 節が続くので動詞は定動詞でなければならない。

37. 解答：B

解説 下線部前の those を後置修飾する形にする。前後関係から修飾部は「調査された」の意であることが分かる。

38. 解答：D

解説 下線部前に the government is があり，後に動詞目的語の a national master plan があるので，能動態の進行形とするのが適切。

39. 解答：C

解説 下線部前に by があるので，下線部動詞以下は名詞句となる。

40. 解答：B

解説 下線部前に have already とあるので，文意も合わせて考え，下線部動詞までで現在完了形を構成していることを見抜く。

訳例　タイの民間部門は，実質カーボンゼロ経済への移行に重要な役割を担っている。タイ政府の年金基金の責任者によれば，「社会的責任と持続可能な利益」は両立しうるという。国連とタイ経済界の最大手企業は，タイの実質カーボンゼロ経済への移行を加速させるべく，ともに手を携えて同国の銀行および金融機関の取り組みを支援している。

金融・銀行部門が企業への投資や資金提供についての判断方法を通じて経済に多大な影響を与えうるという認識がますます高まっており，タイでは国連が政府を支援して，持続可能な金融の重要性に対する認識を高めようとしている。

タイ金融界の指導者らに持続可能なビジネスの採用を奨励することを目的とした国連後援のイベントを前に，国連環境計画のエリック・アッシャー金融イニシアチブ代表が，タイ政府年金基金のスリカンヤ・ヤティプ事務局長，カシコン銀行のカティヤ・インダラヴィジャヤ CEO の２人と UN News で会談した。

エリック・アッシャー：国連環境計画金融イニシアチブは 1992 年，持続可能な金融を基盤に世界の金融部門と組む最初期のパートナーシップとしてスタートしたが，当時それはニッチなテーマだったと言える。何しろ金融機関は樹木の伐採などしないのだし，環境とは何の関わりもない〔と考えられていた〕。

〔だが〕それ以来，融資が実際に影響を与えることが認識されるようになってきた。銀行は，樹木を伐採している顧客に融資を行うかどうかを選べる。だから，銀行の行動や方針は環境に大きな影響を与えることになるわけだ。おふたりの属する組織にとって，持続可能な金融が重要なテーマとなる理由は？

スリカンヤ・ヤティプ：それは，我々の投資判断には，変革をもたらす効果があると考えるから。持続可能なしかたで世界を再構築できれば，環境や社会を保護することはもはや不要になる。

我々は年金基金という機関投資家として，何をどこに投資するかを決めてよい特権を与えられているので，企業としての行動を社会の幅広い目的に合致させることや，長期的な投資利益を求めるよう心がけている。それは我々からすれば，「よい行いによってよい結果を出す」ということになる。社会的責任と持続可能な利益は両立可能だ。

また，現状を考慮して言えば，コロナ禍のために我々みなが受けている極度のプレッシャーの下では，自分の利益を守りたいなら，他の人たちを守らなければならない。

カティヤ・インダラヴィジャヤ：顧客と従業員，納入業者，地域社会など，すべてのステークホルダーを顧慮する必要があるが，時としてそれは，短期的な痛みと長期的な利益の兼ね合いの問題になる。

銀行業界では，2種類のライセンスが求められる。1つは銀行免許で，営業を許可するもの。2つ目は，地域社会から得るべき社会的なライセンス。地域社会が存続できなければ，銀行も存続できないから。

最近の調査によると，環境に配慮していない製品を支持したくないという人が調査対象者の74%を占めている。これは，社会が持続可能な開発の方向へ進んでいることを示している。置いていかれたくなければ，この流れを無視することはできない。

エリック・アッシャー：持続可能な開発に関しては現在，2つの陣営がある。一方の陣営は，危機からの回復を優先し，持続可能性は保留にすべきと言い，他方は，いまこそ持続可能な投資を行い，気候危機に対処して，実質カーボンゼロ経済へ移行するチャンスだと言っている。おふたりのご意見は？

スリカンヤ・ヤティブ：タイでは現在，政府がネットゼロを目標に国家基本計画の策定を進めており，私が知るかぎり，COP26でこの基本計画を発表するはずだ。私は計画の草案をいくつか見たが，多くの企業に影響を及ぼすだろう。提案されている変革としては，より低炭素型の発電への移行，電気自動車産業に対する支援，循環型経済［企業，社会，環境のためになるよう考えられた体系的な経済発展手法アプローチを指す。循環型経済はその設計からして再生可能であり，成長ということを有限な資源を消費することから段階的に切り離すことを目指すもの］などがある。

カティヤ・インダラヴィジャヤ：ネットゼロへの移行は非常に重要で，今後30年以内の目標達成を約束する国や組織も出てきた。つまり，大事だということはみな知っているが，やり遂げるには時間と多くの労力を要するということだ。

カシコン銀行としては，顧客がより持続可能な方法でビジネスを行えるように支援することで，ネットゼロかつ持続可能な成長に参画する用意がある。当行には，それを実現するための方針があり，意思がある。当行ではすでに，目標の一部を達成したが，業界として取り組みを加速し，より多くの仕事をこなす必要がある。責任ある融資は，業務の一部でなくてはならないし，金融機関はより緊密に連携する必要がある。また，企業，規制当局，消費者が持続可能性の問題に関与していくことが必要だ。

スリカンヤ・ヤティプ：私も同じ考えだ。我々は企業市民として，社会に対して責任を負っている。共同で取り組めば大きな声になる。1人では微力でも，みなで力を合わせれば大きな力になるし，可能性は無限だ。

V

以下の文章の中に含まれる語句の意味として文脈上最も近いものを4つの選択肢の中から1つ選びなさい。

41. 解答：C

解説 下線部 strife は多くの英英辞典でも C. bitter disagreement と同様の説明がなされている。

42. 解答：B

解説 下線部に続く that 節は「身を捧げようという人間の衝動を現実には自国の国境でとどまらせがちにするものは」の意。これは B.「国際安全保障に対する潜在的脅威」となる。

43. 解答：B

解説 下線部 temper は act as a neutralizing force to の意。B. counterbalance は neutralize by having an opposite effect の意。

44. 解答：A

解説 下線部の前に patriotism has many other enemies to contend with. とあって，そうした enemies の例として下線部で「世界市民主義」を挙げている文脈を把握すれば，下線部の役割は A.「ナショナリズムの代替物の例を示す」ことだと言える。

45. 解答：D

解説 下線部 plutocrats ＜ plutocrat は someone who becomes powerful because of their wealth の意。これに近いのは D. magnates ＜ magnate

= a wealthy person who is successful in business である。

46. 解答：A

解説 下線部 dominion は control over a country の意。

47. 解答：D

解説 下線部 wrought は動詞 work の過去・過去分詞の古い形。この場合 work は他動詞で，produce as a result の意。これに近い bring about を下線部に合わせて過去分詞形とする。

48. 解答：B

解説 prudence は cautiousness に近い意味であるが，この場合 of highwaymen（追い剝ぎの）という限定が付くので shrewdness in handling matters のようなニュアンスとなる。よって，B. nefarious = morally bad な行動を示唆するものと考えられる。

49. 解答：C

解説 下線部は「もしこれらの快楽がもはや追求されなくなるか，あるいはもはや得ることが不可能になるとすれば，侵略に対して安全を確保する問題は難しいものではなくなるだろう」の意。国家の非合理はここで言われる快楽追及が原因であるから，下線部前半で言われる仮定が実現すればC. のように「非合理に関する議論は終結する」。

50. 解答：A

解説 下線部 amicably は in a peaceful manner の意。これと同義は A. genially = in a pleasant and friendly manner.

訳例　宗教としての愛国主義は，普遍性を欠くため不十分なものである。愛国主義が目指す善は，自国にとってだけの善であり，全人類のものではない。愛国主義がイギリス人に抱かせる欲望は，ドイツ人に抱かせる欲望とは異なる。愛国者に満ちた世界は，争いに満ちた世界となるかもしれない。国というものは，自国の愛国主義を強く信じれば信じるほど，他国が被る損害には異常なほど無関心になるものである。人間がひとたび自分自身の善をより大きな全体の善に従属させることを学んだなら，人類にまで広げていかない正当な理由などあるはずがない。人間の自己犠牲への衝動を現実には自国の国境でとどまらせがちにするものは，〔そこに〕混入した国民としての誇りである。人間はどうしても他国より自国に対して大きな愛を抱くものであり，それゆえ，それを避けたいと願うべき理由はないのである。それは，個人の男女すべてを等しく愛したいと願うべき理由がないのと同様である。しかし，適正な宗教であるなら，我々が正義愛によって愛情の不平等を和らげ，また，人類共通のニーズを実現することで我々の目的を普遍のものとするように導いてくれるだろう。

実際には，愛国心には他にも競合する多くの敵がいる。教育や旅行を通じて外国についてより多くの知識を得るにつれて，世界市民主義が伸張せざるをえないし，社会主義，サンディカリズム，反資本主義運動は一般に愛国主義に反対する傾向がある。というのは，この三者は，現在の国家が主に富裕層の特権を守ることに関心を持つことや，国家間の紛争は多くが少数の富豪の経済的利害がもとで発生するということを人に気づかせるものだから。この種の反対はおそらく一時的なものであり，労働者が権力獲得を目指す闘争における偶発事にすぎない。オーストラリアは労働者が自らの勝利を盤石なものと自負している国ではあるが，愛国主義と軍国主義に満ちている。これは，特権的地位がもたらす便益の分け前に外国人労働者が与《あずか》ることを阻止しようという決意に基づくものである。イギリスが仮に社会主義国となった場合，同様のナショナリズムを生み出す可能性は少なくない。しかし，そうしたナショナリズムは純粋に防衛的なものとなる可能性が高い。外国による侵略の計画は，その方針を採用した国の人命と富に大きな損失をもたらすことから，そのような計画に手を染める者は，私有財産と資本主義国家の制度から得られる力を通じて支配本能が研ぎ澄まされた者以外にはほとんどいないだろう。

国家の過剰な力が現代世界にもたらした悪はきわめて大きく，しかもほとんど認識されていない。国家がもたらす最大の害悪は，戦争における効率化の促進である。すべての国家がその力を増大させるならば，力の均衡に変化は生じず，前よりも勝算が高まる国はどこにもないことになる。そして，攻撃手段が存在する場合，その本来の目的が防御であったとしても，使いたいという誘惑に負けてしまうことが早晩明らかになるだろう。このようにして，国境内部の安全保障を強めた当の措置が，他の国においては不安を高めるのである。国内では暴力を抑制し，対外的には暴力を助長することが国家の本質なのである。国家は，人類と人類に対する我々の義務とについて，まったく人為的な区分を行う。すなわち，ある集団に対しては法によって拘束されるが，他の集団に対して拘束されるのは，ただ追い剝ぎの用心深さのためでしかない。

国家が悪とされるのは，その排除〔の論理〕と次の事実による。その事実とは，国家というものは侵略戦争を仕掛けるときは決まって，殺人と強盗を目的とする人間集団となるということである。現在の体制は非合理である。なぜなら，内と外の無政府状態は必然的に，両方とも正しいか，両方間違っているかのいずれかであるはずだから。この体制が支持されているのは，他国がそれを採用する限り，それが安全への唯一の道であると考えられるからであり，また，善良な共同体の中では得られない勝利の喜びを保証してくれるからである。もしこうした快楽がもはや追求されなくなるか，あるいはもはや得ることが不可能になるとすれば，侵略に対して安全を確保する問題は難しいものではなくなるだろう。

このような状況を改善するための第一歩は，一般市民の側が外交問題に真の関心〔を持つこと〕，そして，国家の威信を理由に一般市民のその他の利益が毀損《きそん》されるのを許してはならないと主張することである。一般市民は戦時には奮起して，誇りのためにすべてを犠牲にすることを厭《いと》わないが，平時には，外交問題も私事と同じく，武力や武力行使の脅しを用いる残忍なやり方によってではなく，原則に従って友好的に解決されるべきであると積極的に理解する傾向を，権力者よりも強く持つだろう。

VI

以下の文章に最も適切に当てはまる単語のペアを
４つの選択肢の中から１つ選びなさい。

51. 解答：C

解説 第１空所は launch/introduce a product を意味する unveil ＞ C. unveiled，あるいは proclaim loudly の意の trumpet ＞ B. trumpeted がよい。第２空所は B. convert，C. revolutionize とも「変える」の意味を基本とするが，C.「革命をもたらす」の方がよい。convert は change something so that it can be used for a different purpose（変換，転換）の意味。

訳例　ハンソン・ロボティクス社（本社・香港）は2016年，ソフィア〔を発表して〕世界を席捲《せっけん》した。ソフィアがその後サウジアラビアの市民権を授けられたことはよく知られている。そして同社はこのほど，最新の発明を発表した。グレース〔と名づけられた〕人型ロボット。同社では医療の革命をもたらすものと期待している。

52. 解答：D

解説 第１空所はB，C，Dが「期間」の意味で候補となる（A. stint は a persons fixed period of work の意で不適）。第２空所は「ある種の，ちょっとした」の意味を持つ成句，D. of sorts を選ぶ。

訳例　バージニア州の病院で自らが新型コロナウィルスと闘う様子を懸命に発信する米国人男性。男性はワクチン接種を受けなかったことを深く後悔している。峠は越えたと思っているが，一時は恐怖におびえ，自分が死んだ場合に備えて準備をしなければと考えていた〔という〕。数人の子供を持つ父親として，病室でビデオ日記のようなものを撮影し，恐ろしいジェットコースターのように衰弱と容体改善〔を交互に繰り返す闘病の様子〕を伝えてきた。

53. 解答：B

解説 第1空所はA，B，Dが候補となる。第2空所は，直前のwhichがlong queuesを指すので，「示す」の意味を持つB. point toが適切。

訳例 ザンビアでは木曜日，〔大統領選挙の〕投票が始まった。エドガー・ルング大統領と最大野党のライバルであるハカインデ・ヒチレマとの一騎打ち。接戦となっており，結果は予断を許さない。〔選挙はザンビアの〕負債が膨らみ，経済が停滞する中〔で行われた〕。投票は午前6時に始まったが，首都ルサカの投票所には長蛇の列ができ，投票率の高さが伺える。

54. 解答：A

解説 第2空所はhave some a lucky opportunityを意味する決まった言い方としてcatch a breakが最適。第1空所pledge > A. pledgedはformally promise to give somethingの意で文脈に合う。ほかは，make a formal and serious promise to do somethingを意味するvow > C. vowedも可能。

訳例 大坂なおみ選手が，来週のテニス大会での賞金を父親の出身地であるカリブ海のハイチで〔行われている〕地震の救援活動に寄付することを約束した。この貧しい国を土曜日に襲った地震を受けて発表した。大坂選手はツイッターで，「ハイチで起きているあの惨状を見ると本当に心が痛みますし，本当に勘弁してくださいという気持ちです」と述べた。

55. 解答：B

解説 第2空所は新型コロナウィルスのデルタ株の感染力の高さを述べた箇所と推測されるので，B.「感染しやすい」が選べる。第1空所はB，C，Dが紛らわしいが，D. lethalities = lethality rate（大まかにいえば，感染者当たりの死者数」）がcase fatality rateと同義であり，B. fatalitiesも同様の意味で使われていると考えられる。これに対してC. mortalities = mortality rateは感染症による単位人口当たりの死者数を表す。

訳例 世界保健機関は，アフリカでのコロナウィルスによる死者が過去1カ月で急増したことを明らかにした。死者の増加率は過去4週間以内で80%となっている。コロナ禍による死者数の悪化と感染率の高さは，コロナウィルス原種よりも死亡率が高いとされる，感染力の強いデルタ変異株が原因となっている。

56. 解答：D

解説　第1空所はD. batter = hit repeatedly with hard blowsが適切。第2空所もD. issuedなら，空所の前から ... evacuation warning was issuedとなり，文意に合う。

訳例　日本の南西部が豪雨に見舞われ，洪水や土砂崩れの恐れがあるため，住民500万人以上に緊急安全確保*や避難指示*が発表された。公共放送NHKによると，佐賀，長崎，福岡，広島各県で100万人以上を対象に，最高段階の避難情報となるレベル5の「緊急安全確保*」が土曜日に発表された。

＊訳注：日本の避難情報の正式呼称を採用した。

57. 解答：A

解説　第1空所はbitterly upsetを意味するAとDが残る。第2空所は，a hollow area in a surface made by a blowを意味するdent > A. dentsが適切。

訳例　アイルランド〔2020年パラリンピック〕代表チームのパトリック・フラナガン選手が「気持ちがめげた」と発言。大会に出場するため東京へ移動の途中，車椅子が壊れていることが分かった〔という〕。ツイッターには，「車輪は回らないほど破損しているし，その他にも多くのへこみや擦り傷がある」と投稿している。

58. 解答：B

解説　第1空所はdeath knellが決まった言い方であることからBが選べる。第2空所もB. lifeboatはこの場合「救済策」の意味で比喩的に使われており，文脈に合う。

訳例　レバノン中央銀行が水曜夜に行った発表は，低迷するレバノン経済に弔いの鐘を鳴らすものと思われた。レバノンで増加する多数の貧困にあえぐ人々の救命ボートと長年考えられてきた燃料補助金が，中止となったのだ。

59. 解答：D

解説　第1空所はfile a lawsuit against ... という頻用される表現の一部だから

Dが選べる。第2空所もD. complaintはa formal statement initiating a lawsuit（訴状）で文意に合う。

訳例　米国から国境を越えてメキシコ国内の犯罪者の手に渡る銃器をめぐり，メキシコは水曜日，銃器メーカー11社を相手取り提訴した。「この洪水は，自然現象でもなければ，銃ビジネスや米国の銃規制法の必然的な結果でもない。被告〔企業各社〕の意図的な行動と商慣行がもたらす予見可能な結果である」と訴状には記されている。

60.　解答：C

解説　第1空所は（組織について）break upを意味するdisband ＞ C. disbandingが適切。第2空所もC. wakeであれば，前後がin the wake of (= following someone or something, especially as a result)のようにつながり文意整合する。

訳例　香港で最大級となる抗議行動を数回にわたって主催した民主派団体，民間人権陣線（CHRF）が日曜日，解散を発表した。国家安全保障に関する包括的な法律〔国家安全維持法〕の施行に伴う一連の市民団体解散〔の流れに加わる〕新たなケースとなった。

VII

下線部の単語や句の意味を最もよく表しているものを
4つの選択肢の中から1つ選びなさい。

61.　解答：D

解説　下線部「原則」の意味に最も近いのは，D. tenets ＜ tenet = a principle, especially main one of a religion or philosophyである。

62.　解答：C

解説　下線部reducible ＜ reduceは，この場合describe something in terms of more fundamental elements，またはconsider a complex system as the sum of its partsの意。よって，C. attributable = regard as arising from a particular cause or sourceが最も近い。

63.　解答：C

解説　下線部は「急進的な」の意味。よって最も近いのはC. progressive = supporting new or modern ideas, e.g. in politics（革新的な）。

64. 解答：B

解説 下線部はthe use of force or threats to make someone do somethingを意味する。よってB. compulsion = the act or state of forcing someone to do somethingが同義。

65. 解答：B

解説 下線部はsomething seen as comparable to ...の意。よって最も近いのはB. counterpart = something that corresponds to or has the same function as something else in a different place or situationである。

66. 解答：C

解説 下線部は「直観的」の意。よってC. instinctive = done without conscious thoughtが最も近い。

67. 解答：D

解説 下線部はmake less intenseの意。最も近いD. diminish = make lessを選ぶ。

68. 解答：A

解説 下線部はamount in essence toの意。同義の表現としてはA. add up to = constitute, amount toが最適。

69. 解答：A

解説 下線部plausibility < plausibleはseeming likely to be trueの意。したがって最も近いのはA. credibility < credible = able to be believed。D. speciousness < speciousも似ているが，「もっともらしいが，実は間違い」というニュアンス。

70. 解答：C

解説 下線部disparagingly < disparagingはcriticizing something as being of little worthの意。よって最も適切なのはC. reprovingly < reproving = expressing disapprovalとなる。

訳例　近年の学術研究においては，国際政治が「社会的に構成されたもの」として記述されているのを目にすることが普通になってきた。批判理論，ポストモダニズム，フェミニズム理論，歴史的制度主義，社会学的制度主義，象徴的相互作用論，構造化理論など，さまざまな社会理論に依拠しながら，国際政治学者は「構成主義」の次の２つの基本原則をますます受け入れるようになった。(1) 人間の結合の構造を決定づけるものは，物質的な力よりも，共有された思想が主であること。(2) 目的を持った行為主体のアイデンティティーと利害は，自然から与えられるよりも，むしろこうした共有された思想によって形作られること。第一のものは，社会生活に対する「観念論的」なアプローチであり，思想の共有を強調する点において「社会的」である。同じ意味において，〔これと〕対立する「唯物論的」な考え方が生物学や技術，あるいは環境を強調するのは社会的ではない。第二のものは，社会構造の創発力を強調するゆえに「全体論的」あるいは「構造論的」アプローチであり，社会構造が個人に還元されるとする「個人主義的」見解と対立する。したがって，構成主義は，一種の「構造的観念論」であるとみることができる。

上記のまとめが示すように，構成主義には多くの形態がある。本書では，そのうちの１つを主張し，それを用いて国際システムの理論化を図りたいと考える。私が主張する構成主義の形態は，特に構造論的社会学と象徴的相互作用論的社会学に依拠する穏健なものである。そのため，唯物論的・個人主義的な見方に重要な点があることを認め，社会調査に対する科学的アプローチを承認する。このような理由から，より急進的な構成主義者からは踏み込み不十分として拒否されるかもしれないが，事実，あっさりした構成主義である。けれども，今日主流の国際関係（IR）研究者の多くが，時として社会的構成の話をすべて「ポストモダニズム」として退けるのに比べれば，はるかに進んでいる。この両極端の間に，哲学的な原則に基づく中道を見いだしたいと私は考える。そして，このことが国際政治を考える上で変化をもたらすことを示したい。

国際システムは社会的な面と構成的な面のいずれにおいても，構成主義にとって難しいテーマである。社会面では，国内政治は大半が規範と法によって統治される一方，国際政治は利己主義と強制力によって支配されているように見える。国際法や国際的な制度は存在するが，この上部構造が権力と利害の物質的基盤に対抗する能力は限られているように思われる。このことは，国際システムがあまり「社会的」な場所ではないことを示唆しており，その領域における唯物論への直観的な支持を与えている。構成の面では，個人に関しては，その社会への依存〔という事実〕から，アイデンティティーが社会によって構成されるとの主張には比較的議論の余地がない。一方，国際政治の主要な行為主体である国家は，自らが組み込まれている社会システムに対してはるかに自律的である。国家の外交政策は，国際システム（社会）よりもむしろ個人の人格に類比される国内政治によって決定されることが多い。アルバニアやミャンマーのように，「自閉症」と呼ばれるほど他国との交流が少ない国家もある。このことは，国際システムが国家を「構成」する上で多くをなさないことを示唆しており，それゆえ，その領域においては個人主義に対して直観的な支持を与える（国家を「個人」として想定する）。ここで根底にある問題は，国際システムの社会構造があまり厚くなく，密でもないことであり，これによって構成主義的な議論の余地が大きく減じられるように思われることである。

今日主流のIR研究は，国家システムに関するこうした個人主義的，唯物論的な結論を大体において受け入れており，ケネス・ウォルツが「新現実主義」を力強く打ち出した『国際政治の理論』が主流となっている。〔新現実主義とは〕国際システムに対するミクロ経済学的アプローチ（個人主義）と，権力および利害を重視する古典的現実主義（唯物論）を融合させた〔理論をいう〕。ウォルツの同書は，〔これと〕一部競合する「新自由主義」理論の生成に一役買った。新自由主義を最も体系的に論じた〔書〕は，ロバート・コヘインの『覇権後の国際政治経済学』であって，同書は新現実主義の個人主義の多くを受け入れながらも，国際機関が権力と利害の影響を（まったく排除することはできないにしても）弱めることは可能であると主張した。新現実主義と新自由主義がきわめて多くの点で一致している事実は，両者の対話の進展に貢献したが，同時にまた，その対話の幅を大きく狭める結果となった。その論争は時として，国家が絶対的利益よりも相対的利益を追求する頻度に関する単なる議論に帰着してしまうように思われるのである。

国際政治に対する唯物論的・個人主義的アプローチは直観的なもっともらしさと優位性を備えているが，それとは逆に，社会理論の立場からこのテーマに関する構成主義的思考と考えられる流派があり，長年多彩に〔展開してきている〕。グロティウス，カント，ヘーゲルによる古典的国際理論の根底には，ある構成主義的世界観があり，世界大戦間のIRにおいて一時支配的であった。現在のIR研究者はその当時の〔構成主義〕をしばしば軽蔑を込めて「理想主義」と呼んでいる。

Ⅷ　文脈上，空所を埋めるのに最も ふさわしいものを4つの選択肢の中から１つ選びなさい。

71.　解答：C

解説　文脈に合うのは「インド南部の最下層民」という原義から，一般にoutcastの意味で用いられる pariah ＞ C. pariahs である。

72.　解答：C

解説　ISがタリバンをどのように見ているかを知っていればC. agentは容易

に選べるが，文脈からも他の選択肢は不適と判断できよう。

73. 解答：A

解説 下線部で終わるセンテンスは米国によるアフガン支配と 1989 年のソ連による同国への侵攻を比較していることから，A. by comparison が適切。

74. 解答：D

解説 下線部前後は「(アフガン政府) はソ連の崩壊によって ______ された」という文脈なので，D. precipitated < precipitate = make something serious happen suddenly or unexpectedly が適切。

75. 解答：A

解説 下線部の前のパラグラフでタリバン代表団のロシア訪問について言われており，下線部の後には同じ月に中国にも代表団が派遣されたことが示されている。これが，問題文執筆時点で seems ... to have been part of a concerted diplomatic push という文意から，上の ... を埋める語句としては A. retrospect による in retrospect が最適。

76. 解答：B

解説 1975 年の南ベトナム撤退に続く第 2 期という捉え方なので，失敗に終わった軍事侵攻を指すのに最もふさわしいものを選ぶ。B. profligacy は careless wastefulness in the use of resources の意味。

77. 解答：A

解説 下線部前センテンス頭から「イランが Great Satan の ______ を喜んでいる」の意なので，最適なのは A. discomfiture = この場合 defeat と解釈するのがよいだろう。Great Satan はイランが用いる米国に対する蔑称。

78. 解答：C

解説 下線部直前に not just America’s foes ... have kept their doors open to the Taliban とあって，下線部後はその例としてパキスタンを挙げてい

るので，前後をつなぐ語としては前述内容を強調・確認する C. Indeed が最適。

79. 解答：B

解説 パキスタンがタリバンに対して行っていた支援を形容する語としては，done in secret を意味する B. clandestine が適切。

80. 解答：D

解説 下線部直前の（Pakistan's）prime minister did not hide his glee at events in Afghanistan, congratulating ... と，下線部に続く Turkey's foreign minister ..."views positively" the messages（from the Taliban）... Turkey is in dialogue with all sides とで言動の性格を比較評価する表現。後者の方が穏当と考えられるので，D. Less effusively ＜ effusive = showing one's pleasure in an excited fashion が適切。

訳例　タリバンは 1996 年から 2001 年までアフガニスタンを支配したが，当時は国際的な嫌われ者となっていた。世界のジハーディストらへの歓待や女性に対する抑圧，中世を想わせるような残虐行為，それに文化破壊によって，世界の大半を遠ざけてしまった。タリバンの自称「首長国」を承認したのは，パキスタン，サウジアラビア，アラブ首長国連邦の 3 カ国だけだったし，その 3 国も，アフガニスタンからアルカイダが指揮して実行させた 9 月 11 日の同時多発テロ後は，たちまち背を向けた。

あれから 20 年を経た今，タリバンは自らの第 2 次政権を，より健全な外交基盤の上にしっかり据えようと決意を固めているようだ。カブール掌握時に流血をほぼ回避したことで，穏健で安定した勢力というイメージを打ち出そうとしている。この動きの中で仲間になりそうにないのが，敵対する武装組織イスラミック・ステートの支持者の一部だ。これら IS 支持者はタリバンを「背教者の民兵」と呼び，さらには愚かにも米国の工作員だとして非難している。タリバンの背教性については，欧米諸国は容易に納得しないだろうが，米国に対して屈辱を与えたことは，中国，イラン，ロシアなど一部の大国がタリバン側に有利に動く結果をもたらした。ただ，これらの国々でさえも，タリバンを極度に警戒している。このカブールの勝者は国際的に広く認められたとはまったく言いがたい。

欧米諸国が自国民や一部の現地スタッフを国外に脱出させようと急ぐ中，中国とロシアはタリバンに守られてカブールに置く大使館の業務を続けており，また，新政権と対話する用意があると表明した。8 月 17 日には，ロシアのドミトリー・ジルノフ大使が外国の高官として初めて，タリバン指導者とカブールで会談を行った。ロシアにもやはりアフガニスタンでの屈辱と失敗の記憶がある。そして，ここ数日の大混乱の光景は，少なくとも1989年のソ連撤退をそれほど悲惨ではなかったと思わせるという（露政府から見ての）メリットがある。ソ連が残したアフガニスタン政府は，ただちに崩壊することはなく，3年間存続した。その瓦解（その後の混乱期を経て最終的にタリバンの政権掌握に至る）を早めた要因は，1991年のソ連の崩壊と同国からの経済支援の停止であった。ロシア政府は，タリバンをテロ組織として指定しながらも，長年にわたって接触を保ち，その勝利に備えた。ロシアは7月，モスクワにタリバンの代表団を迎え入れた。

今となっては，〔次のことは〕政権奪取を前にした協調的な外交努力の一環であったと思われるのだが，その同月にはこのほか，タリバンの実質的指導者であるアブドゥル・ガニ・バラダル師率いる代表団が北京を訪問，中国の王毅外相と会談することを許された。会談は大々的に公表された。中国の国営通信社は米国の困惑を喜び，ある評論家が「米国の戦略的放蕩《ほうとう》の第2期」（第1期は同評論家によれば1975年のサイゴン撤退に終結）と称した〔時代〕の終わりを寿《ことほ》いでいる。

イランもまた，「大悪魔」の挫折をよしとして，今週はカブールとイラン国境に近いヘラートの両方に外交官を置いたままとしている。長年にわたるタリバンへの敵意は近年和らいできており，指導者がタリバンと会談を行っている。イランのエブラヒム・ライシ新大統領は今週，米国の撤退と「軍事的敗北」について祝意を表し，「この国〔アフガニスタン〕に生活と安全，それに永続的な平和を取り戻す機会」だ〔と述べた〕。

これまでタリバンに門戸を開いてきたのは，米国の敵や競争相手だけではない。実際，長い間タリバンを招き入れ，歓待してきた国が1つある。パキスタン〔だ〕。数十年にわたって米国との緊密な関係とタリバンに対する秘密支援を両立させてきた。ウサマ・ビン・ラディンも，タリバン保護下から逃れざるを得なくなるとパキスタンに身を潜めた。そして，同組織〔アルカイダ〕を指導する評議会は，拠点となったパキスタンのバロチスタン州内の都市名にちなんで，現在でも「クエッタ・シューラ」と呼ばれている。これは，パキスタンの軍と治安当局が，インドとの関係がいかんともしがいほど悪化した場合に「戦略的縦深性」を備える上で，アフガニスタンが友好国であることが必要だという強迫観念を抱いていることの現れである。イムラン・カーン首相は，アフガニスタンにおける事態の推移に喜びを隠さず，アフガニスタン国民が「奴隷の足枷《あしかせ》を断った」ことに祝意を表わした。

歓迎の熱烈さでは劣るものの，テュルキエ（トルコ）のメヴリュット・チャヴシュオール外相も，タリバンが送ってきているメッセージを「肯定的に受け止めており」，トルコは全方位的対話を進めていると述べた。タリバンに対してパキスタンが強力に支援するのとは逆に，同じくらい激しく敵対してきたインドでさえ，タリバンとの慎重な協議を開始したと伝えられている。

IX 以下の質問に対し，200～250 語の短いエッセイを英語で書きなさい。

質問文：コロナ禍から世界が復興するには，女性の労働者としての生活を改善することが必要であるが，それはなぜか？　またどのような改善が必要か？

解答例 I will discuss three aspects of women’s working conditions and COVID-19 recovery: pandemic impacts, necessary changes, and improvement implementation.

First, women’s work as unpaid family caregivers has been negatively impacted. “Informal employment” in care, service, and hospitality industries, which traditionally underpay women, also suffers. The International Labor Organization—founded 1919 and UN specialized agency in 1946 mandated to give equal voice to workers, employers, and governments—in “Building Forward Fairer: Women’s rights to work and at work at the core of the COVID-19 recovery”—details ways the pandemic worsened gender equality. While 3% of men’s employment was destroyed, 4.2% of women’s was wiped out in 2020. Of the world’s working-age women, only 43.2% will be employed in 2021 versus 68.6% of working-age men.

Second, necessary changes—gender-responsive policies—must advance. Employment retention benefits; wage subsidies for new hires, with greater subsidy rates for women; care economy investments; quality of women’s pay and working condition improvements; abuse and violence prevention in domestic, informal, and formal employment, including services for victims; and promotion of women into more decision-making positions are among the vital policy measures required.

Third, these improvements—already existing as laws, guidelines, and regulations in most progressive countries—must be immediately implemented internationally to support faster and more complete COVID-19 recovery.

We have not fully recuperated from an injury if serious wounds continue to fester; in a similar way, we understand equality for women must be achieved for the world to fully recover from and improve after the COVID-19 pandemic.

解説 解答例はまず，与えられたテーマに対して，「コロナ禍による影響」，復興に「必要な変化」，「改善の実施」の３つの論点を挙げている。

第２パラグラフは，コロナ禍が女性の労働に及ぼした負の影響について，具体的なデータも挙げつつ詳述している。

第３パラグラフは，「必要な変化」として，ジェンダーに的確に対応した具体的な政策を列挙している。

第４パラグラフは「改善の実施」について，すでに先進国の多くで行われている法規制化を世界的に実施すべきとの考えを提示している。

第５パラグラフはこれまでの論点を踏まえて，コロナ禍からの復興のために女性労働の面で何が必要かを結論づけている。このエッセイ解答例のように，与えられた問いに対して，自分が知る事実や情報をもとにいくつかの論点を立て，順序立てて論じていく方法は，応用範囲が広く，限られた時間内に説得的な文章を組み立てる上で有効である。

訳例 女性の労働条件とコロナ禍からの復興について，コロナ禍による影響，求められる変化，改善の実施の３つの側面から考える。

第一に，無報酬の家政婦・介護者としての女性の仕事にマイナスの影響が出てきた。以前から女性の賃金が低い育児や介護，サービス，接客業における「非正規雇用」も打撃を受けている。国際労働機関（1919年設立，1946年国連専門機関。労働者，雇用者，政府に平等の発言権を与えることを任務とする）は，「より公正な前向きの立て直し：新型コロナウィルスからの回復の中核における女性の働く権利と就労に関わる権利」*の中で，ジェンダー平等がコロナ禍によってどのように後退したかを詳述している。2020年には，男性雇用が全体の3%失われたのに対して，女性雇用は4.2%消失した。世界の労働年齢にある女性の就業率は2021年で43.2%にすぎないのに対し，男性の就業率は68.6%となっている。

第二に，求められる変化，すなわちジェンダーに対応した政策が進むことが必要である。雇用維持給付金や新規雇用者への賃金補助金（女性に対する補助率を高くする），ケア経済への投資，女性の賃金と労働条件の質向上，家庭内，非正規，正規雇用における虐待・暴力の防止（被害者に対するサービスを含む），意思決定を伴うより多くの職種への女性登用といった重要な政策措置が求められる。

第三に，こうした改善は，ほとんどの進んだ国々ではすでに法律や指針，規制の形で実施されているが，コロナ禍からの早期かつ完全な復興を支えるために，国際的にも直ちに実施されなければならない。

ケガの場合でも，深い傷が化膿《かのう》したままでは，完全に回復したとは言えない。それと同じように，世界がコロナ禍から完全に復興し，終息後に改善へと進んでいくためには，女性に対して平等が達成されなければならないと我々は考えている。

＊訳注：ILO 駐日事務所による邦訳書名を採用

2021 年特 A 級第 2 回試験　正解一覧

I									
1. D	2. B	3. C	4. A	5. B	6. C	7. C	8. B	9. B	10. D
II									
11. C	12. B	13. A	14. D	15. C	16. B	17. C	18. B	19. A	20. A
III									
21. A	22. D	23. C	24. C	25. D	26. B	27. A	28. A	29. C	30. B
IV									
31. D	32. B	33. A	34. C	35. A	36. B	37. B	38. D	39. C	40. B
V									
41. C	42. B	43. B	44. A	45. D	46. A	47. D	48. B	49. C	50. A
VI									
51. C	52. D	53. B	54. A	55. B	56. D	57. A	58. B	59. D	60. C
VII									
61. D	62. C	63. C	64. B	65. B	66. C	67. D	68. A	69. A	70. C
VIII									
71. C	72. C	73. A	74. D	75. A	76. B	77. A	78. C	79. B	80. D

2022年

第1回試験

問題

特Ａ級第１次試験問題用紙

特A級

外務省後援

２０２２年度第１回国際連合公用語

英語検定試験 (120分)

受験上の注意

1．問題用紙は試験開始の合図があるまで開いてはいけません。その間に、この**受験上の注意を熟読してください。**

2．**受験番号と氏名を解答用紙（マークシートと作文用紙）**に記入してください。

3．解答用紙の配布は１人１部のみです。複数の配布は致しません。

4．試験開始前は、答案への解答記入は禁止です。

5．マークシートの記入は、１～100までの記入箇所がありますが、この級では１～80までを使います。

6．マークシートの記入は、必ずＨＢ以上の濃い鉛筆を使って該当箇所を黒く塗りつぶしてください。書き間違いの場合は「アト」が残らないように消してください。マークシートは絶対に折ったり曲げたりしないでください。

7．受験級、受験地区、会場番号、受験番号のマークシートへの記入は監督者の指示に従い、間違いなく記入してください。**（裏表紙の「マークシート記入例」参照）**

8．作文は、⑴読みやすい文字をペン、ボールペンまたはＨＢ以上の濃い鉛筆で書いてください。⑵使用語数の200～250語を目安にしてください。

9．試験問題についての質問は、印刷が不鮮明な場合を除き、一切受けつけません。

10．中途退室の際は、マークシートと作文用紙を持って監督者に渡し、他の受験者の迷惑にならないように静かに退室してください。中途退室後の再入室はできません。

11．試験中は他の受験者の妨げとなる行動は慎んでください。また携帯電話等の電源はお切りください。

12．マークシートと作文用紙は監督者に提出し、問題用紙はご自由にお持ち帰りください。

＊試験問題の複製や転載、インターネットへのアップロード等、いかなる媒体への転用を禁止します。

試験結果について

1．第１次試験の結果は2022年6月29日㈬頃に受験申込書に記載された住所に郵送で通知します。

2．その間に住所変更をされた方は、郵便局へ住所変更の届け出を忘れずに行ってください。

3．発表前の試験結果のお問合せには応じられません。

第２次試験について

1．第１次試験合格者には、試験結果発表と同時に試験日時、会場を指定して通知します。

2．第２次試験は2022年7月10日㈰です。特Ａ級（Ａ級との併願を含む）の試験地は**東京と大阪**になります。あらかじめご了承願います。

公益財団法人 日本国際連合協会
http://www.unaj.or.jp/

I. Fill in each of the following blanks with the most appropriate of the four alternatives according to the knowledge and information gained from *New Today's Guide to the United Nations*.

1. <u>The Nobel Lecture delivered by Secretary-General Kofi Annan in Oslo, 10 December 2001</u>

In a world filled with weapons of war and all too often ________ of war, the Nobel Committee has become a vital agent for peace. Sadly, a prize for peace is a rarity in this world.

A. casualties B. words C. burden D. agony

2. <u>Charter of the United Nations</u>

It is not authorized for the United Nations to intervene in matters that are essentially within the domestic jurisdiction of any State, except where enforcement action is necessary with respect to threats to the peace, breaches of the peace, or ________.

A. an outbreak of hostilities B. menace of incursion
C. acts of aggression D. war of invasion

3. <u>Security Council</u>

While other organs of the United Nations may make ________ to governments, the Security Council alone has the power to make decisions which all Member States are obligated under the Charter to accept and carry out.

A. exhortations B. propositions
C. recommendations D. submissions

4. <u>The United Nations System</u>

________ are basically independent of the United Nations and have their own decision-making procedures and budgets.

A. Related agencies B. Coordinating agencies
C. Subsidiary organs D. Specialized agencies

5. <u>United Nations Educational, Scientific and Cultural Organization (UNESCO)</u>

In November 2011, the Obama administration announced the suspension of expenditure to the organization after UNESCO voted to admit ________ as a full member.

A. Montenegro B. Timor-Leste
C. South Sudan D. Palestine

6. **World Intellectual Property Organization (WIPO)**

The World Intellectual Property Organization (WIPO) had its origins in the 1883 Paris Convention for the Protection of Industrial Property and the 1886 _________ Convention for the Protection of Literary and Artistic Works.

A. Berne B. Madrid C. Rome D. Geneva

7. **Doctrinal changes, failures, and present situation of PKO**

"Supplement to An Agenda for Peace" (1995) states that the United Nations can play its role most effectively in PKOs performed on the traditional doctrine and in post-conflict _________.

A. peace preservation
B. peacemaking
C. peacebuilding
D. peace enforcement

8. **Disarmament**

There were two main channels for disarmament by the United Nations. First, the United Nations is a forum for _________ among states, for example, through the General Assembly, its First Committee, the Disarmament Committee and the Security Council.

A. consultation
B. dialogue
C. discussion
D. negotiation

9. **Assistance to Children**

The United Nations International Children's Emergency Fund (UNICEF) focused its attention on the widespread malnutrition, disease and illiteracy afflicting children in the developing world. In _________, the Fund was awarded the Nobel Prize.

A. 1960 B. 1965 C. 1970 D. 1975

10. **Japan and the United Nations - Overview**

Starting in 1978 when _________ was appointed to the position of Under Secretary-General for Public Information, a Japanese candidate has been routinely serving as one of the Under-Secretary-Generals in the UN.

A. Shigeru Oda
B. Yasushi Akashi
C. Genichi Akatani
D. Kotaro Tanaka

II. Choose from among the four alternatives the one that most closely corresponds to the meaning contained in the following passage.

(1) In an environment where the rule of law is non-existent and is always flouted at home and abroad, it is unsurprising that treaties and agreements signed by Ukraine with Russia were worthless pieces of paper during the 2014 crisis. This has increased Ukrainian distrust in Putin's promises. D'Anieri (2019, 258) writes that the 1997 Russian-Ukrainian treaty 'brought little in the way of friendship, opposed as it was by many Russian elites' and the treaty 'had little impact on Ukrainian-Russian relations.' Russia had 'deep and fundamental' disagreements over Ukraine and always insisted that Moscow 'considered a voice in Ukraine as essential' (D'Anieri 2019, 258–259). Ukraine's democratisation signifies the enlargement of western influence into what Russia views as its exclusive sphere of influence. Ukraine's European integration was unacceptable to Russia in 2014, and this remains true today. **(A)**

(2) Ukraine would have to agree to many Russian demands to achieve peace, which would be tantamount to capitulation for many Ukrainians. These demands include relinquishing sovereignty over Crimea and changing its constitution to provide 'special status' to the DNR and LNR. Russia demands that the 35,000-strong security forces of the DNR and LNR be re-organised into a local militia, which would amount to the legalisation of Russian-controlled forces. Ukraine demands the de-militarisation and withdrawal of all foreign forces, but it is impossible for a withdrawal to take place as long as Russia **sticks to the fiction** that it has no security forces in the Donbas. Russia has also rejected returning control over the border to Ukraine until Ukraine meets all of its demands.

(3) Russia seeks a neutral Ukraine that relinquishes its goal of joining NATO and the EU, two objectives that are enshrined in Ukraine's constitution since February 2019. **(B)** Changing the constitution requires a majority two-thirds vote by parliament, which would be impossible and is opposed by large majorities of Ukrainians, who now support membership in both organisations. Support for NATO membership has skyrocketed since 2014 and a high majority would support membership in a referendum. Approximately 69% of Ukrainians would participate in a referendum on NATO membership, of whom 70% would vote in favour, up from 66% in 2017 (Pidsumky 2018: hromadska dumka 2018). In Ukrainian-controlled Donbas, 31% of people support NATO membership, despite miniscule support prior to 2014 (Observations of Public Attitudes in Donbas 2020).

(4) President Zelenskyy's inability to move the peace process forward confirms that neither former President Poroshenko nor 'Ukrainian nationalists' were the obstacles. ①Zelenskyy's decision to withdraw from three contact points on the front line was unpopular. ②With Russian and Russian proxy forces continuing to engage Ukrainian forces on a daily basis, the withdrawals failed to achieve a significant reduction in

hostilities. ③Russian leaders have continued to believe this fallacy after Zelenskyy's election. ④Zelenskyy also oversaw two prisoner exchanges, which earned him good will as a populist exercise, but also criticism. Of those transferred to Russia, six prisoners were Berkut riot police guilty of killing protestors during the Euromaidan. Another was Volodymyr Tsemakh, who had been kidnapped by Security Service of Ukraine special forces in a daring raid and was wanted by the Hague-based Joint Investigations Team due to his involvement in the downing of MH17.

(5) Despite his good will and willingness to compromise, (1) ____________________ the peace process for reasons which are the same as those under Poroshenko. An inability to push the peace process forward points to deeper issues; after all, Zelenskyy is a centrist, Russian-speaking politician from eastern Ukraine who (unlike his predecessor) would have been willing to make difficult compromises. Typically, in Russian policies towards Ukraine, Putin does not attempt to engage with Zelenskyy or adopt compromises, in this case towards the goal of achieving peace. Russian demands towards Kyiv are not modified and Zelenskyy (2) ____________________.

(6) In April 2019, the month Zelenskyy was elected, Putin slapped him twice in the face. **(C)** Russia began issuing passports to residents of Russian-controlled Donbas, forecasting that, by the end of 2020, one million residents of the DNR and LNR would possess them. The residents of Russian-controlled Donbas returned their gratitude and voted for constitutional amendments in the July 2020 Russian referendum. In the same month, Russia introduced sanctions on 140 goods (on top of the 200 goods sanctioned by Russia earlier in December 2018), including coal, crude oil, and oil products, which could no longer be exported to Ukraine.

(7) Stereotypes of a divided Ukraine on the verge of disintegration, and Ukrainians and Russians as very close people were wrong prior to 2014 and are outdated in the face of the tectonic changes that have occurred since then (see Kuzyk 2019). Putin's rehabilitation of Tsarist Russian and White émigré views, which deny the existence of a Ukrainian people and portray Ukraine as an 'artificial' and failed state, annexation of Crimea, and invasion and war with Ukraine have fundamentally changed the Ukrainian-Russian relationship. A pro-Russian 'east' has disappeared, Ukrainians no longer view Russians as their 'brothers,' and Russian soft power in Ukraine has disintegrated. Ukrainian opinion polls show dramatic changes in identity, views of Ukrainian history and relations with Russia.

(8) D'Anieri (2019) believes that the West's goals of seeking to keep Russia satisfied and Ukraine independent are mutually incompatible. **(D)** Putin does not distinguish between integration (on offer in the Eastern Partnership) and membership (which is not). Integration into Europe means that Putin cannot fulfil his destiny of 'gathering Russian lands' because Ukraine would not be part of the Russian World. Russian leaders believe that 'Russian lands,' wrongly included in Ukraine, are being prevented from joining the Russian World by Ukrainian nationalists. With Russian nationalism (imperialism) driving Putin's policies towards Ukraine, it is difficult to see how peace in the Donbas can be achieved. With Putin in power for another 16 years, the policies he has pursued, however counter-productive they have been to Russian goals, will continue towards Ukraine.

11. Which is correct according to the information explicitly stated in Paragraph 1?

A. During the 2014 crisis, the rule of law bolstered the existing treaties and agreements signed by Ukraine with Russia.

B. The 1997 Russian-Ukrainian treaty was disregarded by Russian elites because it had little effect on Ukrainian-Russian relations.

C. Significant disagreements between Russia and Ukraine led the Russian government to avoid involvement in Ukrainian matters.

D. Ukraine's closer alignment with western influences is perceived by Russia as an impermissible threat to its influence in the region.

12. The underlined phrase "sticks to the fiction" in Paragraph 2 is closest in meaning to which of the following?

A. adheres to the motive

B. maintains the fabrication

C. remains dubious of the narrative

D. tolerates the myth

13. Which of the following is correct according to the information presented in Paragraph 3?

A. The Ukrainian constitution states that it will remain neutral in its relations with Russia and will not join NATO and the EU.

B. Prior to 2014, the majority of Ukrainians supported membership of NATO and the EU.

C. Of the Ukrainians who would participate in a referendum, just under 70% would support membership of NATO.

D. The percentage of people in the Donbas region who support NATO has increased notably since 2014.

14. In Paragraph 4, which of the underlined sections, ① to ④, should be omitted because it is either unnecessary or inappropriate there?

A. ①　　B. ②　　C. ③　　D. ④

15. **In the context of the information presented in Paragraph 5, which of the following sets, (A to D), best fits the blanks (1) and (2) in the paragraph?**

A. (1) Zelenskyy has had little impact on (2) has become more like his predecessor

B. (1) Putin was not willing to cooperate with (2) must simply comply

C. (1) Putin declines to adjust his position on (2) has accepted hard compromises

D. (1) Zelenskyy could not achieve major success in (2) is simply expected to abide by them

16. **Which of the following is NOT correct according to the information presented in Paragraph 6?**

A. Following Zelenskyy's election in 2019, Putin took aggressive action against Ukraine.

B. Russia predicted that one million residents would possess its passport by the end of 2020.

C. The majority of people in Russian-controlled Donbas are wary of Russian intentions.

D. Since 2018, Ukraine is no longer allowed to import certain goods from Russia.

17. **Which of the following most accurately represents the author's view according to the information explicitly stated in paragraphs 7 and 8?**

A. Ukraine has always been one step away from collapse and never more so since the dramatic events of 2014.

B. While Putin's extreme views, the annexation of Crimea, and wars have turned most Ukrainians against Russia, in the east, Ukrainian support for Russia remains high.

C. Russian leaders believe that increased EU integration and EU membership are distinguishable and therefore prevent their destiny of 'gathering Russian lands'.

D. Putin's nationalistic policies towards Ukraine will likely continue while he remains in power in spite of their not being in the best interests of Russia.

18. **Which part of the essay, indicated by the capital letters in parentheses, is MOST appropriate for the following sentence?**

NATO is not Russia's only problem; a democratising Ukraine integrating into Europe within the EU's Eastern Partnership is also unacceptable to Russia.

A. (A) B. (B) C. (C) D. (D)

19. Which of the following ideas is explicitly stated in the essay?

A. Russia seeks to legalize the military forces it controls in the DNR and LNR and demands Ukraine gives up sovereignty over Crimea.

B. For many Ukrainians, especially the younger generation, closer integration into the EU is desirable for social and economic reasons.

C. Putin's military aggression in the east has been a key factor in making Ukraine independent of Russian energy.

D. Trade with the EU, which is now the biggest destination for Ukrainian exports, has grown since 2014.

20. If we divide paragraphs (2) to (7) into four main topics, which set, A, B, C, or D, is the most representative?

	Topic 1	Topic 2	Topic 3	Topic 4
A.	(2)	(3)	(4) (5)	(6) (7)
B.	(2) (3)	(4) (5)	(6)	(7)
C.	(2) (3)	(4)	(5)	(6) (7)
D.	(2) (3) (4)	(5)	(6)	(7)

Ⅲ. Choose from among the underlined phrases the one that is grammatically or idiomatically incorrect.

21. **(A)** From electric cars and buses to zero-carbon producing energy sources, new and emerging technologies **(B)** along with innovative policy changes, are critical for combating climate change. **(C)** But to be effective, they must be ensured that transport strategies benefit **(D)** everyone, including the poorest, according to a new UN multi-agency report launched on Tuesday.

22. The massive **(A)** volcanic eruption and tsunami in Tonga followed by another earthquake **(B)** and aftershock just days afterwards, has highlighted **(C)** again the vulnerability of Small Island Developing States (SIDS), a meeting this week convened **(D)** by the Food and Agriculture Organization (FAO) has heard.

23. **(A)** As millions took to the streets of cities around the world **(B)** on Saturday, demanding greater climate action, some countries **(C)** taking part in the COP26 negotiations, making new pledges **(D)** to invest in nature-based solutions and a greener approach to farming.

24. **(A)** Yemen is teetering a new **(B)** "fragmented and bloody" chapter of war as **(C)** military conflict escalates, Special Envoy Hans Grundberg **(D)** told the Security Council on Tuesday, calling for "restraint, de-escalation and dialogue."

25. The UN Secretary-General on Sunday said he was committed **(A)** to ensuring that the Organisation is a place where "youth voices are heard, and their ideas lead", **(B)** as he spent the day in Barbados which tomorrow hosts a major UN conference **(C)** on trade and development, focused on the need to build a global green economy **(D)** and recover equitability from the COVID-19 pandemic.

26. In a UN first, **(A)** a ferocious and talkative dinosaur bursts **(B)** into the iconic General Assembly Hall at UN Headquarters in New York, **(C)** with a special warning for any diplomats who still **(D)** think climate action is for birds.

27. Many migrant domestic workers in Lebanon **(A)** are denied basic human rights, and **(B)** suffered abuse at the hands of their employers. **(C)** Since the worsening economic crisis in **(D)** the country its plight has, if anything, worsened.

28. **(A)** Fuelled by Omicron, more than 15 million new cases of COVID-19 **(B)** were reported around the world **(C)** last week, by far the worst cases reported **(D)** in a single seven day period, the World Health Organization (WHO) informed on Wednesday.

29. Following armed conflict from 1991 to 1994 in Croatia **(A)** and the rest of former Yugoslavia, which triggered **(B)** increased radicalization and hate speech, an independent UN human rights expert **(C)** urged the authorities on Thursday to redouble **(D)** efforts towards full justification for victims and survivors.

30. The Sahel region of Africa should be considered a region of opportunity, **(A)** although the "multiple crises" that people there are enduring. The Sahel is a vast under-populated region **(B)** stretching across Africa from Senegal in the west to Djibouti in the east, **(C)** an area which is being destabilized by terrorism-related conflict, **(D)** the effects of climate change and a lack of development.

Ⅳ.　Choose the answer that uses the most logically and grammatically appropriate form of each underlined infinitive, in whichever manner (transitive, intransitive, participle, or otherwise) it is used, in the context of the following article.

United Nations Security Council sanctions are no longer the "blunt instrument" they once were, having transformed since the 1990s into "a vital tool" that minimizes negative consequences for civilians and States that are not directly being **(31) to target**. That was the main message the Under-Secretary-General for Political and Peacebuilding Affairs, Rosemary A. DiCarlo, conveyed on Monday to the Security Council during Monday's debate on sanctions, focused on the unintended consequences that stem from them, especially in the humanitarian context.

According to Ms. DiCarlo, there are currently 14 Council sanctions regimes in place around the world. These sanctions measures support conflict resolution in Libya, Mali, South Sudan and Yemen; deter unconstitutional changes of government in places like Guinea Bissau; and curb the illicit exploitation of natural resources that fund the activities of armed groups in the Central African Republic (CAR), the Democratic Republic of Congo and Somalia. They also **(32) to constrain** the proliferation activities of the Democratic People's Republic of Korea (DPRK) and the terrorist threat **(33) to pose** by the Islamist terrorist groups (ISIL), Al-Qaida and their affiliates.

According to the UN political affairs chief, however, sanctions "are not an end in themselves. To be effective, sanctions should be part of a comprehensive political strategy, working in tandem with direct political dialogue, mediation, peacekeeping and special political missions", she explained. In recent years, the Security Council has **(34) to try** to avoid adverse consequences for civilian populations and third-party States, Ms. DiCarlo said.

In the case of arms embargoes, for instance, exemptions are routinely granted for the import of non-lethal equipment necessary for humanitarian relief. In the case of travel bans, exemptions are provided for medical or religious reasons or **(35) to participate** in peace processes; exemptions for assets freezes allow payment for food, utilities or medicines. The Security Council has also created standing humanitarian exemptions in Somalia and Afghanistan, as well as case-by-case exemptions in Libya, Yemen and DPRK.

Sanctions are also "continually adjusted" in response to changes on the ground, the political chief said, highlighting how the Council terminated sanctions against Eritrea, and significantly narrowed down the terms of an arms embargo in the CAR. As a result of these changes, only one Member State reported facing "special economic problems" arising from Council sanctions in the last decade.

The last 10 years have also shown that sanctions can do more than limit the influx of arms and ammunition or the financing of armed groups. Almost all regimes now try to uphold international humanitarian standards. In 2020, for example, humanitarian obligations helped release **(36) to abduct** women and children from military bases in South Sudan; in the DRC, it opened space to negotiate the release of children by armed groups.

Sanctions have also become more targeted, with more than 50 individuals and entities placed on lists. That was the case with Sultan Zabin, the director of the Criminal Investigation Department (CID) in Sanaa, Yemen, sanctioned for torture and sexual violence in conflict; and Ahmed Ag Albachar, the self-proclaimed "president of the humanitarian commission" of the restive Kidal region in Mali, for **(37) to obstruct** the delivery of humanitarian assistance. "The imposition of sanctions solely for such acts is a relatively recent and welcome step. Its use sends an unmistakable signal", Ms. DiCarlo argued.

For the Under-Secretary-General, the evolution from comprehensive to targeted sanctions marked a sea change, but there are still concerns. The continued difficulty in reviving the banking process for making humanitarian transfers to the DPRK, since its collapse in 2017, is a prime example of the challenges that arise, she said. "Financial actors and other service providers may impose additional conditions, increase their costs, or simply refuse to provide the requested goods and services, thereby inhibiting the delivery of humanitarian assistance", Ms. DiCarlo said.

Arguing that more can be done, she shared the example of resolution 2615, which was approved late last year to create a humanitarian exemption to help the people of Afghanistan. "Similar standing exemptions in other sanctions regimes could go a long way to respond to the critical needs of civilian populations", she concluded.

Humanitarian affairs chief, Martin Griffiths, also highlighted the exemptions approved for Afghanistan, saying they allowed operations to continue. The humanitarian chief explained that sanctions can be smart and targeted, but compliance is always a daily element in the work of the UN and its partners. "They can **(38) to impact** our logistics, our finances, our ability to deliver. They can lead to humanitarian projects delaying or stalling. And some can threaten the well-being of whole swathes of civilian society", he said. According to Mr. Griffiths, who also acts as the UN's Emergency Relief Coordinator, sanctions applied by Member States themselves often have a wider reach than the ones imposed by the Security Council.

The humanitarian chief then shared some of his concerns, such as difficulties to engage with listed individuals or entities, who sometimes hold significant control over the lives of entire populations. He also said that banks and other commercial operators, aiming to avoid any risk of penalty, can effectively deny services to humanitarian customers; commercial operators that trade food, fuel or other necessities can also decide **(39) to err** on the side of caution, leading to shortages and price rises. Finally, when ministries and departments are run by listed individuals, sanctions can limit the provision of social services and economic stability—a clear unintended consequence.

To mitigate this, the Under-Secretary-General suggested some areas for action. Mr. Griffiths asked the Council to build in comprehensive humanitarian carve-outs in every regime from the outset, rather than the current case-by-case authorization procedures that can be “cumbersome and inefficient.” According to him, these carve-outs and exceptions should be “smoothly **(40)** **to translate** into national legislation”, to lessen the concerns of humanitarian donors, NGOs and private companies.

31. **to target**
A. target B. targeted
C. targeting D. to target

32. **to constrain**
A. to constrain B. constrains
C. constraining D. constrain

33. **to pose**
A. pose B. poses C. posed D. posing

34. **to try**
A. tries B. try C. trying D. tried

35. **to participate**
A. participate B. participated
C. participates D. to participate

36. **to abduct**
A. abduct B. abducted
C. abducting D. abducts

37. **to obstruct**
A. obstruct B. obstructed
C. obstructing D. obstructs

38. **to impact**
A. impact B. impacted
C. impacting D. impacts

39. **to err**
A. err B. erring C. errs D. to err

40. **to translate**
A. translate B. translated
C. translates D. to translate

V. Choose from among the four alternatives the one that most closely corresponds to the meaning contained in the following passage.

The inevitable historical process which **(41) <u>culminated in</u>** the Revolution of March, 1917, has resulted in the collapse of the Russian State. Philosophers, historians and sociologists, in studying the course of Russian life, may have foreseen the impending catastrophe. But nobody could foresee that the people, rising like a tidal wave, **(42) <u>would so rapidly and so easily sweep away all the foundations of their existence</u>**: the Supreme Power and the Governing classes which disappeared without a struggle; the intelligencia, gifted but weak, isolated and lacking will-power, which at first, in the midst of a deadly struggle, had only words as a weapon, later submissively bent their necks under the knife of the victors; and last, but not least, an army of ten million, powerful and **(43) <u>imbued</u>** with historic traditions. That army was destroyed in three or four months.

This last event—the collapse of the army—was not, however, quite unexpected, as the **(44) <u>epilogue</u>** of the Manchurian war and the subsequent events in Moscow, Kronstadt and Sevastopol were a terrible warning. At the end of November, 1905, I lived for a fortnight in Harbin, and travelled on the Siberian Railway for thirty-one days in December, 1907, through a series of "republics" from Harbin to Petrograd. I thus gained a clear indication of what might be expected from a **(45) <u>licentious</u>** mob of soldiers utterly devoid of restraining principles. All the meetings, resolutions, soviets—in a word, all the manifestations of a mutiny of the military—occurred again in 1917 with photographic accuracy, but with greater **(46) <u>impetus</u>** and on a much larger scale.

It should be noted that the possibility of such a rapid psychological transformation was not characteristic of the Russian Army alone. There can be no doubt that war-weariness after three years of bloodshed played an important part in these events, as the armies of the whole world were affected by it and were rendered more accessible to the disintegrating influences of extreme Socialist doctrines. In the autumn of 1918 the German Army Corps that occupied the region of the Don and Little Russia were **(47) <u>demoralized</u>** in one week, and they repeated to a certain extent the process which we had already lived through of meetings, soviets, committees, of doing away with Commanding Officers, and in some units of the sale of military stores, horses and arms. It was not till then that the Germans understood the tragedy of the Russian officers. More than once our volunteers saw the German officers, formerly so **(48) <u>haughty</u>** and so frigid, weeping bitterly over their degradation.

"You have done the same to us; you have done it with your own hands," we said.

"Not we; it was our Government," was their reply.

In the winter of 1918, as Commander-in-Chief of the Volunteer Army, I received an offer from a group of German officers to join our army as volunteers **(49) <u>in the ranks</u>**. The collapse of the army cannot be explained away as the psychological result of defeats and disasters. Even the victors experienced disturbances in the army. The troops did not always obey the orders of their Commanding Officers. Rapid demobilization and the arrival of fresh, partly volunteer elements, altered the situation.

The members of the House of Romanov did not preserve the "idea" which the orthodox monarchists wished to surround with a halo of greatness, nobility and reverence. **(50) I recall the impression of a sitting of the Duma which I happened to attend.** For the first time, Gutchkov uttered a word of warning from the Tribune of the Duma about Rasputin.

"All is not well with our land."

The House, which had been rather noisy, was silent, and every word, spoken in a low voice, was distinctly audible in remote corners. A mysterious cloud, pregnant with catastrophe, seemed to hang over the normal course of Russian history.

41. **Here the words "culminated in" mean**

A. underscored B. engendered
C. embellished D. desolated

42. **This suggests that the author feels _________ by the Russian Revolution.**

A. pacified B. emboldened
C. appalled D. enchanted

43. **Here the word "imbued" means**

A. erected B. permeated
C. exalted D. prefaced

44. **Here the word "epilogue" means**

A. consummation B. impudence
C. stoicism D. duplicity

45. **Here the word "licentious" means**

A. lethargic B. resolute
C. rampant D. depraved

46. **Here the word "impetus" means**

A. divergency B. aggregate
C. fervor D. profundity

47. **Here the word "demoralized" means**

A. apathetic B. benevolent
C. nefarious D. galvanized

48. Here the word “haughty” means

A. disingenuous
B. outlandish
C. gullible
D. disdainful

49. Here the phrase “ in the ranks” means

A. a position in military hierarchy
B. a precarious situation
C. an unofficial military position
D. a duty to perform routine manual labor.

50. The author mentions this personal anecdote in order to

A. present the author’s opinion about how to end the ongoing violence.
B. emphasize the dire consequences of the Romanov’s poor judgment.
C. contrast the morality of the Romanovs with the viciousness of the revolutionaries.
D. describe a captivating speech that positively changed the course of Russian history.

Ⅵ. Choose from among the four alternatives the one that best completes the following sentences.

51. **Indian businesswoman Swati Daga first bought bitcoin in 2017, when the cryptocurrency was trading ________ under $3,000. Her decision to invest in digital currencies was met with ________ by her family, she recalls. But the 33-year-old hasn't regretted her decision. Bitcoin's value has increased 15 times since then.**

A. well - wariness
B. largely - geniality
C. greatly - vindictiveness
D. hard - vigilance

52. **Hong Kong, once ________ as a zero-Covid success story, is now battling a deadly outbreak ________ of the early days of the pandemic, despite having had more than two years to prepare.**

A. glorified - connotative
B. renowned - evocative
C. lauded - reminiscent
D. flattered - insinuative

53. **The United States' largest reservoir is draining rapidly. ________ by extreme, climate change-fueled drought and increasing demand for water, Lake Mead registered its lowest level on record. The lake is ________ to become the focal point of one of the country's most significant climate crises: water shortages in the West.**

A. Afflicted - initiated
B. Plagued - poised
C. Possessed - designated
D. Agitated - labeled

54. **As Russia continues its invasion of Ukraine, various international sports organizations have begun ________ sanctions on the country and its athletes. Various governing bodies have so far either suspended Russian teams from competitions or ________ the country of its right to host events.**

A. allocating- rescinded
B. placing - canceled
C. arranging - revoked
D. imposing - stripped

55. **A crowd gathered in central Seoul last month waving signs and wearing white sashes emblazoned with the words "Vote for Women." Protestors aim to draw attention to the country's widespread sexual violence, ________ gender expectations, and low female representation in boardrooms and in politics as examples of how discrimination against women is still ________.**

A. fortified - replete
B. repressed - endemic
C. entrenched - rife
D. tempered - ubiquitous

56. **North Korea has started work on a sprawling 10,000-apartment residential project as the country embarks on a housing drive in its capital, Pyongyang. Amid major economic _________ brought about by trade sanctions and the Covid-19 pandemic, leader Kim Jong Un attended a long-awaited _________ ceremony at the construction site on Saturday, according to state media reports.**

A. austerity – ice-breaking
B. woes – ground-breaking
C. adversity – earth-shaking
D. rows – ribbon-cutting

57. **The age of a 31-kilometer (19-mile) wide meteorite crater discovered under a kilometer of Greenland ice had long puzzled scientists. The crater, which is one of the world's largest, has now been _________ dated, and it is much, much older than previously thought. In fact, it _________ into the Earth just a few million years after dinosaurs went extinct, about 58 million years ago.**

A. definitively – slammed
B. assuredly – whacked
C. decisively – boomed
D. indubitably – banged

58. **In the first federal trial related to the January 6 riot, a jury in Washington, DC found Guy Reffitt guilty of all five charges he faced. Reffitt, a supporter of then-President Donald Trump when he went to the Capitol on January 6, was charged with five _________, including weapons-related charges. The jury _________ for just under four hours.**

A. allegations – contested
B. indictments – mediated
C. bills – debated
D. counts – deliberated

59. **Russia has _________ its citizens from buying US dollars, completing the isolation of an economy that once had ambitions to join the global club of financial powers. President Putin's _________ to dominate his neighbors, starting with his assault on Georgia in 2008, and continuing with the annexation of Crimea in 2014 and last month's invasion of Ukraine, has shredded what remained of his economic dreams.**

A. ceased – expedition
B. banned – quest
C. stalled – campaign
D. banished – crusade

60. **More than 12,000 years ago, South America was _________ with an astonishing array of ice age beasts—giant ground sloths the size of a car, elephantine herbivores, and a deerlike animal with an elongated snout. These extinct giants are among many animals _________ in an 8-mile-long (13-kilometer-long) frieze of rock paintings in the Colombian Amazon rainforest.**

A. rampant - solidified
B. thronging - canonized
C. teeming - immortalized
D. replete - mummified

Ⅶ. Choose from among the four alternatives the one that best explains each of the underlined words.

We will examine this in greater detail in the later sections of the book, but let us begin by seeing this from the perspective of "leverage" and the role that leverage plays in the ongoing debate over Japan's treatment of the comfort women. In negotiations, we examine the leverage that each side possesses in the process. Leverage leads the opposing side in a conflict to recognize the importance of reaching a settlement. When the treatment of women and girls by the Japanese military came to the surface in the 1990s, it led to a groundswell of righteous **(61) rancor** towards Japan, especially on the part of Koreans. A large portion of the women conscripted to serve as *ianfu*, or comfort women, during WWII came from Korea.

The first recourse that the victims sought beginning in the early 1990s was through the court system. Yet, during the 14-year period between 1991 and 2005, few courts ruled in these women's favor and, if they did, they were **(62) struck down** on a higher level of the justice system both in Japan and in the United States. This prompted intensification of civil society activity. For decades, most Japanese maintained their reserved demeanor on this topic with **(63) inimitable** Japanese politeness. Most Japanese, after all, had a different understanding of this chapter of history than Koreans had. The Japanese had been taught the official Japanese account of historical events—that the comfort women had acted voluntarily as professional prostitutes servicing the military. They had been treated and compensated well for their work and were portrayed as having fulfilled a patriotic duty.

The Korean Council persevered with its understanding of events, using a growing volume of evidence uncovered in previously inaccessible government archives in Japan and the United States. The Korean Council's supporters also successfully **(64) lobbied** for the appointment in 1994 of a special rapporteur to the United Nations Human Rights Commission to investigate the comfort women issue. In 1999 the findings of this extensive UN investigation led to a sharp **(65) rebuke** of Japan for having engaged in massive violations of women's rights. The year 2007 even saw the passage of a non-binding resolution by the United States House of Representatives calling upon Japan to recognize its **(66) culpability**.

Yet the acts most impactful on Japan's **(67) demeanor** on this topic were not based on investigations or legislation. On the occasion of its 1000th Wednesday demonstration on December 14, 2011, the Korean Council erected the statue of a comfort woman directly across from the Japanese embassy in Seoul. The Japanese abandoned their reserved demeanor. They condemned this action and launched a formal protest against Korea, arguing that the statue impaired Japan's dignity and constituted a violation of guidelines and **(68) procedures** that a host country should follow when welcoming an embassy from a member of the community of nations with which it engages in diplomatic relations.

The first memorial to provoke an official response from Japan was created in 2010 not in Seoul but on the grounds of the Palisades Park Municipal Library in New Jersey. Members of the Japanese Diet (Japan's parliament) challenged the historical accuracy and fairness of the allegations that the comfort women system represented a crime against humanity. Without effect, they argued that the women had been volunteers who were well compensated. In establishing a memorial in Palisades Park and in erecting a statue in front of the embassy of Japan, Koreans, intentionally or not, had established powerful leverage that helped to bring Japan, which famously **(69) cringes** at humiliation, to the bargaining table.

Still today, every time a new statue or memorial is erected, whether in Korea, the United States, or Europe, it embarrasses Japan. It provides one additional point of leverage for the Korean Council and other CSOs which call upon Japan to accept responsibility and resolve the problem. For Korea, the problem is about justice for the comfort women and **(70) restoration** of Korea's dignity as a nation. For Japan, the problem is about what they view as unfair national humiliation and a significant loss of "face." In either case, we should be clear that at this stage, the Korean Council, whether the problem is resolved or not, has no intention of seeing the statues come down. The statues and memorials may have never been erected if the problem had been solved earlier, but, now that they are in place, they are thought to represent an important piece of history.

61. **rancor**

A. acrimony B. callousness
C. maliciousness D. spitefulness

62. **struck down**

A. countermanded B. demeaned
C. overruled D. repealed

63. **inimitable**

A. inequitable B. incomparable
C. uncompromising D. uncustomary

64. **lobbied**

A. acquiesced B. coerced
C. obliged D. petitioned

65. **rebuke**

A. relinquishment B. removal
C. reproach D. resignation

66. **culpability**

A. delinquency
B. duplicity
C. guilt
D. misconduct

67. **demeanor**

A. bearing
B. elevation
C. outlook
D. profile

68. **procedures**

A. pacts
B. perplexities
C. processes
D. protocols

69. **cringes**

A. bellows
B. curries
C. grimaces
D. maligns

70. **restoration**

A. reclamation
B. refurbishment
C. reproving
D. revamping

Ⅷ. Fill in each of the following blanks with the most appropriate of the four alternatives as required by the context.

The Biden administration's **(71)** _________ for the Middle East is simple: "end the 'forever wars.'" The White House is preoccupied with managing the challenge posed by China and aims to disentangle the United States from the Middle East's seemingly endless and unwinnable conflicts. But the United States' disengagement threatens to leave a political vacuum that will be filled by sectarian rivalries, **(72)**_________ a more violent and unstable region.

The struggle for geopolitical primacy between Iran's Shiite theocracy and the countries led by Sunni Arabs and, more recently, Sunni Turkey is stoking conflict across the region—eroding social compacts, worsening state dysfunction, and catalyzing extremist movements. Both sides have weaponized religious identity for their own purposes, using it to rally partisans and bolster their influence across the region. As a result, the broader Middle East remains a **(73)** _________ .

Although Iran retains the upper hand, challenges to its position are building across the region. Sunnis have tired of **(74)** _________ extremism, but the anger that fueled the rise of the Islamic State (also known as ISIS) remains undiminished; new insurgencies in the broken parts of the region will undoubtedly harness that rage once more. Sunnis in Iraq, Lebanon, and Syria are increasingly **(75)** _________ moves by Tehran and its allies to tighten their hold on power. And terrorism has emerged in Afghanistan again, as the country slides into chaos in the wake of the Taliban's victory. Without any political process to defuse these tensions, they are bound to erupt in new waves of tumult and bloodshed.

Israel's intervention in these sectarian conflicts on the side of the Sunni powers has only added fuel to the fire. **(76)**_________ Israel's involvement, regional stability is even more subject to the fate of Iran's nuclear program. Washington and Jerusalem are already discussing a "Plan B" if a diplomatic settlement remains beyond reach. This path would place Iran and the United States on a collision course—as well as exacerbate sectarian tensions, deepen societal divisions, and trigger new conflicts from the Levant to Afghanistan.

Washington's desire to do less in the Middle East comes at a time when China and Russia are leaning into the region, a hard-line government in Iran is **(77)** _________ , and the Sunni Arab states are less confident than ever about U.S. security guarantees. Unless the United States paves the way for a more stable regional order—beginning by striking a deal over Iran's nuclear program—it may find itself dragged back into the Middle East's many conflicts despite its best efforts to walk away.

The origins of the rivalry between the Shiites and the Sunnis go back to the very beginnings of Islam, and over the centuries, the two sects have evolved distinct interpretations of Islamic law and religious practice. The strife between the two groups today, however, is rooted not in theology but in a struggle for power. Shiism and Sunnism are prominent identity markers that shape political allegiances in divided societies. The intensity of sectarian fighting has ebbed and flowed over the past two decades, but sectarianism's salience to the region's politics has not waned—nor has the struggle between Iran and its Sunni-led rivals, which both feeds on and fuels this **(78)** ________ . These two forces are different sides of the same coin.

It was the 2003 U.S. invasion of Iraq that allowed Iran to dramatically expand its influence in the Arab world. Ever since the United States brought down the authoritarian regime that guaranteed Sunni-minority rule in Baghdad, Tehran has expertly played on sectarian loyalties to empower a network of armed proxies that now stretches from Lebanon and Syria to Iraq and Yemen, forming what Jordan's King Abdullah once called a "Shiite crescent." **(79)** ________ , Iran has empowered Shiites at the expense of Sunnis across the region and enhanced its own influence over that of rivals such as Saudi Arabia, Turkey, and the United Arab Emirates (UAE).

The Arab world's push for democracy and good government, the so-called Arab Spring, led autocrats, threatened by the prospect of change, to further weaponize sectarianism. Syrian President Bashar al-Assad stoked fear of Sunnis to scare the Syrian Alawite community, to which he belongs and which traces its roots to Shiism, into **(80)** ________ for his regime. In Bahrain and Yemen, rulers justified violent crackdowns by accusing Shiite protesters of being Iranian proxies. Iran and its Arab rivals reinforced this dynamic by arraying themselves behind their respective Shiite and Sunni clients, seeing their coreligionists as tools to protect their regional influence.

71. A. riposte B. dictum
C. argot D. mantra

72. A. stacking the deck against B. bearing the brunt of
C. paving the way for D. drawing the curtain over

73. A. junta B. tinderbox
C. contraption D. rapture

74. A. virulent B. nebulous
C. sporadic D. propitious

75. A. reveling in B. chafing at
C. slobbering over D. barging into

76.	A.	Because of	B.	In addition to
	C.	For lack of	D.	Along with
77.	A.	twiddling its thumbs	B.	sinking to its knees
	C.	digging in its heels	D.	pricking its ears
78.	A.	chagrin	B.	gaffe
	C.	travesty	D.	schism
79.	A.	In doing so	B.	For one thing
	C.	On the whole	D.	Above all
80.	A.	immutable legitimacy	B.	unflinching support
	C.	disruptive innovation	D.	inexhaustible fund

IX. Write a short essay in English of 200-250 words as your answer to the following.

Please discuss a concern you feel is at the heart of the battle against climate change.

マークシート記入例

東京の本会場で特A級を受験する、国連 太郎さん、受験番号が「東京01-10001」、生年月日が「1980年10月24日」の場合の記入例です。

【受験番号/氏名】
それぞれ受験票の記載通りに記入してください。

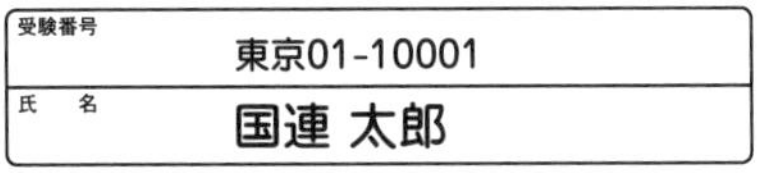

【受験地区】
下段の都道府県部分を塗りつぶしてください。

【会場番号】
都道府県部分に続く２桁の数字を塗りつぶしてください。

【受験番号】
ハイフン（－）以降の５桁の数字を塗りつぶしてください。

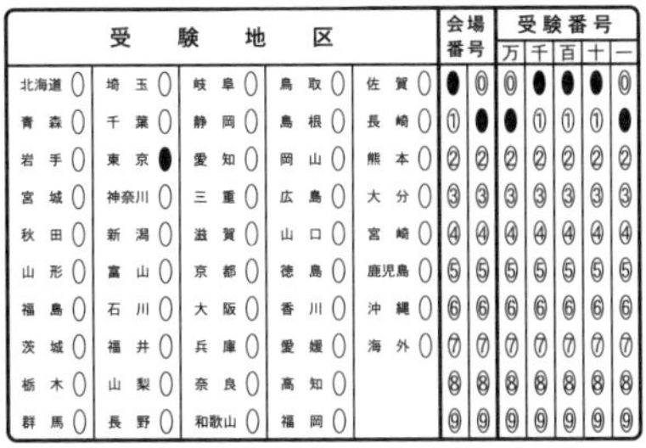

【受験級】
「特A」と記入し、下段の特A級部分を塗りつぶしてください。

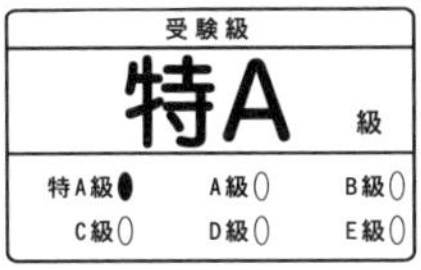

【生年月日】
４桁の西暦・月・日を塗りつぶしてください。
10未満の月・日の十の位は、「０」を塗りつぶしてください。

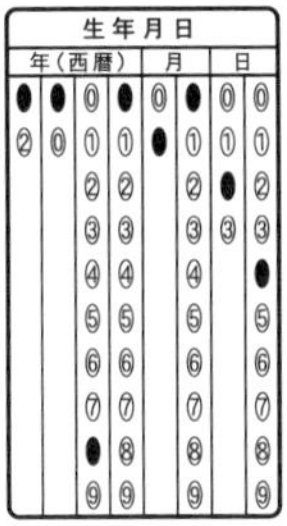

※HB以上の鉛筆を用いてマークをしてください。

※他の地区から会場を変更して受験する場合でも、受験票に記載されている受験地区・会場番号をマークしてください。

2022年
第1回試験
解答・解説

2022年　国連英検特A級第1回試験
解答・解説

＊〔　〕内は訳出上の補足や説明

I 『新 わかりやすい国連の活動と世界』に基づき，
空所を埋めるのに最も適切なものを4つの選択肢の中から1つ選びなさい。

1. 解答：B

訳例　戦争兵器にあふれ，戦争という言葉が蔓延している今日の世界で，ノーベル委員会は，平和実現の上で非常に重要な役割を担うようになりました。残念なことですが，この世界では平和のための賞は大変希少なものです（『新 わかりやすい国連の活動と世界』p.13。以下，書名略）。

2. 解答：C

訳例　国連憲章のいかなる規定も，本質的にその国の国内問題である事項に干渉する権限を国連に与えるものではない。ただし，平和に対する脅威，平和の破壊および侵略行為に関して強制措置が必要な場合は，その限りではない（同 p.44）。

3. 解答：C

訳例　国連の他機関が各国政府に勧告を行うに留まるのに対し，安全保障理事会だけは決定を下す権限を持つ。全加盟国は，国連憲章に基づき，その決定を受け入れ，履行する義務を負う（同 p.55）。

4. 解答：D

訳例　専門機関は，基本的に国連からは独立した国際機関であり，独自の政策決定や予算を有している（同 p.72）。

5. 解答：D

訳例　2011年11月，ユネスコがパレスチナを正式加盟国としてその加盟を認めたことを受けて，オバマ政権はユネスコへの支出を停止することを表明した（同 p.79）。

6. 解答：A

訳例　世界知的所有権機関（WIPO）の母体となったのは，1883年の工業所有権保護に関するパリ条約と1886年の文学的および美術的著作物の保護に関するベルン条約である（同 p.84）。

7. 解答：C

訳例　そのことは，『平和への課題：補遺』（1995年）の中でもはっきりと示され，伝統的な原則に則ったPKOと紛争後の平和構築こそが国連の役割を発揮できる分野である（同 p.107）。

8. 解答：D

訳例　国連による軍縮にはふたつの流れがあった。ひとつは，国連は国々の交渉のためのフォーラムであること，例えば総会を通して，その第一委員会があり，軍縮委員会があり，安全保障理事会がある（同 p.114）。

9. 解答：B

訳例　ユニセフは，開発途上国の子供を苦しめている栄養失調，病気，読み書きができないことの問題に精力的に取り組み，1965年にノーベル平和賞を受けた（同 p.141）。

10. 解答：C

訳例　1978年に任命された赤谷源一事務次長（広報担当）を皮切りに，日本人候補者が恒例的に複数ある国連事務次長職の1つに登用されてきた（同 p.165）。

II

以下の文章の中に含まれる意味に文脈上最も近いものを4つの選択肢の中から1つ選びなさい。

11. 解答：D

解説　A.「2014年の危機の間，法の支配が，ウクライナがロシアと結んだ既存の条約や協定をゆるぎないものにした」は，パラグラフ（1）冒頭から3行目のIn an environment where the rule of law is non-existence and is always flouted at home and abroad, it is unsurprising that treaties and agreements signed by Ukraine with Russia were worthless pieces of paper during the 2014 crisis. に矛盾し，B.「1997年のロシア・ウクライナ条約は，宇露関係にほとんど影響を与えないという理由

でロシア支配層から軽視された」とあるが，「影響を与えなかった」こととロシア支配層の「反対」はそれぞれダニエリの主張の別項目であり，理由として関連しているとは読み取れない。C.「ロシア・ウクライナ間の大きな見解の相違により，ロシア政府はウクライナ問題への関与を避けるに至った」は，7～8行目のRussia had ‘deep and fundamental’ disagreements over Ukraine and always insisted that Moscow ‘considered a voice in Ukraine as essential.’ に矛盾する。D.「ウクライナの西側有力国との緊密な協力体制について，ロシアは，その地域の自国の影響力にとって容認できない脅威と捉えている」は，下から2行目～最後のUkraine’s European integration was unacceptable to Russia in 2014, and this remains true today. と一致する。

12. 解答：B

解説 A.「意思を持ち続ける」，B.「作り話を続ける」，C.「その物語を疑い続ける」，D.「作り話を容認する」の中では，B が適解となる。

13. 解答：D

解説 A.「ウクライナ憲法は，ウクライナがロシアとの関係において中立国であり続け，NATO や EU には加盟しないと述べている」は，パラグラフ(3) 1～2行目の「ウクライナ憲法に2019年2月以来定められている NATO および EU への加盟という2つの目標」と全く逆になっている。B.「2014年以前は，ウクライナ人の多数が NATO や EU への加盟を支持していた」については，4～5行目の large majorities of Ukrainians, who now support membership in both organisations より，2014年以前ではなく「現在」のことであることがわかる。C.「国民投票に参加するウクライナ人のうち，NATO 加盟を支持するのは70%未満にとどまるだろう」は，5～7行目の Support for NATO membership has skyrocketed since 2014 and a high majority would support membership in a referendum. と一致しない。D.「NATO 加盟を支持するドンバス地方の住民の割合は2014年以来顕著に増加している」は下から3～2行目の In Ukrainian-controlled Donbas, 31% of people support NATO membership, despite miniscule support prior to 2014. と一致する。

14. 解答：C

解説 このパラグラフはゼレンスキー大統領の政策（前線からの撤退と重罪人の受刑者交換）への批判を論じており，③のロシアの指導者に関する記述は話の流れに合わない。

15. 解答：D

解説 和平プロセスの不調，ポロシェンコとの比較からパラグラフ（5）の1行目はゼレンスキーのことを述べていることがわかるため，(1) はAとDに絞られる。Aの (2)「前任者と同様になった」というのは，(unlike his predecessor) と矛盾するため，Dが適解となる。

16. 解答：C

解説 A.「2019年のゼレンスキーの当選後，プーチンはウクライナに対して攻撃的な行動に出た」は，パラグラフ（6）の1行目，In April 2019, the month Zelenskyy was elected, Putin slapped his twice in the face. と以降の具体策に一致する。B.「ロシアは，2020年末までに100万人の住民がロシアの旅券を所有すると予測した」は，2～3行目のRussia began issuing passports to residents of Russian-controlled Donbas, forecasting that, by the end of 2020, one million residents of the DNR and LNR would possess them. と一致する。D.「2018年以来，ウクライナはかなりの品目をロシアから輸入できない状態にある」は，5行目～最後のIn the same month, Russia introduced sanctions on 140 goods (on top of the 200 goods sanctioned by Russia earlier in December 2018), including coal, crude oil, and oil products, which could no longer be exported to Ukraine. と一致する。一方，C.「ロシア支配下にあるドンバスの大多数の人々はロシアを警戒している」は，4行目のThe residents of Russian-controlled Donbas returned their gratitude以下に矛盾する。

17. 解答：D

解説 A.「ウクライナは2014年の劇的な出来事からずっと常に変わらずに崩壊寸前である」については，パラグラフ（7）の2～3行目にwrong prior to 2014 ... outdated in the face of the tectonic changes that have occurred since then と書かれていることと矛盾する。B.「プーチンの極端な考え方やクリミア併合，戦争がほとんどのウクライナ人を反ロシアに転じさせてきた一方で，ウクライナ東部ではロシアの支持率が依然として高い」は，(7) の下から 4 〜 3 行目の A pro-Russian ‘east’ has disappeared, Ukrainians no longer view Russians as ‘brothers,’ and Russian soft power in Ukraine has disintegrated. と矛盾する。C.「ロシアの指導者たちは，拡大する EU 統合と EU 加盟は区別することができ，したがって『ロシアの国々をまとめる』という彼らの運命を妨げると信じている」は，パラグラフ (8) 2 〜 4 行目の Putin does not distinguish between integration (on offer in the Eastern Partnership) and membership (which is not). と矛盾する。D.「ウクライナに対するプーチンの国家主義的政策は，それがロシアのための最善策ではないにもかかわらず彼が政権の座にとどまっている限りは，多分継続するであろう」は，(8) の最後から 3 行目〜末の With Putin in power for another 16 years, the policies he pursued, however counter-productive they have been to Russian goals, will continue toward Ukraine. と一致する。

18. 解答：D

解説 A を含む (1) はロシアとウクライナの関係性を概観的に述べており，B を含む (3) はウクライナの NATO 加盟をめぐる憲法改正・国民投票について説明している。C を含む (6) はゼレンスキー政権に対するロシアの対抗策について述べている。D の後に，ウクライナの欧州への統合がいかにプーチン政権にとって不都合であるかが詳しく述べられているため，与えられた文が主題文としてここに入ることが最も適切である。

19. 解答：A

解説 A は，前半「ロシアは DNR と LNR で自らが統制する軍隊を合法化しようとしている」がパラグラフ (2) 4 〜 7 行目の Russia demands that the 35,000-strong security forces of the DNR and LNR be re-organised into a local militia, which would amount to the legalisation of Russian-controlled forces. と，後半がパラグラフ (2) 2 〜 3 行「クリミアに対する主権を放棄すること」と一致する。B.「多くのウクライナ人，

特に若者世代にとっては，EU への緊密な統合は社会的・経済的理由から望ましいものである」，C.「東部におけるプーチンの軍事攻撃はウクライナをロシアの勢力から独立させる重要な要素になっている」，D.「EU との貿易は，いまやウクライナの輸出の最大目標となっているが，2014 年以来成長を続けている」はいずれも言及がない。

20. 解答：B

解説 パラグラフ（2）（3）は，ロシアのウクライナに対する姿勢を述べており，パラグラフ（4）（5）にはロシアに対するゼレンスキーの政策が，パラグラフ（6）にはそれに対するプーチンの対抗措置が，パラグラフ（7）にはウクライナの（現在の）独立性が述べられている。

訳例 (1)　法の支配が存在せず，国内外で常に無視されている環境では，ウクライナがロシアと結んだ条約や協定が 2014 年の危機に際して価値のない紙切れとなったのは驚くに当たらない。このことが，プーチンの約束に対するウクライナ人の不信感を膨らませてきた。〔米国の国際政治学者ポール・〕ダニエリ（2019）は，1997 年のロシア・ウクライナ条約は「実際多くのロシア支配層が反対したように，友好をほとんどもたらさず」，「宇露関係にはほとんど影響を与えなかった」と述べている。ロシアはウクライナに関して「根深く根本的な」異なる見解を持っていたのであり，「ウクライナ国内に発言権をもつこと」をロシア政府が「不可欠と考えている」と常に主張していた。ウクライナの民主化は，ロシアが自国の排他的な影響圏とみなす領域へと西側の影響力が拡大していくことを意味する。ウクライナの欧州への統合は 2014 年当時，ロシアにとって受け入れがたいものであったし，それは現在も変わっていない。(A)

(2)　ウクライナは和平を実現するためにはロシアの多くの要求に応じなければならないだろうが，それは多くのウクライナ人にとって降伏に等しいものとなるだろう。これらの要求には，クリミアに対する主権を放棄することや，憲法改正により DNR〔ドネツク人民共和国〕と LNR〔ルガンスク人民共和国〕に「特別な地位」を与えることなどが含まれる。ロシアは，DNR と LNR の治安部隊 3 万 5,000 人を現地の民兵に再編成することを要求しており，それはロシアが統制する部隊を合法化することになる。ウクライナは外国軍の非軍事化と撤退を要求しているが，ロシアがドンバスにはロシアの治安部隊はいないという虚構に固執するかぎり，撤退は不可能である。また，ロシアは，ウクライナがすべての要求を呑むまで国境の支配権をウクライナに返すことを拒む〔姿勢を貫いて〕きた。

(3)　ロシアが求めているのは，ウクライナ憲法に2019年２月以来定められているNATOおよびEUへの加盟という２つの目標を放棄した，中立国としてのウクライナなのである。(B) 憲法を変更するには，議会の採決で３分の２以上の賛成が必要だが，これは不可能であろうし，しかも現在両方への加盟を支持しているウクライナ人の大多数が反対している。NATO加盟への支持は2014年以降急増しており，国民投票を行えば大多数が加盟を支持するだろう。NATO加盟の是非を問う国民投票が実施された場合，ウクライナ国民の投票率は約69％となり，そのうち賛成票は70％と，2017年〔の調査で示された〕66％を上回るものと予測されている（Pidsumky 2018: hromadska dumka 2018）。また，ウクライナ支配下のドンバス地方では，2014年以前は住民のNATO加盟支持はきわめてわずかであったのに対し，〔現在では〕31％に達している。

(4)　ゼレンスキー大統領が和平プロセスを前に進めることができない事実は，ポロシェンコ前大統領や「ウクライナ民族主義者」がいずれも障害ではなかったことを裏付けるものである。①前線の接触点３カ所から撤退するというゼレンスキーの決断は不評であった。②ロシア軍とロシアの代理勢力が日常的にウクライナ軍と交戦を続ける中で，撤退は戦闘行為の大幅な低減を達成できなかった。③〔削除対象〕ロシアの指導者は，ゼレンスキーの〔大統領〕当選後もこの誤りを信じている。④また，ゼレンスキーは２度の受刑者交換を行った。これは一般大衆向けの策として好感を得たが，批判も浴びた。ロシアに移送された受刑者のうち，６人は機動隊ベルクトの隊員で，ユーロマイダンの際にデモ参加者を殺害した者。そしてもう１人は，ウクライナ特殊部隊の治安隊が大胆な奇襲を行って拉致した人物で，MH17便の撃墜に関わった容疑でハーグの合同調査チームに指名手配されていたヴォロディミル・ツェマフである。

(5)　ゼレンスキーは善意と妥協への意欲に満ちていたが，和平プロセスにおいては，ポロシェンコ政権時代と同じ理由から，大きな成功を収めることができなかった。和平プロセスを進める力を欠くということは，より深い問題を示唆している。何しろゼレンスキーはウクライナ東部出身のロシア語を母語とする中道の政治家であり，（〔ポロシェンコ〕前大統領とは異なり）困難な妥協も厭《いと》わなかったはずなのである。典型的〔な事例を挙げれば〕，プーチンはロシアの対ウクライナ政策においてゼレンスキーと戦争しようとも，妥協（今の場合は和平実現の目標に向けた妥協）をしようともしていない。ロシアのウクライナ政府に対する要求は変わっておらず，ゼレンスキーは単にそれに従うものと考えられている。

(6)　ゼレンスキーが当選した2019年４月，プーチンはゼレンスキーの顔を２度，「平手打ち」した。(C) ロシアが支配するドンバスの住民に対して旅券の発給を開始するとともに，旅券を所持するDNRとLNRの住民は

2020年末までに100万人に達するとの予測〔を発表した〕。ロシア支配下にあるドンバス地方の住民はこれに謝意を示す形で，2020年7月に行われたロシアの住民投票では憲法改正に賛成した。また同月，ロシアは石炭，原油，石油製品など140品目を対象とする制裁を発動（かつて2018年12月にロシアが制裁の対象とした200品目に追加）。これら品目がウクライナへ輸出できなくなった。

(7)　分断されたウクライナが崩壊寸前であるとか，ウクライナ人とロシア人が非常に近い民族であるというステレオタイプは，2014年より前は誤りであったし，それ以降の地殻変動を経ていまや時代遅れとなった。プーチンがウクライナ民族の存在を否定し，ウクライナを「人工的」な破綻国家とするロシア帝政時代のロシア人や白系ロシア人の考え方を復活させたことや，クリミアを併合し，ウクライナに侵攻して戦争を行ったことで，宇露関係は一変してしまった。親ロシア派の「東部」は消滅した。ウクライナ人はもはやロシア人を「兄弟」と見なしておらず，ウクライナにおけるロシアのソフトパワーは崩壊した。ウクライナで実施された各種世論調査の結果を見ると，アイデンティティーやウクライナの歴史に対する認識，それにロシアとの関係に劇的な変化が起きたことが分かる。

(8)　ダニエリは，欧米が目標とする〔ように〕ロシアを満足させ，しかもウクライナを独立国として維持することは，両立不可能と考えている。(D)〔ロシアにとっての問題はNATOだけではない。民主化を進めるウクライナがEUの東方パートナーシップの中で欧州に統合されることも，ロシアには受け入れがたいことなのである。〕プーチンは統合（東方パートナーシップの中で提案あり）と加盟（提案なし）とを区別していない。欧州への統合ということは，ウクライナがロシア世界の一部でなくなることであるから，その場合プーチンは「ロシアの国々をまとめる」という自らの運命を果たせなくなる。ロシアの指導者たちは，ウクライナに間違って含まれている「ロシアの国々」が，ウクライナの民族主義者によってロシア世界に入ることを阻まれていると考えている。ロシアの国家主義（帝国主義）がプーチンの対ウクライナ政策を動かしている以上，ドンバスの平和がいかにして実現されうるかを考えることは困難である。プーチンがあと16年政権を維持すれば，同氏が進めてきた政策は，それがロシアの目標を達成する上でいかに逆効果であったとしても，ウクライナに対して継続されるだろう。

III

文法的，語法的にふさわしくないものを下線の中から１つ選びなさい。

21.　解答：C

解説　be ensured → ensure。they は new and emerging technologies を指し，それらが「確実に～するようにする」という意味になるようにするには，they must ensure ... としなければならない。

訳例　電気自動車やバス，そして CO_2 排出ゼロのエネルギー源など，新技術や新興技術は，革新的な政策変更と並んで，気候変動と闘う上できわめて重要な〔手段となっている〕。ただ，実際に効果を生むためには，これら技術は，輸送戦略が最貧困層を含むすべての人に利益をもたらすよう保証するものでなければならない――火曜日に発表された国連の複数機関による報告書はこう述べている。

22.　解答：B

解説　aftershock → aftershocks。aftershock は可算名詞なので，aftershocks とする。

訳例　トンガで起きた大規模な火山噴火と津波，そしてそのわずか数日後に発生した地震と余震は，小島嶼《しょうとうしょ》開発途上国（SIDS）の脆弱性《ぜいじゃくせい》を改めて浮き彫りにした。食糧農業機関（FAO）が今週招集した会議で報告された。

23.　解答：C

解説　making → made。making の部分は，some countries から始まる節の述語動詞となるため，直前のコンマを削除して made としなければならない。

訳例　世界中の都市で土曜日，〔合わせて〕数百万の人々が街頭に出て気候変動対策の強化を訴える中，COP26 の交渉参加国の一部は，自然を利用した解決策と環境に優しい農業への投資を新たに約束した。

24.　解答：A

解説　teetering → teetering on。teeter は「～に瀕《ひん》している」という意味では自動詞であるため，on, with などを伴う必要がある。

訳例　イエメンは，軍事紛争が激化する中，新たな「分裂した悲惨な」戦争の局面に突入する瀬戸際にある。国連のハンス・グルンドベルク〔イエメン〕特使が火曜日，安保理でこのように訴え，「自制，対立の緩和，対話」を呼びかけた。

25. 解答：D

解説 equitability → equitably。現状は recover が他動詞で「コロナ禍から公平さを取り戻す」となり，意味が通らない。「コロナ禍から回復する」(recover は自動詞) とするためには，equitably (公平に) と副詞にすればよい。

訳例 国連事務総長は日曜日，バルバドスで一日を過ごし，国連が「若者が声を聞いてもらえる場，若者のアイデアが指導的役割を果たす」場となるよう取り組むと述べた。同国では明日，世界規模のグリーン経済構築とコロナ禍からの公平な回復の必要性をテーマに，貿易と開発に関する国連の大きな会議〔第 15 回国連貿易開発会議＝ UNCTAD15〕が開かれる。

26. 解答：D

解説 for birds → for the birds。「くだらない」という表現は be for the birds。

訳例 国連初の試みとして，ニューヨーク国連本部で国連の象徴となっている総会議場に，言葉を話す獰猛《どうもう》な恐竜が乱入し，いまだに気候変動対策をくだらないと思っている外交官らに特別な警告を発する〔という動画が発表された〕。

27. 解答：D

解説 its → their。plight（苦境）は many migrant domestic workers in Lebanon が陥っている状況なので，their plight とすべきである。

訳例 レバノンに〔住む〕多くの移民家事労働者は基本的人権を否定され，雇用主からの虐待に苦しんでいる。レバノンの経済危機が悪化して以来，これら労働者のひどい状況はいずれにせよ悪化している。

28. 解答：C

解説 worst → most。by far（はるかに）に続く部分は more than 15 million new cases という数の多さに呼応するので，the most cases とすべきである。

訳例 オミクロン株〔の広がり〕により，コロナウィルス新規感染者は先週，全世界で 1,500 万人以上が報告された。1 週間の報告感染者数としては飛び抜けて多い数字。世界保健機関（WHO）が水曜日，発表した。

29. 解答：D

解説 justification → justice。justification とすると (victims and survivors に

対する）「正当化」「正当とする証拠」となり不適切であるため，justice（裁判，裁き）とすべきである。

訳例　1991年から1994年にかけてクロアチアと旧ユーゴスラビアのそれ以外の地域との間に起きた武力紛争は，急進化とヘイトスピーチが悪化するきっかけとなったが，これを受けて国連の独立人権専門家〔真実・正義・賠償・再発防止保証推進の特別報告者〕は木曜日，被害者と生存者のために〔犯罪を究明する〕十分な裁きを実現すべく努力を倍加するよう当局に要請した。

30.　解答：A

解説　although → despite。although は接続詞で，後に「主語＋動詞～」が続いて副詞節を作るが，A の the “multiple crisis” 以下は関係代名詞節を含む名詞句であるため，although ではなく，前置詞である despite にすべきである。

訳例　アフリカのサヘル地域は，住民が耐え忍ぶ「多重の危機」〔の存在〕にもかかわらず，チャンスに恵まれた地域と考えるべきだ。同地域は，アフリカ大陸西部のセネガルから東部ジブチまで広がる広大な過疎地で，テロに関係した紛争や気候変動の影響，開発不足によって不安定化が進んでいる。

IV　以下の文章の下線を引いた動詞（原形）について，文脈に沿って論理的，文法的に最も適切な形（他動詞，自動詞，分詞など）を４つの選択肢の中から選びなさい。

31.　解答：B

解説　関係代名詞節 that 以下が「直接的に標的とされている」（受動態の進行形）となるように過去分詞にする。

32.　解答：D

解説　They は前文の主語 These sanction measures であり，ここはその続きで述語動詞の形（原形と同じ）となる。

33.　解答：C

解説　前の the terrorist threat を後置修飾して「～によって引き起こされるテロの脅威」となるように過去分詞にする。

34.　解答：D

解説　提示されている has とともに現在完了の形にするために tried が適当で

ある。

35. 解答：D

解説 ここは medical（医療上の），religious（宗教上の）と並列的に reasons にかかり，「～に参加するために」という意味になるように不定詞にする。

36. 解答：B

解説 「『誘拐された』女性や子どもたち」となるように過去分詞にする。

37. 解答：C

解説 前置詞 for に続く動名詞にし，「『妨害したことで』制裁された」（前に sanctioned が省略されている）となる。

38. 解答：A

解説 助動詞 can に続く原形となる。

39. 解答：D

解説 「～することを決定する」という意味になるように decide に続く不定詞の形をとる。to err on the side of caution は「注意し過ぎるぐらい注意する」の意味。

40. 解答：B

解説 「『速やかに国内法に』移されるべき」という意味になるように，be 動詞とともに受動態の形を作る過去分詞になる。

訳例　国連安全保障理事会の制裁はもはや，かつてのような「鈍器」ではない。1990 年代以降，直接標的としていない民間人や国家への悪影響を最小限に抑える「重要な手段」へと変貌を遂げた――これは〔国連〕政治・平和構築担当事務次長のローズマリー・A・ディカルロ氏が月曜日，〔安保理で行われた〕制裁に関する討議で発表した声明の主要部分である。同討議は，制裁によって（特に人道的な意味で）生じる意図せぬ結果をテーマとしたものだった。

ディカルロ氏によれば，現在，世界各地で実施されている安保理制裁は 14 件にのぼっており，リビア，マリ，南スーダン，イエメンにおける紛争解決を支援するものや，ギニア・ビサウなどにおける憲法に違反する政権交代を抑止するもの，中央アフリカ共和国，コンゴ民主共和国，ソマリアにおける武装グループの活動資金となる天然資源の不正な開発を抑止するものなどがある。また，朝鮮民主主義人民共和国の核拡散活動や，イスラム系テロ組織（ISIL），アルカイダおよびその関連組織がもたらすテロの脅威を封じ込める〔ための制裁〕もある。

しかし，同政治〔・平和構築〕担当事務次長によると，制裁は「それ自体が目的ではない。効果を上げるには，包括的な政治戦略の一環として，直接の政治対話，調停，平和維持，特別政治ミッションと連動したものであるべきだ」という。また近年，安保理は市民や第三国への悪影響を回避しようと努めてきた，と同氏は述べた。

たとえば，武器禁輸の場合，人道援助に必要な非軍事的な装備の輸入には例外が認められるのが通例となっている。渡航禁止の場合は，医療や宗教上の理由，あるいは和平プロセスへの参加という目的がある場合に免除される。さらに，資産凍結では，食料や光熱費，医薬品の支払いが〔凍結の〕免除対象となっている。また，安保理はソマリアとアフガニスタンには常時の人道的免除措置を，またリビア，イエメン，北朝鮮にはケース・バイ・ケースの免除措置を，それぞれ設けている。

同事務次長はまた，制裁は現場の変化に応じて「継続的に調整される」として，安保理が対エリトリア制裁を解除したことや，中央アフリカ共和国に対する武器禁輸の条件を大幅に絞り込んだことを強調した。こうした変更の結果として，過去 10 年間に安保理制裁に起因する「特別な経済問題」に直面したと報告した加盟国は，わずか 1 カ国となっている。

過去 10 年間で，制裁は武器弾薬の流入や武装集団への資金供与を制限する以上の効果をもたらすことも明らかになった。現在では，ほぼすべての政権が国際人道基準の維持に努めている。例えば，2020 年には南スーダンで，誘拐された女性や子どもを軍事基地から解放する上で人道的義務が役に立ったし，コンゴ民主共和国では，武装集団に子どもを解放〔させる〕交渉を行う場が開かれた。

また，制裁は対象をより絞り込むようになり，50 以上の個人と団体が対象に指定されるようになった。例えば，イエメン〔では，首都〕サヌアにある犯罪捜査部のスルタン・ザビン部長が，紛争中に拷問と性的暴力を犯したとして制裁を受けた。また，マリでは，反政府勢力が強いキダル地方で「人道委員会委員長」を自称するアーメド・アグ・アルバチャールが，人道支援を届ける作業を妨害したとして制裁の対象となった。「このような行為に対してのみ制裁を科すのは比較的最近のことであり，歓迎すべき一歩。その運用は明確なシグナルを送るものだ」とディカルロ氏は強調した。

同事務次長にとって，包括的な制裁から対象を絞った制裁への進化は大転換となったが，懸念は依然として残る。北朝鮮へ人道的送金を行うための銀行業務プロセスは，2017年に崩壊して以来ずっと復旧が困難な状況で，〔上の転換を進める中で〕発生する課題の典型例となっている，と同氏は述べた。「金融関係の行為主体やその他のサービス提供者が追加の条件を課したり，コストを上げたり，あるいは単に商品やサービスの提供の求めを拒んだりすることで，人道支援を届けることを妨げる場合がある」(同)。

同氏は，アフガニスタン国民の支援を目的に人道的免除を設けるべく昨年終盤に採択された決議2615号を例に，もっとできることがあるはずだと主張した。そして最後に，「他の制裁においても同様の常時免除措置があれば，民間人の切実なニーズに応える上で大いに役立つだろう」と述べた。

マーティン・グリフィス人道問題担当事務次長も，アフガニスタンに対して承認された免除措置を取り上げ，活動の継続を可能にするものとして強調した。同事務次長は，制裁は高度化し，対象を絞り込んだものとすることができるが，国連と国連の提携先の活動においては，それを遵守することが常に日常的な課題となっている，と説明するとともに，「制裁は，我々の物流管理や財務状態，〔支援を〕届ける能力に影響を及ぼす。人道プロジェクトの遅延や停滞につながることもある。また，一部には，市民社会のすべての年代層の幸福を脅かす恐れがあるものもある」と述べた。グリフィス氏（緊急援助調整官を兼任）によると，加盟国が自ら行う制裁は，安全保障理事会が科す制裁に比べて広い範囲に影響を及ぼすことが多いという。

同人道問題担当事務次長は次に，リストアップされた個人や団体に関与することの難しさなど，いくつかの懸念事項について述べた。そうした個人または団体は，時に国民全体の生活に対して大きな支配力を持つ。同氏はまた，銀行やその他の商業者は，罰則を受けるリスクを回避するために，人道〔支援を行う〕顧客に対してサービス〔の提供〕を事実上拒否することがあるほか，食料や燃料，その他の生活必需品を扱う商業者も，慎重の上に慎重を期そうとするあまり，物不足や価格上昇を招いてしまう場合がある，と述べた。最後に，省庁がリストに挙がった個人によって運営されている場合，制裁によって社会サービスの提供や経済的安定が制限される可能性があるが，明らかにこれは，意図せざる結果である。

このような事態を緩和するため，同事務次長はいくつかの面での取り組みを提案した。グリフィス氏は安保理に対し，「煩雑で非効率的」な現在のケース・バイ・ケースの承認手続きに代えて，すべての制裁措置に最初から包括的な人道的〔例外〕区分を組み込むよう要請した。同氏はまた，人道援助資金の提供者やNGO，民間企業の懸念を和らげるために，こうした〔例外〕区分や免除規定を「速やかに国内法に移す」べきだ，とも述べた。

V 以下の文章の中に含まれる語句の意味として文脈上最も近いものを4つの選択肢の中から1つ選びなさい。

41. 解答：B

解説 「結果的に～になった」などの意味で，B.「生じさせた」と最も近い。Aは「明白にした」，Cは「粉飾した」，Dは「荒廃させた」などの意味。

42. 解答：C

解説 文中の so rapidly, so easily などの表現からも筆者の驚きが感じられる部分である。C.「愕然として」が最もそれを端的に言い得ている。Aは「穏やかな」，Bは「勇気づけられて」，Dは「魅了されて」などの意味。

43. 解答：B

解説 「～が染み渡った」「～に満ちた」などの意味で，B.「行き渡った」「広がった」が最も近い。Aは「直立した」，Cは「得意になった」，Dは「先行した」などの意味。

44. 解答：A

解説 「結末」などの意味で，A.「結末」「終わり」が最も近い。Bは「図々しさ」，Cは「冷静」，Dは「不誠実」などの意味。

45. 解答：D

解説 「不道徳な」「放縦な」などの意味で，D.「腐敗した」「邪悪な」が最も近い。Aは「無気力な」，Bは「決然とした」，Cは「荒々しい」などの意味。

46. 解答：C

解説 「勢い」などの意味で，C.「熱情」が最も近い。Aは「相違」，Bは「集合体」，Dは「深遠」などの意味。

47. 解答：A

解説 「士気を失った」などの意味で，A.「やる気のない」が最も近い。Bは「慈悲深い」，Cは「無法な」，Dは「活気づいて」などの意味。

48. 解答：D

解説 「高慢な」などの意味で，D.「尊大な」が最も近い。A は「不誠実な」，B は「風変わりな」，C は「だまされやすい」などの意味。

49. 解答：A

解説 「軍に属して」などの意味で，A.「軍隊の階級における地位」が最も近い。B は「不安定な状況」，C は「非公式の軍隊の身分」，D は「日々の肉体労働を行う義務」などの意味。

50. 解答：B

解説 ロマノフ朝ロシア帝国の崩壊を肌で感じた経験を述べた部分で，B.「ロマノフ家のひどい判断の末の悲惨な結果を強調する」ために書いたと判断できる。A.「継続している暴力をいかに終息させるかについての筆者の考えを示す」，C.「ロマノフ家の道徳性を革命支持者の不道徳性と対比する」，D.「ロシア史の歩みを良い方向へ変えた魅惑的な演説を描く」などは目的として当たらない。

訳例　1917 年 3 月の革命に至った不可避的な歴史的過程は，ロシア国家の崩壊という結果をもたらした。哲学者や歴史家，社会学者なら，ロシアの生活の変化を研究する中で，迫りくる破局を予見していたかもしれない。しかし，津波のごとく立ち上がった人民が，そのすべての存立基盤をこれほど急速に，そしてこれほど容易に一掃するとは，誰も予見できなかったのである。〔その要素とは〕闘うことなく消滅した最高権力者と統治階級であり，才能はあるが無力で，孤立して意志の力を欠き，最初は死闘の中で言葉だけを武器とし，後には勝者の刃におとなしく屈服した知識人階層であり，そして忘れてならないのは，歴史的伝統を誇る強力な 1,000 万人の軍隊であった。その軍隊は 3，4 カ月後には壊滅してしまった。

この最後の出来事，すなわち軍隊の崩壊はしかし，予想外とまで言えるものではなかった。というのも，日露戦争の結末や，それに続くモスクワ，クロンシュタット，セヴァストポリでの出来事が恐ろしい警告となっていたのだから。1905 年 11 月末，私〔アントーン・デニーキン〕はハルビンに 2 週間滞在した。また，1907 年 12 月にはシベリア鉄道で 31 日間，ハルビンからペトログラードまで，多くの「共和国」を横断する旅をした。こうして私は，自制を促す原則をまったく欠いた放縦な将兵の集団から何が予期されうるのか，それをはっきり示す〔経験〕を得た。あらゆる集会や決議，ソビエト，つまり，軍の反乱を示すあらゆる動きが，1917 年に写真のような正確さで再び生じたのだ。ただし，より激しい勢いとはるかに大きな規模で……。

注意すべきは，このような急激な心理的変化の可能性〔があるということ〕は，ロシア軍だけの特徴ではないということである。3 年間の流血を経た戦争疲れがこれらの出来事に重要な役割を果たしたことは疑いない。全世界の軍隊がその影響を受け，過激な社会主義の教義がもたらす破壊的な影響を受けやすくなったからである。1918 年の秋，ドン川および小ロシア地域を占領したドイツ軍部隊は，1 週間で士気を失い，我々がすでに経験した過程を一定程度繰り返すことになった。すなわち，集会，ソビエト，委員会，そして指揮官の廃止，また，一部の部隊における軍用品や馬，武器の売却という過程である。そのときになってようやくドイツ人はロシア将校の悲劇を理解した。かつてあれほど高慢で冷淡だったドイツ将校が自軍の堕落に激しく涙するのを，わが志願兵は何度も目にしている。

「君たちも我々に同じことをしたのだ。君たち自身が手を下したのだ」と我々は言った。「我々ではない。政府がやったことだ」――それが答えであった。

1918 年の冬，〔当時〕志願軍の総司令官であった私は，ドイツ人将校の一団から，我が軍に志願兵として加わりたいとの申し出を受けた。陸軍の崩壊は，敗北や大惨事がもたらす心理的な結果として説明し去ることはできない。勝者でさえも軍内で騒乱を経験した。部隊が指揮官の命令に必ずしも服さないことがあった。急速な復員，そして新たな人員（一部は志願兵）の参加によって，状況が変わっていった。

ロマノフ家の人々は，正統派君主制主義者が雄偉，高貴，畏敬という後光に好んで包み込もうとした「理念」というものを，もはや護持していなかった。私は，たまたま出席していたドゥーマ〔国会〕の会議の場で受けた印象を思い出す。このとき初めて，グチコフがドゥーマの演壇から，ラスプーチンについて警告の言葉を発したのであった。

「我が国はすべてよしという状況にはありません」。

やや騒々しかった議場は静まり返り，低い声で発せられる一言一言が，離れたところでもはっきり聞き取れた。ロシア史が通常進むべき道の上に，破滅を孕《はら》んだ得体のしれない雲が垂れ込めているようであった。

VI 以下の文章に最も適切に当てはまる単語のペアを4つの選択肢の中から1つ選びなさい。

51. 解答：A

解説 A は，well が under $3,000 の前に付いて「3,000 ドルをかなり下回って」，wariness が by her family の前に付いて「家族から**心配**（された）」となり，意味が通る。B，C，D については，第 2 空所候補の意味の違いから判断できる。

訳例　インドの実業家スワティ・ダガ氏 (33) が初めて暗号通貨ビットコインを購入したのは2017年のこと。当時〔対ドル〕相場は3,000ドルを大きく下回っていた。デジタル通貨に投資しようと決めた〔当時は〕，家族から心配されたという。しかし，その決断を後悔したことはない。ビットコインの価値が当時から15倍も上昇した〔からだ〕。

52.　解答：C

解説　Cは，once **lauded** as ～で「かつて～として称賛された」，**reminiscent** of ～ で「(過去に起きたことを) 思い出させる」となり，意味が通る。他の第1空所候補を見ていくと，Aは「称賛された」と訳せるものの「崇められた」のニュアンスがあり多少大げさ。また，Bは「(秘密などが) 暴露された」，Dは「おだてられた」などの意味。第2空所はB. evocativeは正解reminiscentの同義語として可能。

訳例　一時はゼロコロナの成功例として称賛された香港。〔しかし〕現在はコロナ禍初期を思わせる恐ろしい大流行との闘いを続けている。2年以上の準備期間〔を生かせなかった形だ〕。

53.　解答：B

解説　Bは，**Plagued** by ～ で「～に見舞われ」(plagueは「悩ませる」「苦しめる」などの意味)，be **poised** to ～ で「～する態勢にある」となり，意味が通る。Aは，Afflictedは擬人化表現として可能だが，initiated (始められた) は意味が適切でないと同時に，後に共起する不定詞は「～するために」となるため意味が通らない。Cはpossessed (取りつかれて) の意味が適切でない。Dはagitated (液体を揺り動かされて) の意味がdraughtと矛盾する。

訳例　米国最大の「水がめ」〔ミード湖〕で貯水量が急速に減少している。気候変動に伴う異常な干ばつと水の需要の増加によって，水位は記録に残る中でも過去最低となった。同湖は，米国最大の気候危機に数えられる西部渇水問題の中でも最重要ポイントとなりそうだ。

54.　解答：D

解説　Dは，**impose** sanctions on ～で「～に制裁を課す」，**strip** A of Bで「AからBを奪う」となり，意味が通る。Aは，第2空所候補rescind (ed)（〜を無効にする）の対象は直後の目的語となるため，“rescind the country” では意味が通らない。B は，第 1 空所の placing は可能だが，cancel(ed)（〜を取り消す）は上と同様の理由で適切でない。C の第 1 空所は begun arranging というつながりとなり，すでに制裁が科されつつあるという後半の文意に合わない。revoke(d)（〜を無効にする）は上と同じ理由で文意に合わない。

訳例　ロシアがウクライナへの侵攻を続ける中，さまざまな国際スポーツ団体がロシアとロシア選手に対する制裁を開始した。これまでにも，さまざまな運営組織がロシアチームの出場停止やロシアの大会開催権剥奪などの措置を講じている。

55.　解答：C

解説　C は，**entrenched** gender expectations で「凝り固まった性別による役割の期待」，**rife** は「広まっている」となり，意味が通る。A は，第 2 空所候補の replete が通常ポジティブな意味で用いられる語であることから不適。B は第 2 空所候補の endemic（地方特有の）の意味から文意に合わない。D は第 1 空所候補の tempered（緩和された）がここで gender expectation を形容する語としてふさわしくない。

訳例　先月，ソウル中心部に群衆が集まり，「Vote for Women」と鮮やかな色で書かれた白いたすきをかけ，プラカードを振った。抗議者たちの目的は，韓国に蔓延《まんえん》する性暴力や固定化した性役割期待，それに女性の企業役員や政治家の少なさを〔指摘し〕，女性差別がいまだに広がっている〔ことを示す〕例として人々の関心を集めることだ。

56.　解答：B

解説　B の **woe(s)** は「苦難」，**ground-breaking** ceremony で「起工式」「着工式」となり，意味が通る。A は第 2 空所候補 ice-breaking（緊張をほぐすような）が long-awaited など周囲の文脈にそぐわない（学校用語としての ice-breaking ceremony は新入生の親睦を深めるための活動をいう）。C は，第 1 空所候補 adversity は定冠詞 the を補えば可能だが，第 2 空所候補 earth-shaking は “surprising” のニュアンスを含有するため long-awaited との共起が矛盾する。D の第 2 空所候補 ribbon-cutting は完成した建造物で行われるので at the construction site との共起は不自然。

訳例　北朝鮮は首都平壌で積極的な住宅建設に乗り出し，広大な面積に建物を乱立させるアパート1万戸プロジェクトをスタートさせた。貿易制裁とコロナ禍がもたらした深刻な経済難の中，〔最高〕指導者の金正恩氏が土曜日，建設現場で行われた待望の着工式に出席した。国営メディアが報じた。

57. 解答：A

解説 Aは，be definitively datedで「年代が最終的に算定される」，slam into ～で「～にドシンとぶつかる」となり，意味が通る。Bは第2空所候補のwhackが他動詞のため適切でない。Cの第1空所候補decisivelyは可能（ただしA.のdefinitivelyの方が文脈上より適切）。C, Dの第2空所候補boomed，bangedはこの文脈に対しては口語的すぎる（おどけた）ニュアンスとなる。

訳例 グリーンランドの氷〔河で表面から〕1キロ下に発見された幅31キロ（19マイル）の隕石《いんせき》クレーター。その年代は長い間学会でも謎となっていたが，世界最大級の同クレーターについてこのほど年代が確定され，これまで考えられていたよりもはるかに古いことが判明した。〔具体的には〕この隕石の地球への衝突は，恐竜の絶滅からわずか数百万年後，つまり〔今から〕約5,800万年前〔の出来事だった〕。

58. 解答：D

解説 D. count(s) は「訴因」，deliberateは「審議する」となり，意味が通る。第1空所候補については，Aのallegation(s)，Bのindictmentsが可能。Cのbill（議案，法案）は文意に合わない。第2空所については文脈から，判決に導く裁判の手続きを指すdeliberate(d) が最適。

訳例 〔2021年〕1月6日の暴動に関連する初の連邦訴訟で，首都ワシントンの陪審員団はガイ・レフィット〔被告〕に対し，問われていた5件の罪状すべてについて有罪と判断した。レフィット被告は1月6日の議事堂〔襲撃事件の〕際にドナルド・トランプ大統領（当時）を支持しており，武器関連の容疑など5つの罪状で起訴されていた。陪審の審理時間はわずか4時間弱だった。

59. 解答：B

解説 Bは，ban A from ～ingで「Aが～するのを禁止する」，quest to ～で「～することの追求」となり，意味が通る。Aの第1空所候補cease(d)は「～をやめる，中止する」で意味をなさない。Cの第1空所候補stallは「一時的引き留め」の含意があり，後に続くcompleting the isolation

の文意に合わない。D の第 1 空所候補 banished は「〜を…から追放する，払いのける」などの意味で文意に合わない。第 1 空所については，B の ban 以外にも A，C，D のすべての候補が可能である。

訳例　ロシアは自国民の米ドル購入を禁止することで経済国としての孤立を完成させた。かつては世界の金融大国の仲間入りをする野心を抱いていたのだが……。2008 年のグルジア〔現在はジョージア〕攻撃に始まり，2014 年のクリミア併合，そして先月のウクライナ侵攻と続くプーチン大統領による近隣諸国支配追求の動きは，同大統領が抱いていた経済の夢の残りをもズタズタに砕いてしまった。

60.　解答：C

解説　C は，teeming with 〜 で「〜でいっぱいである」，immortalized は「永遠性を与えられた（太古の昔に描かれ現存している）」となり，意味が通る。A の第 1 空所候補 rampant（はびこっている）は植物の様子を表す形容詞で適当でない。B の第 1 空所候補 thronging は with との群動詞で C と同様の意味を表せるが，第 2 候補の canonize(d)（列聖する，偶像化する）が不適。D は，第 1 候補 replete は可能であるが，第 2 空所候補 mummified（ミイラにされた）が "frieze of rock paintings" の意味と矛盾する。

訳例　〔今から〕1 万 2,000 年以上前，南米には，車ほどの大きさの巨大な地上性ナマケモノや象のような草食動物，細長い鼻を持つ鹿に似た動物など，氷河期の動物たちが驚くほどたくさんいた。コロンビアのアマゾン熱帯雨林にある全長 8 マイル（13km）の横に長い岩窟壁画には，そうした絶滅した巨大生物が数多く描かれている。

Ⅶ

下線部の単語の意味を最もよく表しているものを
4 つの選択肢の中から 1 つ選びなさい。

61.　解答：A

解説　「(根深い) 憎しみ・怨恨」などの意味で，A.「(互いの嫌悪や意見の相違に起因する) 怒りの感情」が最も近い。B は「(他者を意に介さない) 冷淡さ」，C は「(他者を傷つけようとする) 悪意」，D は「(他者を傷つけようとする) 意地の悪さ」などの意味。

62.　解答：C

解説　「無効とされた」などの意味で，C.「却下された」が最も近い。A は「撤回された」，B は「卑しめられた」，D は「廃止された」などの意味。

63.　解答：B

解説　「独特な」などの意味で，B.「比類のない」が最も近い。A は「不公平な」，C は「断固たる」，D は「慣習・慣例に反する」などの意味。

64.　解答：D

解説　「働きかけた」などの意味で，D.「請願した」が最も近い。A は「黙認した」，B は「強要した」，C は「余儀なくさせた」などの意味。

65.　解答：C

解説　「非難」などの意味で，C.「非難」に最も近い。A は「放棄」，B は「排除」，D は「辞職」「断念」などの意味。

66.　解答：C

解説　「有罪性」「有責性」などの意味で，C.「有罪」「責任」が最も近い。A は「怠慢」，B は「不誠実」，D は「非行」などの意味。

67.　解答：A

解説　「態度」などの意味で，A.「態度」「物腰」が最も近い。B は「高尚さ」，C は「見解」，D は「素描」などの意味。

68.　解答：D

解説　「(正式な) 手続き」の意味で，ここでは D.「外交儀礼」が最も近い。A は「協定」，B は「紛糾」，C は「遂行」などの意味。

69.　解答：C

解説　「(恐怖や卑屈さで) すくむ」「畏縮する」などの意味で，この中では C.「しかめつらをする」が最も近い。A は「どなる」，B は「馬ぐしをかける」，D は「中傷する」などの意味。

70. 解答：A

解説 「回復」などの意味で，A.「再生」が最も近い。Bは「改装」，Cは「叱責」，Dは「改造」などの意味。

訳例　これ〔従軍慰安婦について対立する見解がもたらす問題〕については本書の後の部分で詳しく検討するが，まずはこれを「レバレッジ〔交渉上の相対的優位性〕」という観点から捉え，慰安婦に対する日本の対応をめぐる現在続いている議論において，このレバレッジが果たす役割について考えてみよう。交渉の場では，双方が有するレバレッジに対する見極めがなされる。レバレッジは，紛争の相手側に和解に至ることの重要性を認識させるものなのである。1990年代，日本軍による女性や少女の扱いが表面化すると，日本に対する正義の怒りが特に韓国人側で沸き起こった。第2次世界大戦中に慰安婦として徴用された女性の大半は，朝鮮半島出身者であった。

1990年代初めから被害者らが最初に頼りにしたのは裁判制度であった。しかし，1991年から2005年までの14年間，ほとんどの裁判で〔被害者側〕に有利な判決は下されず，また，そうした判決があっても日米両国の上訴審で覆されたことから，市民活動が活発化した。大半の日本人は数十年にわたり，この問題について日本ならではの礼儀正しさをもって控えめな態度を保っていた。結局のところ，大半の日本人はこの歴史の局面について，韓国人とは異なる理解をしていたのである。日本人は歴史事実に関する日本側の公式な解釈を教えられていた。すなわち，慰安婦は軍を客とするプロの売春婦として自発的に働いたものであって，労働に対して十分な待遇と報酬を得，愛国者としての義務を果たしたとする〔説明である〕。

「〔日本軍性奴隷制問題解決のための〕正義記憶連帯」は，かつては閲覧できなかった日米の公文書から明らかとなった膨大な証拠をもとに，粘り強く事実解明を進めた。また，正義記憶連体の支援者らは，慰安婦問題を調査する国連人権委員会特別報告者を任命するよう働きかけを行い，1994年にこれを実現させた。1999年，この国連によるこの広範な調査の結果が〔発表されると〕日本は，女性の権利に対する大規模な侵害を行ったとして厳しく非難されることとなった。2007年には米国下院において，日本に対して責任を認めるよう求める拘束力を持たない決議案が可決された。

しかし，この問題に対する日本の態度に最も影響を与えた行為は，調査や法律に基づくものではなかった。2011年12月14日，正義記憶連帯は1,000回目となる水曜デモを機に，在ソウル日本大使館の真向かいに慰安婦像を設置した。日本は〔それまでの〕控え目な態度を捨ててこれを非難し，韓国側に対して正式な抗議を開始した。同像が日本の尊厳を傷つけるものであり，一国が外交関係を結ぶ国際社会の一員の大使館設置を認める際に従うべきガイドラインと手続きに違反する，と主張したのである。

日本が初めて公式な対応を示すに至った追悼記念物〔碑〕は，2010年，ソウルではなく，ニュージャージー州のパリセーズパーク市立図書館の敷地内に設置されたものであった。慰安婦制度が人道に対する罪であるという主張は歴史的正確さと公正さ〔を欠くとして〕日本の複数の国会議員が異議を申し立てたのである。国会議員らは，慰安婦は志願したものであり，十分な報酬を得ていたと反論したが，むだであった。パリセーズパークに追悼碑を建て，日本大使館の前に像を設置することで，韓国側は意図するにせよしないにせよ，屈辱に身をすくませることで有名な日本を交渉のテーブルに着かせる強力なレバレッジを確立したのである。

いまもなお，新しい像や記念碑が建てられるたびに，その場所が韓国，米国，欧州のいずれであっても，日本は狼狽《ろうばい》する。日本に責任を認め，問題を解決するよう求める正義記憶連帯や他の市民社会団体は，それによってまた1つのレバレッジを得る。韓国にとって，この問題は慰安婦のための〔公正な〕裁き〔の実現〕と，韓国の国家としての尊厳の回復に関わるものである。日本にとっては，同国の見方で言う「不当な国家的屈辱」を受け，「面子」を大きく失ったという問題である。いずれにせよ，現段階ではっきり知るべきは，問題が解決されようがされまいが，正義記憶連帯には像を撤去するつもりがないということである。問題が早期に解決していれば，像や追悼碑が建てられることはなかったかもしれない。しかし現に設置された以上は，重要な歴史的事物になったと考えられる。

VIII 文脈上，空所を埋めるのに最も ふさわしいものを4つの選択肢の中から1つ選びなさい。

71. 解答：D

解説 コロン以下の “end the forever wars” は何かを定義づけられる語を選ぶとすると，D.「スローガン」「お題目」が最も適当である。A は「反撃」，B は「断言」「格言」，C は「隠語」などの意味。

72. 解答：C

解説 the United States’ disengagement が，a more violent and unstable regions をどうする恐れがあるか，と考えれば，C.「～への道を開いてしまう」「～を容易にする」が最も適当である。A は「不正な工作をする」B は「矢面に立つ」，D は「終わりにする」などの意味。

73. 解答：B

解説 ここまでの文脈から，この地域の宗派間対立による紛争や不安定な政情を象徴するような語を選ぶとすると，B.「火薬箱」が最も適当である。Aは「(クーデター後の）軍事政府」，Cは「奇妙な仕掛け」，Dは「有頂天」などの意味。

74. 解答：A

解説 スンニ派の（かつての）「過激主義」を形容する語としてふさわしい語としては，A.「猛毒を持った」「憎悪を持った」が最も適当である。Bは「不明瞭な」，Cは「散発的な」，Dは「慈悲深い」などの意味。

75. 解答：B

解説 Tehran（＝イラン）と同盟国の権力強化の動きに対するスンニ派の対抗意識は文脈的に明らかなので，その態度として最も適当なのは，B.「～に苛立っている」となる。Aは「～を大いに喜んでいる」，Cは「猫かわいがりする」，Dは「～（話など）に割り込んでいる」などの意味。

76. 解答：A

解説 スンニ派側に付いたイスラエルの介入と，敵対するイランの核開発計画との相関を考えれば，その介入が計画促進の「要因」となると考えられるため，A.「～が原因で」が最も適当である。Bは「～に加えて」，Cは「～の不足のために」，Dは「～と協力して」などの意味。

77. 解答：C

解説 米国の中東への関与縮小，スンニ派アラブ諸国の米国への不信ということから，イランの強硬路線政府の態度としては，C.「自己の主張を譲らずにいる」が最も適当である。Aは「(退屈のあまり）両手の親指をくるくる回している（のらくらしている)」，Bは「がっくり膝をついている」，Dは「聞き耳を立てている」などの意味。

78. 解答：D

解説 which以下の関係詞節の先行詞はthe struggleであり，それが「養分とし，また油を注いだもの」として最も適当なのは，D.「(両者の）分裂」

である。A は「無念」，B は「失策」，C は「こじつけ」などの意味。

79. 解答：A

解説 このパラグラフの前半でイランの勢力拡大が描かれているが，当該部分は，勢力拡大を基にしたその発展がさらに述べられているので，A.「そうすることで」が最も適当である。B は「1 つの理由には」，C は「概して」，D は「とりわけ」などの意味。

80. 解答：B

解説 scare A into 〜（A を脅して〜をさせる）の表現の中で使われており，for his regime（彼の政権に対する）に意味的・文法的につながる最も適当なものは，B.「揺るぎない支持」になる。A は「不変の正当性」，C は「分裂を伴う刷新」，D は「無尽蔵の資金」などの意味。

訳例　バイデン政権の中東に対する持論は単純である。「『永遠の戦争』を終わらせる」というものだ。ホワイトハウスは中国が突き付ける難題への対処に追われており，中東の終わりの見えない、そして勝ち目もなさそうな紛争から米国を引き離そうとしている。しかし，米国が関与をやめれば，そのあとに政治的空白が残され，それを埋めるように宗派間対立が生じて，この地域における暴力の激化や不安定化をお膳立てしてしまう恐れがある。

イランのシーア派による神政国家と，スンニ派アラブ人（最近ではスンニ派テュルキエ＝トルコ）が率いる国々との間の地政学的優位をめぐる争いによって，地域全体にわたって紛争がかき立てられており，それが社会的合意を毀損し，国家機能不全を悪化させ，過激派運動をエスカレートさせる結果を招いている。双方とも自己の目的のために宗教的アイデンティティーを武器としてきた。そしてそれを利用して支持者を集め，地域全体に影響力を強めてきた。その結果，拡大中東地域は今なお「火薬箱」のままである。

イランは優位を保っているものの，その地位に挑戦する動きが地域全体に広がりつつある。スンニ派は「猛毒」のような過激主義にうんざりしているが，「イスラミックステート」(ISIS) 台頭のもととなった怒りは薄れてはおらず，地域内の破綻した部分部分に生じている新たな反政府活動がその怒りを再び利用することは間違いない。イラク，レバノン，シリアのスンニ派は，イランとイランの同盟国が権力を強化しようとする動きにますます苛立ちを感じている。またアフガニスタンでは，タリバンの勝利に続いて国が混乱に陥り，テロリズムが再び台頭してきた。これらの緊張を和らげる政治的プロセスがなければ，新たな騒乱と流血の事態が相次いで勃発するに違いない。

イスラエルがスンニ派勢力の側に付いてこうした宗派間紛争に介入したことは，ただ火に油を注ぐ結果となった。イスラエルが関与することで，地域の安定はイランの核開発計画の行方にいっそう左右されることになる。米国とイスラエルの両国政府は外交的解決に至らない場合に備え，すでに「プランB」の議論を進めている。この方向はイランと米国を衝突コースに乗せるだけではない。それは，宗派間の緊張を激化させ，社会の分断を深め，レバント〔東部地中海沿岸地方〕からアフガニスタン〔にわたる地域〕に新たな紛争をもたらすだろう。中東への関与を縮小しようとする米国政府の意向〔が明らかになったが，それ〕は折しも中国とロシアが中東に接近し，イランの強硬政権が主張を一歩も譲らず，スンニ派アラブ諸国が米国の安全保障に対して信頼をなくしつつある最中《さなか》のことである。米国は，まずはイラン核開発計画をめぐる合意を結ぶことを手始めに，より安定した地域秩序を実現する道を切り開かないかぎり，せっかく手を引く苦労をしながら，再び中東の多くの紛争に巻き込まれることにもなりかねない。

シーア派とスンニ派の対立の起源はイスラム教の最初期にまでさかのぼり，両派は数世紀にわたってイスラム法と宗教的慣習について〔それぞれ〕独自の解釈を発展させてきた。しかし，現在の両派の争いの根は，神学的な問題というより，むしろ権力闘争にある。シーア派とスンニ派は，分断された社会において〔異なる〕政治信条を形成する際立ったアイデンティティーマーカー〔自他を思想的に区別する標識〕となっている。宗派間抗争は過去20年間に激化したり沈静化したりしたが，この地域の政治に対して宗派主義が持つ際立った重要性は衰えていないし，この分裂を養分としつつ，それに油を注ぐイランとスンニ派主導の敵国との間の闘いも鎮まってきてはいない。この2つの勢力は同じコインの裏表なのである。

イランがアラブ世界での影響力を飛躍的に拡大しえた要因は，2003年の米国によるイラク侵攻であった。〔イラクでは〕少数派のスンニ派による統治を〔首都〕バグダッドで担保していた権威主義的政権を米国が打倒して以来，イラン政府は，宗派に対する忠誠心を巧みに利用して，レバノンおよびシリアからイラク，イエメンまで広がる武装した代理者〔親イラン派〕のネットワークを強化し，かつてヨルダンのアブドゥラ国王が言ったように「シーア派の三日月地帯」を形成してきた。これによってイランは，地域全体のスンニ派を犠牲にしてシーア派に力を与え，サウジアラビア，トルコ，アラブ首長国連邦などの敵対する国々に対して影響力を高めてきた。

アラブ世界が民主化とよい統治を推進しようとする動き（いわゆる「アラブの春」）は，変化が起きるかもしれないと怯《おび》えた独裁者たちが宗派対立をさらに武器として利用するという結果を招いた。シリアのバシャル・アル・アサド大統領は，スンニ派に対する恐怖心を焚《た》きつけることでアラウィー派（アサド氏自身が属する宗派で，シーア派から分かれた一派）を脅し，政権への揺るぎない支持を得た。バーレーンとイエメンでは，支配層がシーア派の抗議者らをイランの代理人だとして非難し，暴力的な弾圧を正当化した。イランと，イランに敵対するアラブ諸国は，シーア派とスンニ派のそれぞれの「顧客」の背後に陣取り，同じ宗派に属する人々を地域における自陣営の影響力を守る道具と見なすことで，この力動的関係を補強したのである。

IX

以下の質問に対し，200～250語の短いエッセイを英語で書きなさい。

質問文：気候変動との闘いの核心だと感じる懸念事項について論じよ。

解答例 I think adaptation, following acceptance and accommodation, is the central theme in the battle against human-caused climate change.

By “acceptance” I mean scientific evidence now enables most people to accept human-caused climate change as a real and urgent peril.

By “accommodation” I mean most people understand they must change their lives to ensure a sustainable future for life on Earth.

By “adaptation” I mean concrete action to reverse climate change, utilizing science and driven by global recognition (acceptance) and commitment (accommodation) with regional approaches, must begin immediately. For example, the United Nations University’s Institute of Environment and Human Security (UNU-EHS) has devised such action strategies in real-world partnerships—with San Pedro Sula, Honduras, a large industrial city; the Afar and Somali regions of Ethiopia; and Can Tho, a city in southern Viet Nam—as case studies using a technique called Economics of Climate Adaptation (ECA) to craft the most advantageous and cost-effective plans tailor made for each part of the world.

As policy-makers and leaders learn how their region can adapt in the most cost-effective ways, specific recommendations and benefits, and the numbers of people and millions of dollars to be saved—for example, $6 million investment preventing $300 million in damages in the ECA-based forecast for Can Tho city—are detailed in Economics of Climate Adaptation recommendations.

I conclude the economics of climate adaptation are central to the battle against human-caused climate change for two reasons: all initiatives for environmental sustainability require adaptation and cost-effectiveness is always a concern.

解説　第1パラグラフでは，「(気候変動に対して) 受容し，順応し，さらに適応することが重要だ」という自らの主張を明確に述べている。第2パラグラフで，「受容」とは気候変動の危機を認識することであるということ，第3パラグラフで，「順応」とは気候変動に合わせて生活を変えることであるということを定義づけている。続く第4パラグラフで，「適応」が気候変動を反転させる具体的な行動と定義され，具体的な取り組み（国連大学と諸外国の行動戦略）について紹介している。第5パラグラフは，「適応」の費用対効果の重要性について，例を挙げて詳しく述べている。そして第6パラグラフで，費用対効果を考慮した「適応」の実現のためには，気候変動適応経済学が中心的役割を果たすと結論付けている。

訳例　人間がもたらした気候変動との闘いにおいて，適応は，受容や順応に続く中心的なテーマだと思う。

「受容」とは，科学的な証拠によって大多数の人が，人間がもたらした気候変動を現実的かつ差し迫った危険として認めることができるようになったということをいう。

「順応」とは，地球上の生命に対して持続可能な未来を確実に実現するために，大半の人が生活を変える必要を理解していることを指す。

「適応」とは，科学を活用するとともに，世界的な認識（受容）と地域的アプローチを伴う真剣な取り組み（順応）が牽引《けんいん》する形で，気候変動を反転させる具体的な行動を直ちに開始しなければならないことを意味する。たとえば，国連大学環境・人間の安全保障研究所（UNU-EHS）では，実際のパートナーシップ（ホンジュラスの大工業都市サン・ペドロ・スーラ，エチオピアのアファール地方とソマリ地方，ベトナム南部の都市カントーと提携）の下，気候適応経済学（ECA）という手法を用いて，そうした行動戦略を考案してきた。〔これは〕世界各地で最も有利で費用対効果の高い計画を地域にぴったり合う形で策定するケーススタディとなるものである。

地域がどうすれば最も費用対効果の高い方法で適応できるかを，その地域の政策立案者や指導者が知ることが〔できる〕よう，具体的な提言や利益，それに救われる人の数や節約できる100万ドル単位の資金（例えば，カントー市に関するECA予測では600万ドルの投資で3億ドルの損害を防ぐ〔ことが可能〕）が，気候適応経済学を用いた提言書の中に詳述されている。

結論としては，人間がもたらした気候変動との闘いにおいて中心的な役割を果たすものは，以下の2つの理由から気候適応経済学であると考える。すなわち，環境の持続可能性実現のための取り組みにはすべて適応が要求されること，費用対効果が常に関心事となること〔の2つである〕。

2022年特A級第1回試験　正解一覧

Ⅰ

1. B　2. C　3. C　4. D　5. D　6. A　7. C　8. D　9. B　10. C

Ⅱ

11. D　12. B　13. D　14. C　15. D　16. C　17. D　18. D　19. A　20. B

Ⅲ

21. C　22. B　23. C　24. A　25. D　26. D　27. D　28. C　29. D　30. A

Ⅳ

31. B　32. D　33. C　34. D　35. D　36. B　37. C　38. A　39. D　40. B

Ⅴ

41. B　42. C　43. B　44. A　45. D　46. C　47. A　48. D　49. A　50. B

Ⅵ

51. A　52. C　53. B　54. D　55. C　56. B　57. A　58. D　59. B　60. C

Ⅶ

61. A　62. C　63. B　64. D　65. C　66. C　67. A　68. D　69. C　70. A

Ⅷ

71. D　72. C　73. B　74. A　75. B　76. A　77. C　78. D　79. A　80. B

2022年
第2回試験
問題

特A級第１次試験問題用紙

特A級

外務省後援

２０２２年度第２回国際連合公用語

英語検定試験（120分）

受験上の注意

1．問題用紙は試験開始の合図があるまで開いてはいけません。その間に、この**受験上の注意を熟読しておいてください。**

2．**受験番号と氏名を解答用紙（マークシートと作文用紙）**に記入してください。

3．解答用紙の配布は１人１部のみです。複数の配布は致しません。

4．試験開始前は、答案への解答記入は禁止です。

5．マークシートの記入は、１～100までの記入箇所がありますが、この級では１～80までを使います。

6．マークシートの記入は、必ずＨＢ以上の濃い鉛筆を使って該当箇所を黒く塗りつぶしてください。書き間違いの場合は「アト」が残らないように消してください。マークシートは絶対に折ったり曲げたりしないでください。

7．受験級、受験地区、会場番号、受験番号のマークシートへの記入は監督者の指示に従い、間違いなく記入してください。**(裏表紙の「マークシート記入例」参照)**

8．作文は、⑴読みやすい文字をペン、ボールペンまたはＨＢ以上の濃い鉛筆で書いてください。⑵使用語数の200～250語を目安にしてください。

9．試験問題についての質問は、印刷が不鮮明な場合を除き、一切受けつけません。

10．中途退室の際は、マークシートと作文用紙を持って監督者に渡し、他の受験者の迷惑にならないように静かに退室してください。中途退室後の再入室はできません。

11．試験中は他の受験者の妨げとなる行動は慎んでください。また携帯電話等の電源はお切りください。

12．マークシートと作文用紙は監督者に提出し、問題用紙はご自由にお持ち帰りください。

＊試験問題の複製や転載、インターネットへのアップロード等、いかなる媒体への転用を禁止します。

試験結果について

1．第１次試験の結果は2022年11月24日㈭頃に受験申込書に記載された住所に郵送で通知します。

2．その間に住所変更をされた方は、郵便局へ住所変更の届け出を忘れずに行ってください。

3．発表前の試験結果のお問合せには応じられません。

第２次試験について

1．第１次試験合格者には、試験結果発表と同時に試験日時、会場を指定して通知します。

2．第２次試験は2022年12月11日㈰です。特Ａ級（Ａ級との併願を含む）の試験地は**東京と大阪**になります。あらかじめご了承願います。

公益財団法人 日本国際連合協会
http://www.unaj.or.jp/

I. Fill in each of the following blanks with the most appropriate of the four alternatives according to the knowledge and information gained from *New Today's Guide to the United Nations.*

1. **United Nations Headquarters**

The Security Council held its first meetings in its new chamber early in ________, and in October of the same year, the Assembly convened for the first time in the new General Assembly Hall.

A. 1949　B. 1950　C. 1951　D. 1952

2. **Secretariat**

Under ________ of the Charter of the United Nations, each Member State undertakes to respect the exclusively international character of the responsibilities of the Secretary-General and the Staff and not to seek to influence them in the discharge of their duties.

A. Article 33　B. Article 41
C. Article 68　D. Article 100

3. **International Maritime Organization (IMO)**

The IMO's policy making body is the Assembly, in which all 174 IMO member States (as of August 2018) and one associate member, ________, are represented.

A. Tokelau　B. Hong Kong
C. Macau　D. Puerto Rico

4. **Origins of peacekeeping**

Peacekeeping Operation (PKO) is one of the United Nation's activities for maintaining international peace and security. The PKO of the United Nations is innovative because there are no specific ________ in the Charter of the United Nations.

A. stipulations　B. provisions
C. mandates　D. commissions

5. **The United Nations Global Compact**

The United Nations Global Compact (UNGC) is a framework for voluntary efforts by companies and stakeholders to act as good citizens while making their commitments to ________ principles on human rights, labor, environment and anti-corruption.

A. five　B. ten　C. twelve　D. twenty

6. **Food Problems**

Approximately ________ million people worldwide were still suffering from chronic malnutrition in 2014-2016. The SDGs accordingly include the goal of ending famine and malnutrition by 2030.

A. 75 B. 167 C. 432 D. 793

7. **Population Questions**

In 1970 the General Assembly designated 1974 as the World Population Year and it held the World Population Conference in ________ in August 1974, where the World Population Plan of Action was adopted.

A. Vienna B. Geneva C. Bucharest D. Berne

8. **Assistance to Refugees**

The legal status of refugees is defined in two international treaties: the 1951 Convention Relating to the Status of Refugees and its 1967 ________ , which defines the rights and duties of refugees.

A. Protocol B. Covenant C. Entente D. Pact

9. **Judicial Settlement of Disputes**

The International Criminal Court (ICC) was established by the Rome Statute in 1998 and began work in ________ . The ICC has jurisdiction to prosecute individuals who commit genocide, war crimes and crimes against humanity as defined in the Rome Statute.

A. 2002 B. 2003 C. 2004 D. 2005

10. **Japan's Relationship with UN Specialized Agencies**

From the late 1960s through the early 1970s when a proposal made by then Secretary-General ________ to establish a United Nations University (UNU) was deliberated in the UN, major powers like the U.S., the U.K., France, and the Soviet Union were all reluctant to approve the idea because they saw no urgent need in it.

A. Kurt Waldheim B. Javier Pérez de Cuéllar
C. Dag Hammarskjöld D. U Thant

II. Choose from among the four alternatives the one that most closely corresponds to the meaning contained in the following passage.

(1) With 22 million residents in 2010, the Xinjiang Uyghur Autonomous Region (XUAR) is China's largest and westernmost region rich in natural resources such as oil, gas and uranium. It is also a connectivity hub across Eurasia, and crucial to the renewal of the ancient Silk Road. The region encourages the development of China's new Silk Road Economic Belt, which is part of the Belt and Road Initiative put forward by President Xi Jinping. Since the founding of the People's Republic of China (PRC), Beijing has attempted to incorporate Xinjiang into the Chinese state through land reform and the building of infrastructure.

(2) Although China's constitution states that ethnic groups are equal, China maintains quite a paternalistic attitude towards its minorities. The Constitution also guarantees their freedom of religion; however, religions must accommodate socialism (Saunders 2017) because Beijing fears their interference and requires religious organisations to register with the Religious Affairs Bureau. Since religion equals ignorance, Uyghur are also considered to be primitive, thieves and increasingly as terrorists (Kantian 2007, 64, 73), while those Uyghur who receive Chinese education are criticised by other Uyghur for sacrificing their culture (Kantian 2007, 17) in exchange for better economic opportunities.

(3) The concept of security that China applies to Xinjiang mirrors a realist definition of national security as the preservation of China's national territory and institutions. The region constitutes a security concern for the Chinese Communist Party (CCP) because its independence would likely threaten the territorial integrity of the PRC by triggering other autonomous regions, such as Tibet, to push for independence. ______________, ethnic and religious dimensions become subordinate to national unity. The use of violence is required to suppress any opposition to a unified China based on Han nationalism, and the economic dimension has become a major tool in the repressive measures. **(A)** China acknowledges separatism as the main threat to Xinjiang's stability. ① It blames hostile foreign forces, mainly the US, for backing Human Rights, minority rights, the spreading of democratic values, and the insurgency in Xinjiang (e.g., through the World Uyghur Congress). ② However, rioters are traditionally indigenous, though increasingly embedded in global jihad networks. ③ The Chinese Communist Party (CCP) fears an independent Xinjiang because it would likely trigger independence movements in other regions, such as Tibet. ④ Therefore, China implements a pervasive surveillance system, the increasing militarisation of the region, repressive policies towards Uyghur, and 'forced Hanicisation' of Xinjian (Laruelle 2012, 179). This has made the ratio of Turkic-speaking Muslims drop from around 90% of the population at the end of the 1940s (Forbes 1986, 6) to roughly half in the 2010s (Han and Paik 2017, 39).

(4) China's strategy adopts **a carrot and stick approach**. Strike Hard security campaigns address political unrest, criminal activities and religious movements under the same banner. In 2017, the provincial government expanded a 2015 regulation forbidding Muslim names as 'overly religious' (Feng 2017). Passports have been seized (Hornby 2016), Muslim dress codes forbidden, and long beards banned (Reuters 2017). In 2017, the Hotan/Hetian prefecture issued a directive outlawing the teaching of Uyghur language at school, including secondary school (Sulaiman 2017), and the XUAR Working Guidelines on the Accurate Registration and Verification of Population introduced biometric collection scheme for Xinjiang's residents from 'DNA samples, fingerprints, iris scans and blood types' (Haas 2017). **(B)**

(5) China's repression of Uyghur culture and religion also breeds resentment. The prohibition of formal religious education under the age of 18 and of informal religious education even if given privately by parents (Wayne 2008, 105) did not eradicate fundamentalism. Rather, these measures increased Uyghur's rancour. Cultural and religious constraint triggers violent protests (Purbrick 2017, 241) with Uyghur reaching the Middle East or Turkey to study and/or fight for Islam. **(C)** Though China's strategic partnership with Egypt, Saudi Arabia, Turkey, and Iran does not stop trade with Muslim countries, it does complicate China's relations with these countries. Therefore, by fearing the support of Muslim countries for Uyghur separatists, Beijing plays down 'proliferation concerns and supplies arms and problematic technology to them at generous prices' (Horner 2002, 44).

(6) Economic development in the region has also played a crucial role in Beijing's approach. Yet, (1) __________________, economic opportunities benefit Han residents disproportionally, and favourable policies to attract Han enhance competition for land and water. Xinjiang per capita income remains behind the national average and the growing wealth gap between Han settlers concentrated in towns and Uyghur concentrated in underdeveloped rural areas (2) __________________. The World Uyghur Congress argues that development policies such as the opening of the Northwest to trade with Central Asia, the development of the Western regions, and more recently the Belt and Road Initiative all result in the marginalisation of the Uyghur (WUC 2016, 2).

(7) While China pushes for economic development in Xinjiang, tight media control and cyber-surveillance constrain the region's economic growth: access to the Internet is pervasive and control exceptionally extensive. **(D)** This explains why Xi Jinping called again for setting up a 'Great Wall of Steel' in Xinjiang (Reuters 2017). The militarisation of Xinjiang is increased by the use of new technology such as the use of drones. In 2013, the regional government ordered China Aerospace Science and Technology Corporation drones for targeting terrorists. It requested drone pilots after 100 people were killed in violence that erupted in Xinjiang in 2014 when Muslims reacted against the security measures during the Ramadan (Tatlow 2014).

Furthermore, counter-terrorist efforts include the use of drones and tracking devices on vehicles based on China's Beidou navigation satellite system (Phillips 2017).

(8) China's security policy towards Xinjiang will push regional development further as well as push further repressive policies, and there is no real alternative for Uyghur to the dilemma of either resisting or sinicising.

11. Which is correct according to the information <u>explicitly stated</u> in paragraphs 1 and 2?

A. Xinjiang is an independent province rich in resources that President Xi Jinping has long wanted to incorporate into the Chinese state.

B. Xinjiang is crucial to the renewal of the ancient Silk Road, initiated at the founding of the People's Republic of China, and redevelopment of the new Silk Road Economic Belt.

C. China has a paternalistic attitude towards its minorities, guaranteeing freedom for all religions through registration with the Religious Affairs Bureau.

D. There is division among the Uyghur regarding abandoning their own culture in exchange for improved economic opportunities that Chinese education might offer.

12. According to the information presented in Paragraph 3, which of the following expressions best fits the blank in that paragraph?

A. Apropos B. Ergo
C. Hitherto D. Notwithstanding

13. In Paragraph 3, which of the underlined sections, ① to ④, should be omitted because it is either unnecessary or inappropriate there?

A. ① B. ② C. ③ D. ④

14. The underlined phrase "a carrot and stick approach" in Paragraph 4 is referring to which of the following?

A. biometric collection schemes and ethnic repression

B. economic development and strict security campaigns

C. national unity and the banning of religious symbols

D. strategic partnerships and the prohibition of religion

15. **In the context of the information presented in Paragraph 6, which of the following sets, (A to D), best fits the blanks (1) and (2) in the paragraph?**

A. (1) besides security measures (2) has led to economic migration

B. (1) despite Xinjiang's economy improving (2) inflames social tensions

C. (1) in spite of increasing repression (2) has narrowed in recent years

D. (1) while the region's economy declines (2) intensifies discord among people

16. **Which of the following is correct according to the information presented in Paragraph 7?**

A. Muslims reacted violently against security measures during Ramadan because Xi Jinping set up a 'Great Wall of Steel' in Xinjiang.

B. The militarisation of Xinjiang includes new technology in counter-terrorism such as drones and tracking devices based on China's Beidou navigation satellite system.

C. Violence that erupted in Xinjiang in 2014, led the regional government to order China Aerospace Science and Technology Corporation drones for targeting terrorists.

D. While control over the Internet and cyber-surveillance constraints are extensive, economic development in Xinjiang has flourished.

17. **Which part of the essay, indicated by the capital letters in parentheses, is MOST appropriate for the following sentence?**

Although security measures and censorship made it difficult to have reports on Xinjiang unrest, officers admit there are incidents.

A. (A) B. (B) C. (C) D. (D)

18. **Which of the following is explicitly stated in the essay?**

A. Although other Muslim minorities live in Xinjiang, the Uygur issue dominates regional security concerns because the Uyghur are the largest minority.

B. Beijing cultivates relations with Muslim countries through the arms trade to obtain support for its policy in Xinjiang and to deter them from supporting the Uyghur's cause.

C. The Uyghur issue is gaining importance within Al Qaeda and domestic and international dimensions are increasingly entangled.

D. While separatist and Islamist movements flourished in poor areas of Xinjiang, poverty was not the only root of terrorism as rich Muslims also embraced it.

19. **Which of the following is <u>NOT</u> correct according to the information presented in the essay?**

A. China's security policy in Xinjiang leaves the Uyghur with only two alternatives.

B. Disallowing Uyghur children to learn about religion was an ineffective measure.

C. Repressive policies have substantially reduced the ratio of Turkic-speaking Muslims.

D. To suppress opposition to unity based on Han nationalism, violence is unnecessary.

20. **If we divide paragraphs (2) to (7) into four main topics, which set, A, B, C, or D, is the most representative?**

	Topic 1	Topic 2	Topic 3	Topic 4
A.	(2) (3)	(4)	(5) (6)	(7)
B.	(2) (3)	(4) (5)	(6)	(7)
C.	(2)	(3) (4) (5)	(6)	(7)
D.	(2)	(3)	(4) (5)	(6) (7)

Ⅲ. Choose from among the underlined phrases the one that is grammatically or idiomatically incorrect.

21. At the end **(A)** of her official visit to China, the first such trip in 17 years, UN rights chief Michelle Bachelet **(B)** announced new areas of engagement between her office and the Chinese Government **(C)** on rights issues, and summarized **(D)** many rights issues raised during her six-day May mission.

22. The "enormous challenges" faced by the northeastern Nigerian **(A)** state of Borno, which include a continuing terrorist insurgency, need to **(B)** be recognized by the international community to create what the UN Secretary-General has called **(C)** a "state of hope and a state of reality", in a region where **(D)** he said did not live up to its reputation for "terrorism, violence, displacement or despair."

23. **(A)** A deal reportedly made by the United Kingdom to send some migrants **(B)** for processing and relocation to the Central African nation of **(C)** Rwanda, is at odds with States' responsibility to **(D)** take care of those in need for protection, the UN refugee agency, UNHCR, said on Thursday.

24. More than 70 percent of South Sudan's **(A)** population will struggle to survive the peak of the annual 'lean season' **(B)** this year, as the country grapples unprecedented **(C)** levels of food insecurity caused by conflict, climate shocks, COVID-19, **(D)** and rising costs, the UN's World Food Programme (WFP) warned on Friday.

25. Top UN officials on Tuesday **(A)** gathered with government and civil society representatives to **(B)** draw attention to the scourge of violence against women **(C)** worldwide who are involved in politics, which is increasingly seeing women parliamentarians, human rights defenders **(D)** and electoral observers silent, and intimidated.

26. **(A)** The top UN political affair official urged the Security Council **(B)** on Friday to be united in its response to the Democratic People's Republic of Korea's (DPRK) **(C)** latest intercontinental ballistic missile launch – the country's first long-range test since 2017 – **(D)** as delegates met on Friday afternoon in emergency session, to discuss the matter.

27. **(A)** For ten weeks into the war in Ukraine, UN humanitarians on Friday **(B)** said that they were urgently ramping up efforts to provide vulnerable children **(C)** with specialist and psychosocial support, amid "tremendous" mental health **(D)** needs and ongoing dangers linked to the Russian invasion and sexual and gender-based violence.

28. The explosive growth of extractive operations around the world **(A)** often plays out on indigenous people's lands without their **(B)** consent, causing irreparable harm to their livelihoods, cultures, languages and lives, speakers told the Permanent Forum on Indigenous Issues on Monday, **(C)** as it opened its 2022 session amid calls to respect their free, prior **(D)** and informed consent on the existent decisions uprooting their communities.

29. Countries already under pressure from the economic **(A)** fall-out of the COVID-19 pandemic risk seeing the same economic turmoil **(B)** and human misery as Sri Lanka, with the war in Ukraine **(C)** dragging on, when the international community agrees to radical financial **(D)** measures to help countries saddled with debt, the UN said on Thursday.

30. **(A)** The chances of seeing unprecedented temperatures of 40 degree Celsius (40° C) **(B)** or more in the UK could be up to 10 times more **(C)** likely in the current climate under a "natural **(D)** climate unaffected by human influence," the World Meteorological Organization (WMO) declared on Monday.

Ⅳ. Choose the answer that uses the most logically and grammatically appropriate form of each underlined infinitive, in whichever manner (transitive, intransitive, participle, or otherwise) it is used, in the context of the following article.

Trying the gravest crimes, involving victims, ensuring fair trials, complementing national tribunals: in its first 20 years of existence, the International Criminal Court has made notable progress in its crucial mission. Ahead of the 20th anniversary of the Court on 1 July 2022, here are five ways the ICC is **(31) to help** build a more just world.

1) Trying the gravest crimes: The ICC was created with "millions of children, women and men" in mind who "have been victims of unimaginable atrocities that deeply shock the conscience of humanity". It is the world's first permanent, treaty-based, international criminal court to investigate and prosecute perpetrators of crimes against humanity, war crimes, genocide, and the crime of aggression. During its first 20 years, the ICC has tried and resolved cases of significance for international justice, shedding light on the crimes of **(32) to use** child soldiers, destruction of cultural heritage, sexual violence, or attacks on innocent civilians. Through its judgments in exemplary cases, it builds authoritative case law: 31 cases were opened; judges have **(33) to pronounce** 10 convictions and four acquittals. The Court has 17 ongoing investigations into some of the world's most violent conflicts, such as the Democratic Republic of the Congo, Central African Republic, Georgia, and Ukraine.

2) Involving victims: The Court does not only **(34) to try** and punish those responsible for the most serious crimes, but also ensures voices of the victims—those who have suffered harm as a result of the commission of any crime within the Court's jurisdiction—are heard. More than 10,000 victims of atrocities have participated in all stages of ICC judicial proceedings, and the Court maintains direct contact, through outreach programs, with communities **(35) to affect** by crimes within its jurisdiction. The Court also seeks to protect the safety and psychological integrity of victims and witnesses. Although victims cannot bring cases, they can bring information to the Prosecutor, including to decide whether to open an investigation. The ICC Trust Fund for Victims is currently making the Court's first orders on reparations a reality. Through its assistance programs, the Fund has **(36) to provide** physical, psychological and socio-economic support to more than 450,000 victims.

3) Ensuring fair trials: All defendants are presumed innocent until proven guilty beyond reasonable doubt before the ICC. Each defendant is entitled to public and impartial proceedings. At the ICC, suspects and accused persons have critical rights, including: to be informed of the charges; to have adequate time and facilities to prepare their defence; to be tried without undue delay; to freely choose a lawyer; to receive exculpatory evidence from the Prosecutor. Among these rights is the right to follow the proceedings in a language the accused fully understands; amongst others. This has led to the Court hiring specialized interpreters and translators in more than 40 languages, and sometimes using, simultaneously, four languages during the same hearing. In its first 20 years, participants were faced with a diversity of new substantive and procedural challenges, miles away from the crime scenes. In addition, the crimes prosecuted by the ICC are of a specific nature and often mass crimes requiring large amounts of evidence as well as substantial and effective efforts **(37) to ensure** the safety of the witnesses. The proceedings are complex and a great number of matters must be resolved in providing support at all levels over the course of a case.

4) Complementing national courts: The Court does not replace national courts. It is a court of last resort. States have primary responsibility to investigate, try and punish perpetrators of the most serious crimes. The Court steps in only when States are unwilling or unable to genuinely address allegations of serious crimes under the Court's jurisdiction. Serious violence is escalating rapidly around the world. The Court's resources are limited; it can only **(38) to deal** with a small number of cases simultaneously. The Court works hand in hand with national and international tribunals.

5) Building more support for justice: With the support of 123 States Parties, from all continents, the ICC has **(39) to establish** itself as a permanent and independent judicial institution. But, unlike national judicial systems, the Court does not have its own police. It depends on the cooperation of states, including to implement its arrest warrants or summonses. Nor does it have territory to relocate witnesses at risk. The ICC is thus largely dependent on the support and cooperation of States. As the Court marks its 20th birthday, it implores all States to renew their support by providing political and financial support, arresting suspects and freezing their assets, adopting implementing legislation that enacts key Rome Statute provisions in national legislation, and by **(40) to sign** voluntary cooperation agreements including relocation agreements for ICC witnesses. The ICC requests joint and renewed commitment of the international community to increase justice and reconciliation for all.

31. **to help**

A. help　B. helping　C. helped　D. to help

32. **to use**

A. to use　B. used　C. uses　D. using

33. **to pronounce**

A. prounounce　　B. to pronounce

C. pronounced　　D. pronouncing

34. **to try**

A. tries　　B. try　　C. trying　　D. tried

35. **to affect**

A. to affect　　B. affect　　C. affects　　D. affected

36. **to provide**

A. provide　　B. provided　　C. provides　　D. providing

37. **to ensure**

A. to ensure　　B. ensured　　C. ensures　　D. ensure

38. **to deal**

A. dealt　　B. to deal　　C. deal　　D. dealing

39. **to establish**

A. establish　　B. establishes

C. establishing　　D. established

40. **to sign**

A. to sign　　B. signing　　C. sign　　D. signs

V. Choose from among the four alternatives the one that most closely corresponds to the meaning contained in the following passage.

(41) The history of human growth and development is at the same time the history of the terrible struggle of every new idea heralding the approach of a brighter dawn. In its tenacious hold on tradition, the Old has never hesitated to make use of the foulest and cruelest means **(42) to stay** the advent of the New, in whatever form or period the latter may have asserted itself. Nor need we retrace our steps into the distant past to realize the enormity of opposition, difficulties, and hardships placed in the path of every progressive idea. The rack, the thumbscrew, and the knout are still with us; so are the convict's garb and the social wrath, all conspiring against the spirit that is serenely marching on.

A thorough perusal of the history of human development will disclose two elements in bitter conflict with each other. Elements that are only now beginning to be understood, not as foreign to each other, but as closely related and truly harmonious, if only placed in proper environment: the individual and social instincts. The individual and society have waged a relentless and bloody battle for ages, each striving for supremacy, because each was blind to the value and importance of the other. **(43) The individual and social instincts,—the one a most potent factor for individual endeavor, for growth, aspiration, self-realization; the other an equally potent factor for mutual helpfulness and social well-being**.

The explanation of the storm raging within the individual, and between him and his surroundings, is not far to seek. The primitive man, unable to understand his being, much less the unity of all life, felt himself absolutely dependent on blind, hidden forces ever ready to mock and taunt him. Out of that attitude grew the religious concepts of man as a mere speck of dust dependent on superior powers on high, who can only be appeased by complete surrender. All the early **(44) sagas** rest on that idea, which continues to be the Leit-Motif of the biblical tales dealing with the relation of man to God, to the State, to society. Again and again the same motif, man is nothing, the powers are everything.

Religion, the dominion of the human mind; Property, the dominion of human needs; and Government, the dominion of human conduct, represent the stronghold of man's enslavement and all the horrors it entails... "Property is robbery," said the great French Anarchist, Proudhon. **(45) Yes, but without risk and danger to the robber**. Monopolizing the accumulated efforts of man, property has robbed him of his birthright, and has turned him loose a **(46) pauper** and an outcast. Property has not even the time-worn excuse that man does not create enough to satisfy all needs. The A B C student of economics knows that the productivity of labor within the last few decades far exceeds normal demand a hundredfold. But what are normal demands to an abnormal institution? The only demand that property recognizes is its own **(47) gluttonous** appetite for greater wealth, because wealth means power; the power to subdue, to crush, to exploit, the power to enslave, to outrage, to degrade. America is particularly boastful of her great power, her enormous national wealth. Poor America, of what avail is all her wealth, if the individuals comprising the nation are wretchedly poor? If they live in **(48) squalor**, in filth, in crime, with hope and joy gone, a homeless, soilless army of human prey.

Real wealth consists in things of utility and beauty, in things that help to create strong, beautiful bodies and surroundings inspiring to live in. But if man is doomed to wind cotton around a spool, or dig coal, or build roads for thirty years of his life, there can be no talk of wealth. What he gives to the world is only gray and hideous things, reflecting a dull and hideous existence,—too weak to live, too cowardly to die. Strange to say, there are people who **(49) extol** this deadening method of centralized production as the proudest achievement of our age. They fail utterly to realize that if we are to continue in machine subserviency, our slavery is more complete than was our **(50) bondage** to the King. They do not want to know that centralization is not only the death-knell of liberty, but also of health and beauty, of art and science, all these being impossible in a clock-like, mechanical atmosphere.

41. **This sentence suggests that the author holds a ________ worldview.**

A. conservative B. neoliberal
C. progressive D. cynical

42. **Here the phrase "to stay" means**

A. to maintain B. to halt
C. to accomodate D. to reinforce

43. **This sentence suggests that the individual and society are**

A. complementary forces.
B. aligned in their goals.
C. uneven in their powers.
D. mutually exclusive.

44. **Here the word "sagas" means**

A. theories B. legends
C. societies D. concepts

45. **This sentence functions in the passage to**

A. further clarify a point made in the previous sentence.
B. draw a conclusion based on evidence.
C. reject a point made in the previous sentence.
D. respond to a question posed previously in the paragraph.

46. **Here the word "pauper" means a person who is**

A. destitute
B. jubilant
C. resentful
D. unscrupulous

47. **Here the word "gluttonous" means**

A. oafish
B. gutsy
C. delectable
D. insatiable

48. **Here the word "squalor" means**

A. despondency
B. impoverishment
C. delinquency
D. disillusionment

49. **Here the word "extol" means**

A. denigrate
B. acquiesce
C. laud
D. jettison

50. **Here the word "bondage" means**

A. vindication
B. animosity
C. wariness
D. fealty

Ⅵ. Choose from among the four alternatives the one that best completes the following sentences.

51. Attacks at the massive Zaporizhzhia nuclear power plant in Ukraine have _________ as fighting continues in Ukraine's south. This has sparked concerns about the _________ of nuclear disaster, leading the United Nations' watchdog and world leaders to demand that a mission be allowed to visit the site and assess the damage.

A. cropped up - acumen B. ramped up - specter
C. steamed ahead - phantom D. forged ahead - apparition

52. Chinese planes are firing rods into the sky to bring more rainfall to its crucial Yangtze River, which has dried up in parts, as _________ of the nation fall into drought and _________ with the worst heat wave on record.

A. swaths - grapple B. fragments - fiddle
C. chunks - clash D. scraps - reckon

53. Some 27 ships loaded with grain have left Ukraine's Black Sea ports since August 1 under an export deal _________ by the United Nations and Turkey, which has laid "the _________ for a permanent peace environment," Turkey's Defense Minister said in a speech on Saturday.

A. adjudicated - boardwalk B. conciliated - landmass
C. brokered - groundwork D. intervened - platform

54. Military-ruled Myanmar plans to import Russian gasoline and fuel oil to _________ supply concerns and rising prices, a junta spokesperson said. Russia is seeking new customers for its energy in the region as its biggest export destination, Europe, will _________ an embargo on Russian oil in phases later this year.

A. soothe - levy B. relax - commence
C. lift - inaugurate D. ease - impose

55. Hong Kong has recorded its sharpest annual drop in population. Though authorities attributed some of it to a "natural" decrease — more deaths than births — experts said the figures also reflected an ongoing _________ that has accelerated in the past few years amid periods of massive social _________ that have included anti-government protests and the coronavirus pandemic.

A. migration - upturn B. withdrawal - turmoil
C. exodus - upheaval D. departure - outbreak

56. **For many South Koreans, China's display of the hanbok dress during the Olympics opening ceremony _________ a particularly sensitive nerve — although the controversy may not be immediately apparent to outside observers.[…] The outrage of South Koreans reflects growing animosity toward what many South Koreans feel is China's _________ of history.**

A. hit – fudge
B. bashed – mangling
C. smacked – bending
D. struck – distortion

57. **William Ruto has emerged the winner of a tense and _________ fought contest for Kenya's presidency. Ruto, who has served as deputy president since 2013, _________ a stunning defeat against his chief opponent, veteran politician Raila Odinga.**

A. fiercely – dealt
B. brutally – handed out
C. emphatically – pulled out
D. decisively – bestowed

58. **A judge in southern India has ruled a woman wore "provocative" clothing, _________ dismissing her sexual assault complaint, causing public _________ in the country, where violence against women and girls make frequent headlines.**

A. literally – uproar
B. effectively – outcry
C. practically – upset
D. incidentally – holdout

59. **Pope Francis has spoken of his "sorrow, indignation and shame" over the Catholic Church's role in the abuse of Canadian Indigenous children in residential schools. Indigenous leaders have long called for a papal apology for the harm _________ for decades on Indigenous children, who suffered abuse and the _________ of Indigenous culture in the country's residential schools.**

A. contracted – deletion
B. lavished – cancellation
C. inflicted – erasure
D. infringed – censure

60. **There's one thing that the two candidates locked in a bad-tempered battle to be Britain's next prime minister agree on: Brexit has nothing to do with any of the _________ facing the UK right now. That much was clear from an answer to a question the pair were posed in a televised debate last week, which came in the middle of _________ at the approaches to the Port of Dover in southeast England, which raised the ire of many holidaymakers.**

A. lulls – hurdles
B. quirks – clogging
C. dregs – blockage
D. woes – gridlock

VII. Choose from among the four alternatives the one that best explains each of the underlined words.

If there is one quote that **(61) encapsulates** politics, we need to look no further than a remark by Ernest Benn (1875–1954) 'politics is the art of looking for trouble, finding it everywhere, diagnosing it incorrectly and applying the wrong remedies'. Politicians have an **(62) uncanny** ability to find trouble, misunderstand the problem and apply an incorrect response. One of the repeated political failures is a reluctance to interpret a situation from an alternative perspective. Many conflicts could have been prevented by adopting this mindset. If there is one theme that occurs time and time again throughout this book, it is surely found in that wise observation from Benn.

My interest in global politics was forged during the turbulence of the Cold War. The battle of ideologies marked an **(63) epic** struggle for the future of mankind. Like others of my generation, I had a ring-side seat to a seemingly new chapter of history. That which had been such a dominant feature of my formative years (such as the prospect of nuclear annihilation) changed overnight. The fall of the Berlin Wall in 1989 felt like the end of the ideological contest between Capitalism and Soviet Communism. The social experiment of creating a new utopia appeared to have failed its people, or at least that was the dominant narrative I was presented with. It was a time in which the news presented in 'The West' was coloured by a **(64) heady** sense of optimism. The war was over, capitalism was in the ascendancy and democracy was spreading its reach throughout the world. In the words of an often cited and heavily contested theorist of the time, we had reached 'The end of history' (Fukuyama 1992). Liberal democracy emerged victorious, and the future seemed to be tinged with freedom and happiness. By the time the liberal 'democratic peace thesis' was presented to me during an undergraduate lecture, the correlation between the spread of liberal democracy and peace made perfect sense. How times have changed. That optimism has since been **(65) decimated** by populism, pandemics and protectionism. The world seems to be a much darker place now, and it is to that reality we must all now face.

The unmistakable drift away from liberal democracy is a **(66) prescient** reminder that there are no final victories in politics. The liberal optimism that characterised the early 1990s has been buried under the weight of history. There are several developments within international relations that have overturned the optimism of that time. The rise of the self-styled 'strong man', the existential threat posed by Covid-19, the poisonous character of tribal politics and the prospect of a trade war now shape the **(67) contour** of the debate. The concepts and theories that captured the zeitgeist of a previous era must be reassessed for the modern world.

Such a dramatic **(68) turnaround** reminds us that there is always the potential for events to overturn cosy assumptions. Equally, there are no final defeats in politics. For instance, the rise of populist politicians has witnessed a revival in nationalist (and even quasi-fascist) sentiment. The contest of ideas is an ever-present feature of the political arena, and this clash of ideas has the capacity to reinvent itself from one era to the next. Borrowing language from economics, there is an **(69) inherent** competition between international actors over scarce resources. Inevitably, this will shape the behaviour of states and non-state actors. Equally, the dynamics of a 'glocal' (a portmanteau of 'global' and 'local') commons often generate some level of cooperation and coexistence. Frankly, nothing is deterministic in the political realm.

In order to properly comprehend the subject, there are a number of misconceptions that need highlighting before we can fully explore what makes up global politics. For instance, the argument that 'Americans are from Mars, and Europeans are from Venus' is overly simplistic and now somewhat dated (Kagan 2004). In reality, the United States is a **(70) bastion** of both hard power and soft power. In contrast, the European Union (EU) has expanded its military capacity in recent years. The description of the latter as a civilian actor has been overtaken by events. Once again, we are reminded how events can overturn long-held assumptions.

61. **encapsulates**

A. criticizes　　B. epitomizes
C. denigrates　　D. maligns

62. **uncanny**

A. erudite　　B. peculiar
C. run-of-the-mill　　D. uncompromising

63. **epic**

A. bombastic　　B. grandiloquent
C. haughty　　D. monumental

64. **heady**

A. ardent　　B. fervent
C. intoxicating　　D. zealous

65. **decimated**

A. admonished　　B. exterminated
C. obliterated　　D. rebuked

66. **prescient**

A. errant　　B. forbidding
C. innocuous　　D. prophetic

67. **contour**

A. curvature　B. frame
C. sketch　D. template

68. **turnaround**

A. about-face　B. contravention
C. deviation　D. stumbling block

69. **inherent**

A. inbred　B. indelible
C. instinctual　D. intrinsic

70. **bastion**

A. bulwark　B. disciple
C. embankment　D. missionary

Ⅷ. Fill in each of the following blanks with the most appropriate of the four alternatives as required by the context.

In July, a popular uprising in Sri Lanka toppled the government and sent its president scurrying into exile. The revolt had been brewing for months in the wake of the country's economic implosion, but it still caught observers off-guard. In **(71)** ________ scenes, protesters took over the presidential palace, swam in the pool, dined in the kitchen, traipsed around the bedrooms, and held stylized meetings in the conference rooms.

Such images from Sri Lanka stunned cash-strapped economies across South Asia, a turbulent region plagued by unstable governments, **(72)** ________ nationalism, violent extremism, and the unsettling consequences of China's expanding influence. From Dhaka to Islamabad, governments in the region have looked at the chaos in Colombo and wondered if they might be next.

Sri Lanka's dire situation stemmed from the collapse of its economy in the midst of spiking commodity prices and a staggering debt crisis. It offers a bitter lesson to other **(73)** ________ economies in similar situations, especially those that, like Sri Lanka, rely excessively on China. Including Sri Lanka, 42 middle- and low-income countries, such as Djibouti, Kyrgyzstan, Laos, and Zambia, have reportedly taken on significant debt obligations to China worth over ten percent of GDP. The debacle in Sri Lanka is particularly chastening for Pakistan, a country that is heavily dependent on Chinese loans. Pakistan has **(74)** ________ much of its hope for development to courting Chinese investment. But despite rising borrowing costs, Pakistani leaders still believe the country's wager with China is worth it. If they are wrong, the relationship with China threatens to leave Pakistan vulnerable to rising political turmoil in the midst of an already dangerous economic downturn.

(75) ________ the country's size, the stakes are even bigger in Pakistan than they were in Sri Lanka. Pakistan is home to the world's fifth-largest population and a $340 billion economy. In the last six years, economic productivity has fallen to record lows, domestic revenues and foreign reserves have shrunk, the currency has depreciated, unemployment is soaring, and political corruption has increased. The country's total foreign debt has nearly doubled since 2016, reaching a monumental $131 billion. Alarm bells are ringing even as Pakistan's bickering leaders refuse to listen.

Scrambling to avoid a default, Pakistan has now been on a borrowing spree to fund its expenditures and meet its debt repayments. In June, Pakistan's shaky new government borrowed another $2.3 billion from China to **(76)** ________ its foreign reserves. It also negotiated the continuance of a $6 billion bailout package with the International Monetary Fund, which involved raising fuel prices and electricity tariffs, deeply unpopular measures that prompted a public backlash. The government has tried to get Pakistanis to accept the reality of straitened times, urging them to cut back on drinking tea to help reduce the country's outstanding $600 million bill for tea imports.

(77) ________ these short-term measures could buy Pakistan time, they will not ensure its economic self-reliance. Pakistan risks an outcome far more dangerous than Sri Lanka; its politics have become increasingly turbulent in recent years thanks to the actions of its leaders, an overreaching military, and a deeply polarized population. A growing **(78)** ________ of Pakistani leaders, subscribing to a brand of Islamic nationalism, has made Islamist militant groups increasingly mainstream; others are fanning dangerous anti-American sentiments to win public support. **(79)** ________ of grievance may explode as ordinary Pakistanis become poorer and angrier.

Any consideration of Pakistan's parlous financial situation must involve China; Islamabad owes nearly a quarter of its foreign debt to Beijing. But no Pakistani leader has dared to question the country's unequal relationship with its neighbor to the north, silencing any criticism of China. Pakistan is quick to upbraid its neighbor India for attacks against and the **(80)** ________ of India's minority Muslim population, but it has refused to condemn China's gross mistreatment of the Muslim Uyghur population.

71. A. surreal B. grotesque
C. nightmarish D. halcyon

72. A. mercurial B. spurious
C. bilious D. toxic

73. A. floundering B. solidary
C. polarized D. corrupt

74. A. meditated B. hitched
C. envisaged D. justified

75. A. Regardless of B. Along with
C. Thanks to D. In spite of

76. A. divvy up B. square up
C. shore up D. ante up

77. A. Unless B. Once
C. Whenever D. Although

78. A. mendicant B. cadre
C. denizen D. neophyte

79. A. The launch pad B. A powder keg
C. A gunport lid D. The flash point

80. A. marginalization B. neutralization
C. enervation D. trivialization

Ⅸ. Write a short essay in English of 200-250 words as your answer to the following.

Discuss a specific function of the WHO and use a particular current situation as an example of how the WHO is fulfilling this role.

マークシート記入例

東京の本会場で特A級を受験する、国連 太郎さん、受験番号が「東京01-10001」、生年月日が「1980年10月24日」の場合の記入例です。

【受験番号/氏名】
それぞれ受験票の記載通りに記入してください。

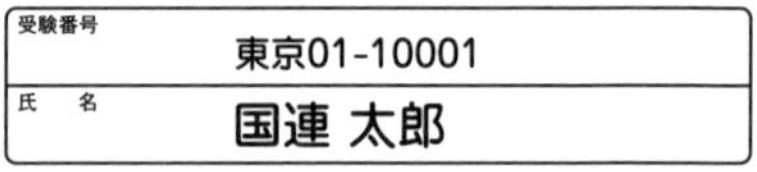

【受験地区】
下段の都道府県部分を塗りつぶしてください。

【会場番号】
都道府県部分に続く２桁の数字を塗りつぶしてください。

【受験番号】
ハイフン（－）以降の５桁の数字を塗りつぶしてください。

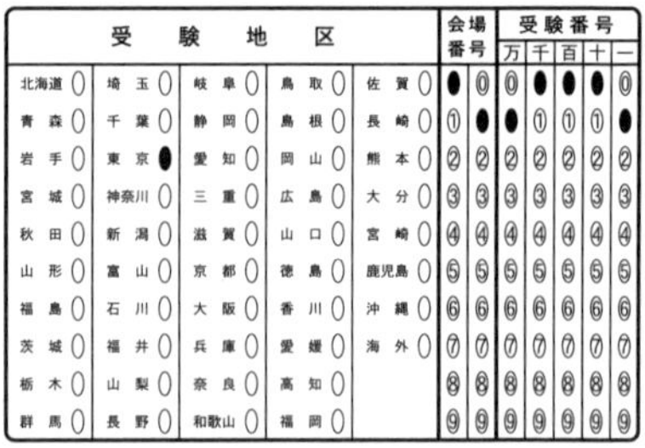

【受験級】
「特Ａ」と記入し、下段の特Ａ級部分を塗りつぶしてください。

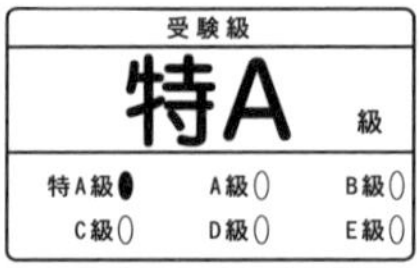

【生年月日】
４桁の西暦・月・日を塗りつぶしてください。
10未満の月・日の十の位は、「０」を塗りつぶしてください。

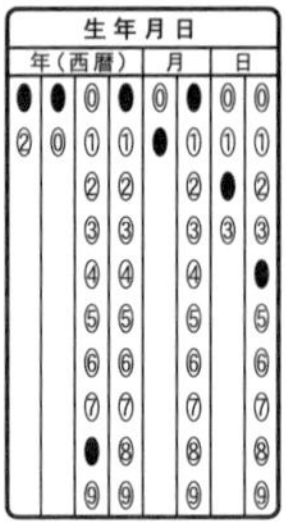

※HB以上の鉛筆を用いてマークをしてください。

※他の地区から会場を変更して受験する場合でも、受験票に記載されている受験地区・会場番号をマークしてください。

2022年
第2回試験

解答・解説

2022年　国連英検特A級第2回試験
解答・解説

＊〔　〕内は訳出上の補足や説明

I 『新 わかりやすい国連の活動と世界』に基づき，
空所を埋めるのに最も適切なものを4つの選択肢の中から1つ選びなさい。

1. 解答：D

訳例　1952年早々に，新議場で第1回安全保障理事会が開かれ，同年10月には新しい総会議場において初めての国連総会が招集された（『新 わかりやすい国連の活動と世界』p.46。以下，書名略）。

2. 解答：D

訳例　国連憲章第100条に従い各加盟国は，事務総長および職員の責任がとりわけ国際的な性質のものであることを尊重し，その職務活動に対して影響力を行使しないよう義務づけられている（同p.61）。

3. 解答：B

訳例　IMOの政策を決定するのは総会で，174カ国（2018年8月）のIMO全加盟国と准加盟国である香港の代表で構成されている（同p.83）

4. 解答：B

訳例　平和維持活動（PKO）は，国際平和と安全の維持に努める国連の活動の一環であるが，国連憲章上，明文の規定を持たない点で革新的なものであ〔る〕（同p.104）。

5. 解答：B

訳例　国連グローバル・コンパクト（UNGC）は，企業やステークホルダーが，人権，労働，環境および腐敗防止の10原則について，自らのコミットメントを示し，社会の良き一員として行動する自発的な取り組みのための枠組みである（同p.118）。

6. 解答：D

訳例 2014年から2016年においても，世界では約7億9千3百万人が慢性的な栄養不良に苦しんでおり，SDGsにおいても，「2030年までに飢餓と栄養不良を終わらせる」という目標を掲げている（同p.140）。

7. 解答：C

訳例 1970年に総会は，1974年を世界人口年に指定するとともに，同年8月に世界人口会議をブカレストにおいて開催した。同会議では世界人口行動計画が採択された（同p.141）。

8. 解答：A

訳例 難民の法的地位は，1951年の「難民の地位に関する条約」と，難民の権利および義務を規定した1967年の議定書の2つの国際条約によって規定されている（同p.143）。

9. 解答：A

訳例 国際刑事裁判所（ICC）は，1998年にローマ規程により設立され，2002年から活動を開始した。ICCは，ローマ規程に示されたジェノサイド罪，戦争犯罪，人道に対する罪を犯した個人の訴追について管轄権を持つ（同p.147）。

10. 解答：D

訳例 1960年代末から1970年代初頭に亘って，ウ・タント国連事務総長（当時）の発案で国際連合大学（略称，国連大学）の設置が国連のなかで審議されていた際，米英仏ソなどの大国は同大学を不要不急のものと見なし，その設立を渋っていた（同p.169）。

II 以下の文章の中に含まれる意味に文脈上最も近いものを4つの選択肢の中から1つ選びなさい。

11. 解答：D

解説 パラグラフ（2）の最後に，those Uyghur who receive Chinese education are criticised by other Uyghur for sacrificing their culture in exchange for better economic opportunities. とあることから，正しい内容文はD.「中国の教育がもたらすより良い経済機会と引き換えに独自の文化を見捨てることに関して，ウイグル人の中に不和がある」。

12.　解答：B

解説　下線部直前のThe region constitutes a security concernと直後のethnic and religious dimensions become subordinate to national unity.の間に，原因・結果の関係が存在する。よって，B.「したがって」が正解。

13.　解答：C

解説　中国にとって分離主義は脅威と述べたあと，①中国が外国の敵対勢力を非難。②しかしながら，実際反乱を起こしているのは先住民（ウイグル民族）である。④したがって，中国はそこで広範囲な監視を行っている，とすれば文脈的にしっくりくる。③の「中国共産党は，新疆《シンキョウ》が独立すると，チベットなど他の地域の独立運動の引き金になる可能性が高いため，その事態を恐れている」は，パラグラフ（3）3～5行目のThe region constitutes a security concern for the Chinese Communist Party (CCP) because its independence would likely threaten the territorial integrity of the PRC by triggering other autonomous regions, such as Tibet, to push for independence.を言い換えているに過ぎない。

14.　解答：B

解説　carrot and stickとは「アメとムチ」という意味。パラグラフ（4）の冒頭に, Strike Hard security campaigns address political unrest, criminal activities and religious movements under the same banner.，パラグラフ（6）の冒頭に，Economic development in the region has also played a crucial role in Beijing's approach.とある。よって，a carrot and stick approachが指すのは，B.「経済発展と厳しい治安強化キャンペーン」。

15.　解答：B

解説　下線部（1）は，冒頭のEconomic development in the region has also played a crucial role in Beijing's approach. Yet, ... economic opportunities benefit Han residents disproportionallyから，経済発展が必ずしも新疆の先住民のためになってないことがわかるので，B.「新疆の経済が改善しているにもかかわらず」。下線部（2）は，the growing wealth gap between Han settlers concentrated in towns and Uyghur concentrated in underdeveloped rural areasが主語なので，両者の関係性がこじれていることを示すB.「社会的緊張を高めている」が適切。

16. 解答：B

解説 パラグラフ（7）の4行目にThe militarisation of Xinjiang is increased by the usc of new technology such as the use of drones，最後の文にcounter-terrorist efforts include the use of drones and tracking devices on vehicles based on China's Beidou navigation satellite systemとあるので，この段落の内容に適切なのは，B.「中国の〔衛星測位システム〕「北斗衛星導航系統」に基づくドローンや車両搭載型追跡装置といったテロ対策の新技術も，新疆の軍事化に含まれる」。

17. 解答：D

解説 パラグラフ（7）の2～3行目にある，access to the Internet is pervasive and control exceptionally extensiveを受けて，挿入文のsecurity measures and censorship made it difficult to have reports on Xinjiang unrestが，挿入文のofficers admit there are incidentsを受けて，（D）直後のThis explains why Xi Jinping called again for setting up a 'Great Wall of Steel' in Xinjiangがあると考えると文意に合う。よって，正解はD。

18. 解答：B

解説 パラグラフ（5）の最後から3～2行目に，by fearing the support of Muslim countries for Uyghur separatists, Beijing plays down 'proliferation concerns and supplies armsとあることから，このエッセイで述べられているのは，B.「北京は武器貿易を通じてイスラム諸国との関係を深め，新疆ウイグル自治区の政策への支持を得るとともに，ウイグル人への支援を抑止している」。

19. 解答：D

解説 Aはパラグラフ（8）に，Bはパラグラフ（5）の1～4行目に，Cはパラグラフ（3）の最後に書かれているが，D.「漢民族主義に基づく統一への反対を抑圧するためには，暴力は不要である」は本文のどこにも書かれていない。

20. 解答：D

解説 パラグラフ構成を概観すると，(2) が「ウイグル人の被差別的な境遇」，(3) が「自治区の独立を阻止する政策」，(4) (5) が「厳しい締め付けの具体例とその余波」，(6) (7) が「自治区の経済対策とテロ対策」という構成になっている。よって，トピック別に分類するとDが正解。

訳例 (1) 新疆ウイグル自治区は，2010年の人口が2,200万と，中国最大かつ最西端に位置する地域で，石油，ガス，ウランなどの天然資源が豊富〔なことで知られる〕。また，ユーラシア大陸を横断する交通の要衝であり，古代シルクロードを復活させる上で不可欠の地域でもあり，習近平国家主席が提唱する「一帯一路」構想の一環である，中国の新しいシルクロード経済ベルトの発展を後押ししている。中華人民共和国（中国）の建国以来，中国政府は土地改革やインフラ整備を通じて，新疆を中国の国家に組み入れようとしてきた。

(2) 中国は憲法で「各民族は平等」と定めているものの，少数民族に対してはかなり父権主義的な態度をとっている。憲法は少数民族の信教の自由も保証しているが，宗教は社会主義を認めなければならない（Saunders 2017)。なぜなら，中国政府は宗教による干渉を恐れ，宗教団体に対して国家宗教事務局への登録を義務付けているからである。また，宗教が無知と等しい〔と考えられている〕ために，ウイグル人は粗野〔な人間〕，あるいは泥棒と思われ，テロリストと見なされることもますます多くなる(Kantian 2007)。一方，中国の教育を受けるウイグル人は，他のウイグル人から，より良い経済機会と引き換えにウイグル文化を犠牲にしていると批判される（Kantian 2007)。

(3) 中国が新疆に適用している安全保障の概念は，国家安全保障についての現実主義的な定義（すなわち，中国の国土と制度の維持という定義）を反映している。中国共産党にとって，この地域の独立は，チベットなど他の自治区の独立を誘発し，中国の領土的一体性を脅かす可能性が高いため，安全保障上の懸念事項である。したがって，民族や宗教の次元は，国家の統一より下位に位置づけられるのである。漢民族主義に基づく統一中国へのあらゆる反対を抑圧するために暴力の行使が必要となっており，経済的次元が抑圧措置の主要な手段となってきた。(A) 中国は，分離主義が新疆の安定に対する主な脅威であることを認めている。①〔そして〕米国を中心とする敵対的外国勢力が人権や少数民族の権利，民主的価値観の普及，それに（世界ウイグル会議などを通じて）新疆ウイグル自治区の反政府活動を支援していると非難している。②しかし暴徒は，グローバルなジハードネットワークにますます組み込まれつつあるとはいえ，伝統的には先住民である。③〔削除対象〕中国共産党は，新疆が独立すると，チベットなど他の地域の独立運動の引き金になる可能性が高いため，その事態を恐れている。④そのため，中国は新疆ウイグル自治区に広範な監視体制を敷き，地域の軍事化をますます進めるとともに，ウイグル人に対する抑圧政策や「強制的な漢民族化」を実施している（Laruelle 2012）。これにより，テュルク語を話すイスラム教徒の人口比率は，1940年代末の約90%（Forbes 1986）だったものが，2010年代には約半分にまで〔減少した〕（Han and Paik 2017）。

(4)　中国の戦略はアメとムチ方式を採っている。治安強化を目指す「暴力的テロ猛撃キャンペーン」〔打擊恐怖活動専項行動〕は，政情不安，犯罪活動，宗教運動に1つの旗印を揚げて対応するもので，自治区政府は2017年，イスラムの人名を「過度に宗教的」として禁じた2015年の規制を拡大した（Feng 2017）。パスポートが押収されたほか（Hornby 2016），イスラムの服装規定が禁止され，長いひげを生やすことも禁止された（Reuters 2017）。2017年，ホータン県は，中学校を含む学校におけるウイグル語教育を非合法化する指令を出し（Sulaiman 2017），新疆ウイグル自治区「人口の正確な登録と検証に関する作業ガイドライン」は新疆の住民に対する「DNA検体，指紋，虹彩スキャン，血液型」からの生体情報収集計画を導入した（Haas 2017）。(B)

(5)　中国によるウイグルの文化や宗教に対する弾圧はまた，怨恨を生む〔要因〕ともなっている〕。〔年齢〕18歳未満での正式な宗教教育の禁止や，親が個人的に行う場合も含めた非公式の宗教教育の禁止（Wayne 2008）によっては，原理主義は根絶されなかった。むしろ，こうした措置によってウイグル人の怨恨は強まった。文化的・宗教的制約が暴力的な抗議行動のきっかけとなり（Purbrick 2017），ウイグル人はイスラム教を学ぶため，またはイスラム教のために戦う目的で中東やトルコへ渡った。(C) 中国〔が〕エジプト，サウジアラビア，トルコ，イランと〔の間に結んだ〕戦略的パートナーシップは，イスラム諸国との貿易を止めるものではないとはいえ，確かにそれは中国とこれらの国々との関係を複雑なものにしている。つまり中国政府は，イスラム諸国によるウイグル分離主義者に対する支援を恐れるあまり，「拡散の懸念を軽視して，武器や問題のある技術を気前よい価格で〔イスラム〕諸国へ供給している」（Horner 2002）のである。

(6)　また，この地域の経済発展も中国政府のアプローチの中で重要な役割を果たしてきた。けれども，新疆の経済が改善しているにもかかわらず，経済的機会からメリットを受ける者は漢民族住民に偏っており，漢族を呼び込むための有利な政策によって土地と水をめぐる競争が激化している。新疆の1人当たりの住民所得は全国平均を下回っており，また，都市部に集中する漢族移住民と発展が遅れた農村部に集中するウイグル族との貧富の差が拡大することで社会的緊張が高じている。世界ウイグル会議は，中央アジアとの貿易に向けた北西部の開放や，西部地域の開発，また最近では一帯一路構想といった開発政策はいずれも，ウイグルの周辺化をもたらすと主張している（WUC 2016）。

(7)　中国が新疆の経済発展を推し進める一方で，厳しいメディア規制とインターネット監視がこの地域の経済成長を制約しているのであって，インターネットの利用は広く浸透しているが，規制もきわめて広範囲に及んでいる。(D)〔治安維持措置や検閲のため，新疆ウイグル自治区の騒乱に関する情報入手は困難であるが，当局は事件の発生を認めている。〕習近平が新疆に「鉄の長城」を建設するよう再び呼びかけた理由もここにある（Reuters 2017）。新疆の軍事化は，ドローンなど新技術の活用によって強化されている。2013年，自治区政府は中国航天科技集団有限公司に対し，テロリストを標的とするドローンを発注した。また，2014年には，新疆のイスラム教徒がラマダン期間中の治安維持措置に反発して発生した暴力事件で100人が死亡したことを受けて，ドローン操縦士〔の派遣〕を要請した（Tatlow 2014）。さらにテロ対策として，中国の〔衛星測位システム〕「北斗衛星導航系統」に基づくドローンや車両搭載型追跡装置の利用も行われている（Phillips 2017）。

(8)　中国の新疆に対する安全保障政策は，地域の発展をさらに推し進めると同時に，抑圧的な政策をさらに推し進めることになる〔ことから〕，ウイグルにとっては抵抗するか中国化するかというジレンマに代わる現実的な選択肢はないのである。

III

文法的，語法的にふさわしくないものを下線の中から1つ選びなさい。

21．解答：D

解説　many rights issues → the many right issues。直前の right issues を指すので，定冠詞が必要。

訳例　国連のミシェル・バチェレ人権高等弁務官（UNHCHR）は，〔UNHCHRとして〕17年ぶりとなる中国公式訪問の最後に，人権高等弁務官事務所と中国政府との間で人権問題に関して新たに取り組む分野を発表するとともに，5月中に行われた6日間の訪中で提起された多くの人権問題についてその概要を述べた。

22. 解答：C

解説 where → which。did not live up to ... は主語が欠けた不完全文なので，関係代名詞にしなくてはならない。

訳例 ナイジェリア北東部のボルノ州が直面している「巨大な問題」には，テロリストの反乱が継続していることも含まれるが，国連事務総長が言う「テロ，暴力，強制退去，絶望」の「評判倒れ」となる地域に「希望の州にして現実の州」(同) を生み出すためには，〔こうした難問〕を国際社会が認識することが必要だ。

23. 解答：D

解説 in need for → in need of。be in need of ... で「～を必要としている」という意味の熟語。

訳例 英国が数名の移住者を中央アフリカのルワンダに移送した上で手続きを行い，ルワンダに移住させる目的で〔ルワンダとの間で〕結んだとされる取引について，国連難民高等弁務官事務所は木曜日，この取引は保護を必要とする人々を引き受けるという加盟国の責任と相いれない，と述べた。

24. 解答：B

解説 grapples → grapples with。grapple は with を必要とする自動詞。

訳例 南スーダンは紛争，気候変動，コロナ禍，コストの上昇がもたらす過去に例のないほどの食料不安を抱えており，今年の「端境期」の底は人口の 70% 以上が必死で生き延びる状況が予測される。国連世界食糧計画 (WFP) が金曜日，警鐘を鳴らした。

25. 解答：D

解説 silent → silenced。women parliamentarians, human rights defenders and electoral observers を修飾する単語として適切なのは，prevent from speaking を意味する silence の過去分詞。

訳例 国連高官らが火曜日，政府や市民社会の代表者らと一堂に会し，政治に携わる女性に対して世界中で暴力が蔓延《まんえん》している現状に注意を喚起した。政治の世界では，女性議員や人権擁護者，選挙監視員らが口を封じられたり，威嚇されたりすることがますます増えている。

26. 解答：A

解説 affair → affairs。political affairs で「政治事情」という意味になる。

訳例　〔ローズマリー・A・ディカルロ〕国連政治〔・平和構築〕担当事務次長は金曜日，安全保障理事会に対し，朝鮮民主主義人民共和国（北朝鮮）による先日の大陸間弾道ミサイル発射（北朝鮮として2017年以来初の長距離試射）に一致して対応するよう呼びかけた。同日午後，この問題を協議するため〔安保理〕各国代表が集まった緊急会合〔で述べた〕。

27.　解答：A

解説　For→トル。「ウクライナでの戦争が始まって10週間になるが」という意味なので，継続的な期間を表すforは不要。

訳例　ウクライナでの戦争が始まって10週間となる金曜日，国連〔ユニセフ〕は，〔ウクライナでは〕ロシアによる侵攻や性的暴力，ジェンダー暴力に伴う，とてつもなく大きな精神衛生ニーズ〔が発生している〕ほか，危険な状態が続いている〔ことから〕，弱い立場に置かれた子どもたちに専門家による心理社会的支援を施す取り組みを緊急に強化していると述べた。

28.　解答：D

解説　existent → existential。「存続に関わるような決定」という文意なので，aliveと同義のexistentではなく，relating to existenceを意味するexistentialにしなくてはならない。

訳例　世界各地で爆発的に成長している採掘事業は先住民の土地で同意なしに行われている場合が多く，先住民の暮らしや文化，言語，生命に取り返しがつかない損害を与えている――「先住民問題に関する常設フォーラム」の2022年会合が開かれた月曜日，参加者らはこのように訴えるとともに，先住民のコミュニティーを根底から覆し，存続に関わるような決定については，先住民の自由意志に基づく事前の説明と同意を尊重するよう呼びかけた。

29.　解答：C

解説　when → unless。radical financial measuresに国際社会が同意すれば，スリランカと同じ悲惨な状況は避けられるかもしれない，という文意なので，Countries ... risk seeing the same ... when the international community agrees to radical financial measuresでは適さない。

訳例　コロナ禍の経済的余波による圧力にすでにさらされている国々は，ウクライナでの戦争が長引く中，負債を抱えた国々を支援する抜本的な財政支援策に国際社会が合意しないかぎり，スリランカと同様の経済混乱に陥り，国民は悲惨な状況に見舞われる恐れがある。〔アヒム・シュタイナー〕国連〔開発計画

（UNDP）総裁〕が木曜日，述べた。

30. 解答：C

解説 under → than。10 times more likely から，この文が比較級で，a “natural climate unaffected by human influence” が比較対象になっていることから than が必要になる。

訳例 現在の気候の下では，英国内で40℃超のかつてない気温が観測される確率は，「人間の影響を受けていない自然な気候」の場合に比べて最大10倍に高まる可能性がある──世界気象機関（WMO）が月曜日，明らかにした。

IV 下線を引いた動詞（原形）の最も適切な変化形（他動詞，自動詞，分詞など）を示している1語動詞または語句を4つの選択肢の中から1つ選びなさい。

31. 解答：B

解説 ICCの現在の活動について述べているので，ここは現在進行形にする。

32. 解答：D

解説 直前に前置詞があるので，動名詞にする。

33. 解答：C

解説 31 cases were opened が過去形で，その後の判決について述べられているので，現在完了にする。

34. 解答：B

解説 現在形の否定文なので，動詞の原形にする。

35. 解答：D

解説 direct contact ... with という構造になっていることに着目。目的語の communities とは受け身の関係が成立しているので過去分詞にする。

36. 解答：B

解説 ICC被害者信託基金のこれまでの実績について述べている箇所なので，現在完了にする。

37.　解答：A

解説　下線部を含む英文の補語はof a specific nature and often mass crimes。その後に，requiringの目的語としてlarge amounts of ... と substantial and effective efforts の 2 つの名詞句が続いている。よって，下線部以降は efforts を修飾していると考え，不定詞を選ぶ。

38.　解答：C

解説　下線部には述語動詞が入る。助動詞の後なので，動詞の原形。

39.　解答：D

解説　The ICC が a permanent and independent judicial institution というのは事実なので，B.「確立しなければならない」は不可。直前に has があるので，現在完了にする。

40.　解答：B

解説　直前に前置詞 by があるので，動名詞にする。

訳例　最も重大な犯罪を裁き，被害者の参加を実現し，公正な裁判を確保し，各国の法廷を補完する：設立から 20 年の歳月を経る中で，国際刑事裁判所 (ICC) はその重要な使命の遂行に大きな進歩を遂げてきた。2022 年 7 月 1 日の設立 20 周年に向けて，ICC がより公正な世界の建設に貢献している 5 つの面〔について紹介する〕。

1）**最も重大な犯罪を裁く**：ICC は，「人類の良心に深刻な衝撃を与える，想像を絶する残虐行為の犠牲となった」「何百万人もの子ども，女性，男性」を念頭に置いて設立された。人道に対する罪，戦争犯罪，ジェノサイド，侵略罪の加害者を捜査・起訴する，条約に基づく世界初の常設の国際刑事裁判所だ。設立以来これまで 20 年の間，ICC は国際司法にとって重要な事件を審理して解決し，少年兵の使用や文化遺産の破壊，性的暴力，あるいは無辜《むこ》の市民への攻撃などの犯罪に光を投じてきた。ICC は典型的な裁判における審判を通じて，権威ある判例法を構築している。これまで裁判となった事件は 31 件。うち 10 件に有罪，4 件に無罪が宣告された。〔現在は〕コンゴ民主共和国，中央アフリカ共和国，ジョージア，ウクライナなど，世界で最も暴力的な紛争について，17 件の捜査を続けている。

2）**被害者の参加**：ICC は，最も重大な犯罪の責任者を裁き，処罰するだけでなく，ICC の管轄内で起きた犯罪の結果として被害を受けた人々の声を聴くことも徹底して行っている。残虐行為の被害者で，ICCの司法手続きのすべての段階にこれまで参加した人は1万人以上にのぼる。ICCは対外支援活動を通じ，管轄内で犯罪の被害を受けたコミュニティーとの間で直接的な関係を維持している。また，被害者や証人の安全と心理的統合性の保護にも努めている。被害者は提訴はできないが，検察官に情報を提供することはできる（捜査開始の可否決定のための情報など）。ICC被害者信託基金（TFV）は現在，ICCとして初めての〔被害者〕賠償命令を現実のものとしつつある。TFVがこれまで支援プログラムを通じ，身体的，心理的，社会経済的支援を提供した被害者の数は，45万人以上にのぼる。

3）**公正な裁判の確保**：被告人はすべて，ICCにおいて合理的な疑いの余地なく有罪であると証明されるまで推定無罪とされる。各被告は公開の公平な裁判を受ける権利がある。ICCにおいて容疑者および被告人は次のような重要な権利を有する：容疑について知らされること，弁護の準備をする十分な時間と施設を持つこと，不当な遅延なく裁判を受けること，自由に弁護士を選ぶこと，検察官から無罪を証明する証拠を受け取ることなど。これらの権利の中には，被告人が十分に理解できる言語で審理を受ける権利も含まれる。このため，ICCでは40言語以上の専門の通訳・翻訳者を雇用し，場合によっては同じ審理で4言語を同時に使用することもある。これまでの20年間で，参加者は事件の現場からはるかに遠く離れた場所で，実質的にも手続き的にも多岐にわたる新しい課題に直面した。さらに，ICCが訴追する犯罪は特殊な性質を持つものであり，また，多くの場合，大量の証拠のほか，証人の安全確保のため実効ある多大な努力を必要とする集団犯罪である。訴訟手続きは複雑で，しかも訴訟が進む中，あらゆるレベルで支援を行うに当たって，きわめて多くの問題を解決しなければならない。

4）**国内裁判所を補完する**：ICCは，各国の裁判所に代わるものではなく，最後の手段として〔位置づけられる〕。最も重大な犯罪の加害者を捜査し，裁き，処罰する第一の責任は各国家が負うもので，ICCが介入するのは，ICCの管轄内で発生した重大犯罪の申し立てに国家が真摯《しんし》に対応しようとしない場合，あるいは対応できない場合に限られる。深刻な暴力は世界中で急速に激化している。ICCの資源は限られており，同時に扱える事件はほんのわずかだ。〔そのため〕ICCは国内裁判所や国際法廷と手を携えて活動している。

5）**司法に対する支持を拡大する**：全大陸の123の締約国の支持により，ICCは恒久的で独立した司法機関としての地位を確立した。しかし，各国の司法制度のように自前の警察を持たず，逮捕状や召喚状の執行を含め，各国の協力に頼っている。また，危険にさらされている証人を移送して〔受け入れる〕領土も持たない。このように，ICCは各国の支援と協力に大きく依存している。そして，20歳の誕生日を迎えるに当たり，すべての国に対し，政治的・財務的支援の提供や，容疑者の逮捕と容疑者の資産凍結，ローマ規程の主要条項を国内法に定める実施法の採択，およびICC証人の移送協定を含む自主的な協力協定の締結により支援を強化することを要請している。ICCは，国際社会がすべての人に対する正義と和解の促進に向けて新たな共同の誓約を行うことを求めている。

V 以下の文章の中に含まれる語句の意味として文脈上最も近いものを4つの選択肢の中から1つ選びなさい。

41. 解答：C

解説 下線部は「人類の成長と発展の歴史は同時にまた，明るい夜明けの到来を告げるあらゆる新しい思想〔が闘った〕恐ろしい闘いの歴史でもある」という意味なので，著者の世界観はfavoring social reformを意味するC. progressive。

42. 解答：B

解説 このstayは他動詞でpreventを意味する。よって，B. haltが正解。

43. 解答：A

解説 下線部は「個人の本能と社会の本能――一方は個人の努力，成長，願望，自己実現のための最も強力な要因であり，他方は相互扶助と社会福祉を成り立たせる，同じく強力な要因である」という意味なので，この文は，個人と社会はA.「お互いを補完しあう存在」であることを示唆している。

44. 解答：B

解説 下線部はa long story of heroic achievementを意味する。よって，B. legendsが正解。

45. 解答：A

解説 すぐ上のProperty is robberyに対して，「そのとおり。ただし，その窃盗を働く者にリスクと危険は及ばない」と，言いたいことをさらに具体的にしている。よって，正解はA。

46. 解答：A

解説 下線部は，a very poor personを意味する。よって，A. destituteが正

解。

47. 解答：D

解説 下線部は，greedy を意味する。よって，同義の D. insatiable が正解。

48. 解答：B

解説 下線部は，dirtiness を意味する。選択肢の中で一番近いのは，deterioration と同義の B. impoverishment。

49. 解答：C

解説 下線部は，praise enthusiastically を意味する。よって，C. laud が正解。

50. 解答：D

解説 下線部は，slavery を意味する。よって，a vassal's sworn loyalty to a lord を意味する D. fealty が正解。

訳例　人類の成長と発展の歴史は同時にまた，明るい夜明けの到来を告げるあらゆる新しい思想〔が闘った〕恐ろしい闘いの歴史でもある。古いものは伝統に固執するあまり，いかなる形や時代において新しいものが己《おのれ》を主張したとしても，その出現を阻止すべく最も卑劣かつ最も残酷な手段を用いることを決してためらわなかった。また，あらゆる進歩的な思想の行く手に立ちはだかる反対や困難，苦難の甚だしさを悟るには，自らの足跡を遠い過去へと辿《たど》る必要もない。拷問台，親指ねじ締め具，鞭打ちの刑はいまだに存在しているし，囚人服や一般社会の憤怒も同様であって，〔これらは〕すべて，静穏に進みゆく精神に対して陰謀を企てているのである。

人類の発展の歴史を徹底的に読み解けば，互いに激しく対立する２つの要素が明らかになる。それは，いまようやく理解され始めたのであるが，適切な環境に置かれさえすれば，互いに異質ではなく，むしろ密接に関連し，真に調和する〔２つの〕要素，すなわち，個人の本能と社会の本能である。個人と社会は，いずれも他方の価値と重要性に盲目であったために，各々が優位に立とうとして，長きにわたって執拗で血なまぐさい闘いを繰り広げてきたのである。個人の本能と社会の本能――一方は個人の努力，成長，願望，自己実現のための最も強力な要因であり，他方は相互扶助と社会福祉を成り立たせる，同じく強力な要因である。

個人の内部において，また個人とその周囲の環境との間において，吹き荒れている嵐についての説明は，簡単に見つけられる。原始人は己の存在を理解することができず，ましてやすべての生命が一体であることは理解できないため，常に己を嘲り，詰《なじ》ろうとしている盲目の隠れた力に己は絶対的に依存していると感じていた。そのような態度から，人間は高きところにいます卓越した諸力に依存する単なる１つの塵《ちり》であり，その力を鎮めるにはまったき服従によるほかないとする宗教的な考えが生まれたのである。初期の英雄物語はすべてこの考えに基づくものであり，それは神，国家，社会に対する人間の関係を扱う聖書の物語のライトモチーフであり続けている。人間は無であり，かの諸力がすべてであるというモチーフが，何度も繰り返される。

宗教，すなわち人間の心の支配と，財産，すなわち人間の欲求の支配，そして政府，すなわち人間の行為の支配とは，人間の隷属〔を維持する〕砦であり，隷属に伴うすべての恐怖を表すものである。「所有は窃盗である」。フランスの偉大なアナーキスト，プルードンはそう言った。そのとおり。ただし，その窃盗を働く者にリスクと危険は及ばない。人間の努力の蓄積を独り占めすることで，財産は人間から生得権を奪い，貧民やのけ者になるに任せた。財産は，人間がすべてのニーズを満たすだけのものを作り出していないという陳腐な言い訳さえしない。ここ数十年の労働生産性が通常の需要の100倍をはるかに上回っていることは，経済学の初学者でも知っている。しかし，異常な制度にとって正常な需要とは何だろうか。財産が認識する唯一の需要は，より大きな富を求める己の貪り食うような欲望である。なぜなら，富とは力，すなわち，服従させる力，粉砕する力，搾取する力，隷属させる力，侵害する力，相手の価値を引きずり下ろす力のことだからである。米国は，己の大きな力，巨大な国富をとりわけ誇りとしている。哀れな米国よ，国を成す諸個人が惨めなほどに貧しければ，それだけの富があったとて何の役に立とう。国民が不潔，汚物，犯罪にまみれ，希望も喜びもなく暮らす，住む家を持たない，土地を奪われた，〔他人の〕餌食となる人間の集団であるならば……。

真の富とは，有用で美しいもの，強く美しい身体や，住んで活力が湧いてくるような環境を形づくるのに役立つものの中に存する。けれども，もし人間が人生の30年もの歳月にわたって，綿を糸巻きに巻いたり，石炭を掘ったり，道路を作ったりする定めならば，富など話にもなるはずかない。人間が世に与えるものは，灰色で醜悪なものばかりで，退屈で醜悪な存在を映し出すだけである。あまりに虚弱で生きることもできなければ，あまりに臆病で死ぬこともできない。不思議なことに，この死を招くような集中生産方式を，現代の最も誇るべき成果として礼賛する者らがいる。その者らは，もし我々が機械に従属し続けるならば，我々の奴隷状態は，王に束縛されていた時代よりも徹底したものとなることにまったく気づかない。また，集中化（中央集権）が自由のみならず，健康や美，芸術や科学の弔鐘でもあることを知ろうとしない。これらはいずれも，時計のような機械万能の環境の中では存立できないのである。

VI 以下の文章に最も適切に当てはまる単語のペアを4つの選択肢の中から1つ選びなさい。

51. 解答：B

解説 第1空所は as fighting continues という文脈と Attacks とのコロケーションから sharply increased in level を意味する B. ramped up が正解。第2空所は concerns about the ... of nuclear disaster から threat と同義の B. specter を選ぶ。

訳例 ウクライナの巨大なザポリージャ原子力発電所。ウクライナ南部で戦闘が続く中，同原発への攻撃が激化している。このため，原子力災害の発生が懸念され，国連の国際原子力機関や世界の指導者たちは，監視団による現地訪問と被害調査を認めるよう要求している。

52. 解答：A

解説 第1空所は ... of the nation に着目すると，broad areas を意味する A. swaths しか残らない。第2空所は ... with the worst heat wave on record から A. grapple が正解。

訳例 中国では，広大な地域が干ばつとなるほか，記録に残る中で最悪の熱波に見舞われる中，重要な〔取水源〕で，すでに一部が干上がっている長江〔流域〕の降水量を増やすため，航空機〔を使って〕空に〔ヨウ化銀〕ロッドを打ち込む〔対策が講じられ〕ている。

53. 解答：C

解説 第1空所は an export deal ... by the United Nations and Turkey の文脈と国際情勢の基礎知識から C. brokered が正解。B. conciliated には act as a mediator の意味もあるが，受け身では使用できない。第2空所は laid the ... for a permanent peace environment の内容と laid とのコロケーションから preliminary work を意味する C. groundwork が正解。

訳例 トルコの〔アカル〕国防相は土曜日に行った演説の中で，8月1日以降，穀物を積んだ輸送船約27隻が黒海に面するウクライナの港を出航したと述べた。国連とトルコが仲介した輸出協定に基づくもので，〔同国防相はこれにより〕「恒久的な平和的環境を築く基礎」が作られたとしている。

54. 解答：D

解説 第 1 空所は ... supply concerns and rising prices に着目すると，make something less strict を意味する B. relax と同義語の D. ease が候補になる。第 2 空所は ... an embargo on Russian oil から A. levy と D. impose が候補に残る。

訳例 ミャンマー軍事政権の報道官によると，同国は供給不安と価格高騰を緩和するため，ロシアからのガソリンと燃料油の輸入を計画している。ロシアは，最大の輸出先である欧州が今年後半から段階的にロシア石油の禁輸を実施することから，エネルギーの新たな販路を同地域に求めている。

55. 解答：C

解説 第 1 空所は香港の急激な人口減少の原因について書かれているので，a situation in which a lot of people leave a particular place at the same time を意味する C. exodus が最適。第 2 空所は massive social ... that have included anti-government protests and the coronavirus pandemic から，B. turmoil と C. upheaval が候補になる。

訳例 香港が年間で過去最大となる人口減少を記録した。当局は，出生数より死亡数が多くなる「自然減」が一因との見方を示しているが，専門家によると，反政府デモやコロナウィルスの大流行など大きな社会的混乱期の中で数年前から加速し，現在も続く国外脱出も数字に表れていると指摘する。

56. 解答：D

解説 第 1 空所は hit (or strike) a nerve で evoke a strong emotional response を意味する A. hit と D. struck が候補になる。第 2 空所は growing animosity toward what many South Koreans feel is China's ... of history から，a misleading change in facts を意味する D. distortion が正解。

訳例 オリンピック開会式で中国が〔朝鮮半島の伝統衣装である〕チマチョゴリ（韓服）を使用したことは，多くの韓国人にとって，逆鱗《げきりん》に触れるものだった――ただ，この論争は外部からはただちに理解しにくいかもしれない〔……中略……〕。韓国人の怒りは，中国による歴史の歪曲《わいきょく》だと多くの韓国人が感じている事態に対する反感の高まりを映すものだ。

57. 解答：A

解説 第1空所はa tense and ... fought contestから，A. fiercelyとB. brutallyが候補になる。第2空所は ... a stunning defeatから inflict と同義の A. dealt が正解。

訳例　緊迫の激戦となったケニアの大統領選で，ウィリアム・ルト氏が勝利を収めた。2013年から副大統領を務めたルト氏〔の当選は〕，最大の対立候補であるベテラン政治家，ライラ・オディンガ氏にとっては思わぬ敗北となった。

58. 解答：B

解説 第1空所は ... dismissing her sexual assault complaint から actually but not officially or explicitly を意味する B. effectively とその同義語の C. practically が候補に残る。第2空所は a strong expression of public disapproval or anger を意味する B. outcry が正解。C. upset は an unexpected result や the state of being unhappy を意味し，outcry のように世論の強い反発を表現する単語ではない。。

訳例　インド南部の一裁判官が，ある女性〔についての判断で〕「挑発的な」服を着ていたとして女性からの性的暴行の訴えを事実上退けた。インドでは女性や少女に対する暴力がしばしば大きく報じられているだけに，〔この判断は〕世論の反発を招いた。

59. 解答：C

解説 第1空所は the harm ... for decades on Indigenous children から，cause something painful を意味する C. inflicted を選ぶ。第2空所は the ... of Indigenous cultureから，getting rid of somethingを意味する C. erasure が正解。A. deletion も同義だが，対象は something written or stored in a computer に絞られる。

訳例　ローマ教皇フランシスコは，〔カトリック教会が運営していた〕寄宿学校でカナダ先住民の子どもたちに対して行われた虐待に教会が果たした役割について，「悲しみ，憤り，恥」〔を感じる〕と述べた。カナダ国内の寄宿学校で虐待を受け，先住民族の文化を抹殺された先住民族の子どもたちに対して何十年にもわたって加えられた危害については，先住民の指導者らが長年，ローマ教皇の謝罪を求めてきた。

60. 解答：D

解説 第1空所は the ... facing the UK right now から，things that cause sorrow or distress を意味する D. woes が正解。第2空所は ... at the approaches to the Port of Dover から，deadlock と同義の D. gridlock が正解。

訳例 英国の次期首相の座を射止めようと感情的な闘いを繰り広げている2人の候補。しかし意見が一致していることが1つある。英国の EU 離脱は同国がいま直面している苦境とは無関係という見方だ。先週のテレビ討論会で2人に投げられた質問に対する答えからもそのことだけは明らかだ。討論会は，イングランド南東部にあるドーバー港へ通じる道路で大渋滞が発生し，多くの行楽客の怒りを買う中で行われた。

VII 下線部の単語や句の意味を最もよく表しているものを4つの選択肢の中から1つ選びなさい。

61. 解答：B

解説 この encapsulate は express the essential features of something succinctly を意味するので，represent と同義の B. epitomizes が正解。

62. 解答：B

解説 uncanny は strange と同義なので，B. peculiar が正解。

63. 解答：D

解説 この epic は exceptionally long and arduous を意味するので，very important, especially due to years of work を意味する D. monumental が正解。

64. 解答：C

解説 この heady は exhilarating と同義なので，C. intoxicating が正解。

65. 解答：C

解説 この decimate は drastically reduce the strength or effectiveness of something を意味するので，destroy と同義の C. obliterated が正解。

66. 解答：D

解説 prescient は predictive と同義なので，D. prophetic が正解。

67. 解答：B

解説 contour は outline と同義なので，B. frame が正解。

68. 解答：A

解説 turnaround は an abrupt or unexpected change を意味するので，a complete change を意味する A. about-face が正解。

69. 解答：D

解説 inherent は existing in something as an essential attribute を意味するので，D. intrinsic が正解。

70. 解答：A

解説 この bastion は stronghold と同義なので，A. bulwark が正解。

訳例　政治というものを簡潔に示した言葉があるとすれば，アーネスト・ベン（1875～1954）の次の言葉以外にはないだろう。「政治とは，厄介ごとを探し回り，それを至るところに見つけ，誤った診断を下し，間違った治療を行う技術である」。政治家は厄介ごとを発見し，問題を誤解し，誤った対応をする不思議な能力を持っている。政治の失敗の中で頻繁に繰り返される例として，状況を別の視点から考えることをしたがらないということがある。そういう物の考え方をするだけで未然に防ぐことができたと考えられる紛争はあまたある。本書を通じて何度も繰り返し出てくるテーマがあるとすれば，それはきっとベンのあの名言に見つかるはずである。

私が地球政治に関心を持ったのは，冷戦という激動の時代であった。このイデオロギーの戦いは，人類の未来をかけた壮大な闘争であった。自分の同世代の他の人たち同様，私も歴史の新しい 1 ページと思われる事態をリングサイドで見聞きしていた。私の成長期にあれだけ支配的だった（核兵器による人類滅亡の可能性など）が一夜にして変わってしまったのである。1989 年のベルリンの壁の崩壊は，資本主義とソビエト共産主義との間のイデオロギー競争に終止符を打つもののように感じられた。新しいユートピアを創るという社会的実験は，〔ソ連〕国民を失望させたように思われた。というより，少なくともそれが私が接した有力な言説であった。「西側」で報道されるニュースが性急な楽観主義人を酔わせるような楽観的意識，感覚，見方に彩られていた時代であった。戦争は終わり，資本主義が優位となり，民主主義が世界中に広がりつつあった。当時よく引用され，激しい論争の的となった理論家の言葉を借りれば，我々は「歴史の終わり」に到達したのであった（Fukuyama 1992）。自由民主主義が勝利を収め，未来は自由と幸福に彩られているように見えた。学部の講義でリベラル派の「民主的平和論」が提示されるころには，自由民主主義の広がりと平和との相関関係は完璧に納得できるものだった。時代は何と大きく変わったことだろう。その楽観主義はその後，ポピュリズムやパンデミック，保護主義によって大打撃を受けている。世界はいまやずっと暗いところのように思われるし，我々はみなその現実に向き合わなければならない。

自由民主主義からの明らかな離反は，政治に最終的な勝利というものはないということを予見的に示す警告となっている。1990 年代前半を特徴づけたリベラルな楽観主義は，歴史の重みの中に埋没してしまったのであり，国際関係の中に当時の楽観主義を覆すような変化がいくつか見られる。「強い男（実力者）」を僭称《せんしょう》する者たちの台頭やコロナ禍がもたらす〔人類〕存続に対する脅威，同族政治の有害な性格，貿易戦争の見通しなどが，現在では議論の枠組みを形成している。以前の時代の時代精神を捉えた概念や理論を現代世界〔に役立てる〕ため再評価する必要がある。

こうした劇的な転換は，好都合な前提が現実の事態によって覆される可能性が常に存在することを想い起させる。同様に，政治には最終的な敗北というものも存在しない。たとえば，ポピュリスト政治家の台頭とともに，ナショナリスト的（さらには準ファシスト的）な感情の復活が目撃されてきた。思想の競合は政治の場に常に存在するものであり，この思想の衝突は 1 つの時代から次の時代へ向けて自らを発明し直す能力を持っている。経済学の言葉を借りれば，希少資源をめぐって国際的な行為主体間に競争が内在しているのであり，このことから必然的に，国家と非国家主体の行動が形作られることになる。同様に，「グローカル」（「グローバル」と「ローカル」から作られた合成語）コモンズの力学から，しばしばある程度の協力と共存が生まれる。率直に言って，政治の領域には決定論的なものは何もない。

このテーマを正しく理解するためには，地球政治を構成するものについて十分に探求する前に，指摘しておかねばならない誤解がいくつかある。例えば，「米国人は〔ローマ神話で軍神を意味するマールスから名付けられた〕火星の人，欧州人は〔同じく平和の女神ウェーヌスに由来する〕金星の人」という議論は，過度に単純化されたもので，現在ではやや時代遅れとなっている（Kagan 2004）。現実には，米国はハードパワーとソフトパワーの両方の砦であり，これに対して，欧州連合（EU）は近年，軍拡を進めてきている。後者を文民行為主体と規定していたものが，事実によって覆されたのである。長年通用してきた前提も事実によって覆ることがあるということを改めて思い知らされる。

VIII 文脈上，空所を埋めるのに最もふさわしいものを4つの選択肢の中から１つ選びなさい。

71. 解答：A

解説 protesters took over the presidential palace, swam in the pool, ... and held stylized meetings in the conference roomsの場面は，very strange and difficult to understandを意味するA. surrealで説明できる。

72. 解答：D

解説 a turbulent region plagued by ... nationalismに着目して，D. toxicが正解。ここでは比喩的な意味で使われている。A. mercurial (= capricious) は人の性質を表し，C. biliousはnauseous, bad-tempered, distastefulといった単語に言い換えられるが文脈に合わない。

73. 解答：A

解説 直後のsimilar situationsはSri Lanka's dire situationを指すので，struggling financiallyを意味するA. flounderingが正解。

74. 解答：B

解説 Pakistan, a country that is heavily dependent on Chinese loansとPakistan has ... much of its hope for development to courting Chinese investmentからfastenと同義のB. hitchedが正解。

75. 解答：C

解説 ... the country's size, the stakes are even bigger in Pakistan than they were in Sri Lanka.のあとに，Pakistan is home to the world's fifth-largest population and a $340 billion economy.とあることから，パキスタンの規模がスリランカよりも大きいことがわかる。よって，due toと同義のC. Thanks toが正解。

76. 解答：C

解説 borrowed another $2.3 billion from China to ... its foreign reservesから，support something that is likely to failを意味するC. shore up

が正解。

77. 解答：D

解説 these short-term measuresは時間稼ぎにはなっても，its economic self-relianceにはつながらない，という文脈なので，D. Althoughが正解。

78. 解答：B

解説 A growing ... cadre of Pakistani leadersから，small groupを意味するB. cadreが正解。

79. 解答：B

解説 ... of grievance may explode as ordinary Pakistanis become poorer and angrierから，a situation that is dangerous and that could become violentを意味するB. A powder kegが正解。

80. 解答：A

解説 upbraid its neighbor India for attacks against and the ... of India's minority Muslim populationから，A. marginalizationが正解。upbraidはreprimandと同義。

訳例　スリランカで7月，民衆蜂起が起きて政府が倒され，大統領が急遽《きゅうきょ》亡命した。反乱は，スリランカの経済破綻をきっかけに数カ月前からくすぶっていたが，それでも観測筋の意表をつくもので，デモ参加者らが大統領官邸を占拠。プールで泳いだり，キッチンで食事をしたり，あるいは寝室を歩き回る，会議室で模擬会議を開くなど，現実離れした場面〔が報じられた〕。

スリランカから流れたこうした映像は，南アジア全域の資金繰りに苦しむ国々に衝撃を与えた。南アジアは，不安定な政府や，有害なナショナリズム，暴力を伴う急進主義，そして中国の影響力拡大に伴う不安材料に悩まされる激動の地域だ。ダッカからイスラマバードに至るまで，この地域の各国政府はスリランカ政府の混乱を見て，次は我が身かと不安に駆られている。

スリランカの悲惨な状況を招いたのは，商品価格の高騰と膨大な債務危機の中で起きた経済崩壊だ。経済が低迷する他の国々，特にスリランカのように中国に過度に依存している国々にとって，苦い教訓となっている。スリランカを含め，ジブチ，キルギスタン，ラオス，ザンビアなど42の中・低所得国が，GDPの10%を超える多額の債務を中国に負っていると報じられている。スリランカの惨状がとりわけ厳しい戒めとなったのは，中国の融資に大きく依存しているパキスタンだ。パキスタンは，中国からの投資誘致に発展の望みを託してきた。しかし，借入コストの高騰にもかかわらず，パキスタンの指導者層は中国に賭ける価値があるといまだに信じている。それが誤りだった場合，中国との関係によってパキスタンは，それでなくとも危険な経済不況のただ中で政治的混乱の激化に見舞われる恐れがある。

パキスタンは国としての規模の大きさから，その危険度がスリランカに比べていちだんと高い。世界第5位の人口と3,400億ドルの経済規模を誇る。過去6年間で経済生産性は記録的な低水準まで落ち込み，国内歳入と外貨準備高は縮小，通貨は下落した。また，失業率は急上昇中，政治腐敗が拡大してきた。対外債務総額は2016年からほぼ倍増し，1,310億ドルという途方もない額に達している。反目しあう指導者たちが聞く耳を持たない中で，警鐘が鳴り続けている。

債務不履行を回避すべく奔走するパキスタン。現在，支出を賄い，債務返済を果たすためにまた借金を重ねている。パキスタンの不安定な新政府は6月，外貨準備を補強するため中国からさらに23億ドルを借り入れた。また，国際通貨基金との間で60億ドルの救済措置の継続を交渉したが，これは燃料価格と電気料金の引き上げを伴うきわめて不人気の対策で，国民の猛反発を招いた。政府は，窮乏化の時代の現実をパキスタン国民に受け入れさせようと，紅茶輸入の未払代金6億ドルを減らすため紅茶の飲用を控えて協力するよう呼びかけている。

こうした短期的な対策は時間稼ぎにはなるが，経済的自立の確保にはつながらない。パキスタンは，スリランカよりもはるかに危険な結末を迎えるリスクを抱えている。パキスタンの政治は近年，指導者や〔政治的影響力が〕強すぎる軍，そして深く分断された国民の行動のために，ますます混乱の度を増してきている。パキスタン指導者層の中でイスラム・ナショナリズムの一派を信奉する幹部集団が数を伸ばすことで，イスラム過激派組織がますます主流になる一方，国民の支持を得るために危険な反米感情をあおる指導者もいる。パキスタンの庶民が貧しくなり，怒りが増すにつれて，不満の火種が爆発する可能性がある。

パキスタンの危うい財政状況を検討するには，必ず中国を含めて考えなければならない。パキスタン政府の対外債務は対中国が4分の1近くを占めている。しかし，パキスタンの指導層は北の隣国との不平等な関係にあえて疑問を投げかけようとせず，中国への批判があっても封じ込めてしまう。パキスタンは，隣国インドに対しては，インド国内の少数民族であるイスラム教徒に対する攻撃や疎外についてただちに非難するが，中国によるイスラム教ウイグル族に対する過酷な虐待については非難しようとしないのだ。

IX 以下の質問に対し，200～250 語の短いエッセイを英語で書きなさい。

質問文：WHO の具体的な機能を 1 つ取り上げて論じ，WHO がその役割をどのように果たしているかを，現在の特定の状況を例に挙げ説明せよ。

解答例 I will discuss the WHO's role regarding mental health and the Ukraine conflict as a present-day example of UN involvement in this issue.

Creating a worldwide health association was an important topic at the 1945 meeting to form the United Nations; the WHO was constituted April 7th, 1948 to address global health concerns, including emotional stress from conflicts and disasters.

Presently, the WHO's 13th general program of work 2019 – 2023 concentrates on creating three billion measurable impacts for one billion more people to secure: 1) universal health coverage, 2) protection from health emergencies, and 3) better health and general well-being.

Connecting emergencies with mental health, a March 2022 WHO report—reviewing 129 studies in 39 countries that suffered wars or calamities in the last decade— noted 22% of the population developed mental health disorders.

With regard to the Ukraine conflict, on July 28, 2022 Ukraine's First Lady, Olena Zelenska, highlighted the response from the WHO in providing experts and services to combatants and noncombatants facing war trauma. The UN officer on mental health in the Ukraine WHO Country Office noted how they created a new mental health service model—Community Mental Health Teams—to coordinate and deliver better services under more demanding conditions. Effective emergency responses include services of clinical psychiatric specialists as well as community self-help and social support.

Ultimately, the Ukraine example underlines two beneficial outcomes: more resilient multi-level mental health care and broader understanding of the need for mental health as a condition of general good health.

解説　WHO の機能について事実を述べつつ，その役割についてまとめるとよい。

第 1 パラグラフでは，精神衛生とウクライナ紛争をテーマとして提起している。

第 2 パラグラフでは，精神衛生について，WHO が設立された当初の目的に紛争や災害による感情ストレスも含まれていたことを示している。

第 3 パラグラフでは，第 13 次総合事業計画 2019 ～ 2023 における 3 つの取り組みについて触れている。

第 4 パラグラフでは，緊急時における精神衛生上の障害について言及している。

第 5 パラグラフでは，ウクライナ紛争について，戦争のトラウマに苦しむ人々に専門家やサービスを提供する事例，コミュニティー・メンタルヘルス・チームの設立，そして緊急時における支援システムについて述べている。

第 6 パラグラフでは，結論として，多層的精神衛生医療と精神衛生の必要性への理解という 2 つの有益な成果がウクライナでは示されたと締めくくっている。

訳例　精神衛生とウクライナ紛争に関する WHO の役割を，この問題に国連が関与している現在の事例として考察する。

国連設立を議論した 1945 年の会議では，健康に関する世界的な協会を設けることが重要な議題となり，紛争や災害による感情ストレスを含む世界的な健康問題に対処する目的で 1948 年 4 月 7 日，WHO が設立された。

現在，WHO の第 13 次総合事業計画 2019 ～ 2023 では，〔「3 つの 10 億目標」を掲げ，以下の 3 つの項目について〕それが受けられる人を 10 億人増やすための測定可能な影響を生み出すべく集中して取り組んでいる。1）国民皆保険制度，2）健康上の緊急事態からの保護，3）健康増進および一般的な幸福状態。

緊急事態と精神衛生を関連づけた 2022 年 3 月の WHO 報告書――過去 10 年間に戦争や災害を被った 39 カ国における 129 件の研究を概観したもの――では，人口の 22%が精神衛生上の障害を発症していると指摘している。

ウクライナ紛争に関しては，2022 年 7 月 28 日，ウクライナのオレナ・ゼレンスカ大統領夫人が，戦争のトラウマを負った戦闘員や非戦闘員に専門家を紹介し，サービスを提供する WHO の対応に注目する〔発言を行っている〕。WHO ウクライナ事務所の精神衛生担当国連職員は，より厳しい状況下でもサービスの調整と提供を改善できるよう，新たな精神衛生サービスモデルとしてコミュニティー・メンタルヘルス・チームを設けたと述べた。効果的な緊急対応としては，臨床精神医学の専門家によるサービスやコミュニティーの自助努力や社会的支援などがある。

結論としては，ウクライナの例は，より強靭《きょうじん》な多層的精神衛生医療と，一般的な健康の条件として精神衛生が必要であることへの幅広い理解という，2つの有益な成果を上げている〔と言える〕。

2022年特A級第2回試験　正解一覧

Ⅰ

1. D	2. D	3. B	4. B	5. B	6. D	7. C	8. A	9. A	10. D

Ⅱ

11. D	12. B	13. C	14. B	15. B	16. B	17. D	18. B	19. D	20. D

Ⅲ

21. D	22. C	23. D	24. B	25. D	26. A	27. A	28. D	29. C	30. C

Ⅳ

31. B	32. D	33. C	34. B	35. D	36. B	37. A	38. C	39. D	40. B

Ⅴ

41. C	42. B	43. A	44. B	45. A	46. A	47. D	48. B	49. C	50. D

Ⅵ

51. B	52. A	53. C	54. D	55. C	56. D	57. A	58. B	59. C	60. D

Ⅶ

61. B	62. B	63. D	64. C	65. C	66. D	67. B	68. A	69. D	70. A

Ⅷ

71. A	72. D	73. A	74. B	75. C	76. C	77. D	78. B	79. B	80. A

2次試験（面接テスト）について

2次試験は，特A級およびA級の1次試験合格者を対象に，第1回目は7月中旬の日曜日，第2回目は12月中旬の日曜日に実施されます。

特A級は外国人面接官1名，日本人面接官1名との2対1でのインタビュー，A級は外国人面接官と1対1でのインタビューです。面接時間は，特A級が15分，A級が10分です。A級については会場によりSkype等によるオンライン面接となる場合もあります。また面接テストの内容は公正な評価を行うため，すべて録音（オンライン面接の場合は録画）され，一定期間試験記録として保管されます。

外国人面接官は，インタビュアーとしての研修を受け，最終審査に合格した英語のネイティブスピーカーです。外国人面接官の選抜には，国籍や人種のバランスも考慮されています。日本人面接官は，外務省大使OBなど外交実務経験者，または大学教授です。大使経験者は英語を駆使し，なおかつ世界で活躍した人々であり，大学教授はTOEIC® 満点，国連英検特A級合格，通訳案内業国家試験合格など，公的に英語力を証明できる資格を持ち，なおかつ国際舞台で活躍している人々です。

2次試験では，まず面接シート（INTERVIEW SHEET）に事前に必要事項を英語で書き，入室と同時に面接シートを面接官に渡します。受験者が記入したくないと思う事項については書く必要はありません。面接シートは次ページのとおりです。面接シートの目的の1つは，受験者にとって身近な話題からインタビューを始め，リラックスした雰囲気で試験を行うことですから，面接の話題にしてほしいような内容はぜひ記入しておきましょう。受験者が着席すると面接が始まります。国連英検の面接官はインタビュアーとしての訓練を受けた専門家ですから，受験者が落ち着いて面接を受けられるように配慮しています。多くの場合，受験者にとって話のしやすい身近な話題から会話が始まり，質問は徐々に国際事情へと発展します。特定のトピックについて数分間のスピ−チをするといったことはないため，自分にとって興味があり，得意とする分野に話題を導くことができれば有利となるでしょう。ただ，面接官は国際事情に詳しいので，日頃から海外のニュース（CNN, BBC など）や UN News に親しみ，幅広い知識を身につけておくことが必要不可欠です。

面接シート
INTERVIEW SHEET

受験級 Class	受験記号・番号

Name	
氏名	

【記入上の注意 Notes】
1．下記の各項目を英語で記入して下さい。ただし、答えたくない項目は記入しなくて構いません。
2．記入された内容や記入量によって、試験の採点が影響されることはありません。

a. Family 家族（例：Father,Mother,Two brothers,One Daughter）
b. Home Address 現住所（区、市、郡まで。例：Nerima-ku,Tokyo）
c. Occupation 職業（例：Student,Office worker,Housewife,Bank clerk）
d. Special Qualifications 特技（例：Computer）
e. Education 教育（専攻のみ。例：Western History,Economics）
f. Hobbies,Interests,Special Concerns 趣味・興味を持っていること（例：Tennis,World Peace）
g. Your Favorite Authors 好きな作家・愛読書（例：Dickens,B.Russell）
h. Persons You Respect 尊敬する人物（例：My Father,Lincoln）
i. Foreign Countries Visited 海外経験（なければ None,あれば場所、時期、期間、目的）
j. Foreign Countries You Want to Visit 訪れたい国（例：India,Ireland）

国連英検の面接では，ただ単に国際事情の知識があるだけでは不十分です。日本人として，日本が国際社会でどのように行動したらよいか，どのようにすれば国際貢献できるのかといった視点から，理路整然かつ論理的に話ができる必要があります。付け焼刃の国際事情の知識ではとても太刀打ちできません。広く浅く議論を無難にこなせる分野だけではなく，深い議論が可能な分野もいくつか持っていることが必要です。

面接において，日本との関係が希薄な国際事情について詳しく問われることはあまりありません。たとえ面接官が外交実務経験の豊富な大使経験者であっても，世界中の国際会議などで講演を常に行っている大学教授であっても，あくまで日本と日本人という視点からの質問が中心となります。

２次試験の評価方法は，以下の４分野（合計７項目，括弧内は配点の割合）についてそれぞれ 10 段階で採点され，配点の割合に準じた得点の総合点＝総合評価で合否が判定されます。

特Ａ級は総合評価で８点以上，Ａ級は７点以上が合格です。

Examiner' s analysis of candidate' s strengths and weaknesses (Circle on number between 1 and 10 for each area of ability, adding "+" if desired.)					
Level of Strength / Area of Ability	Weak	Middle Range	Strong	Weight	Office Use
1) Comprehension	1 2 3	4 5 6 7	8 9 10	25.00%	
2) Speaking: Pronunciation	1 2 3	4 5 6 7	8 9 10	25.00% (6.25%)	
Fluency	1 2 3	4 5 6 7	8 9 10	(6.25%)	
Structure	1 2 3	4 5 6 7	8 9 10	(6.25%)	
Vocabulary	1 2 3	4 5 6 7	8 9 10	(6.25%)	
3) Communication	1 2 3	4 5 6 7	8 9 10	25.00%	
4) Knowledge (International Affairs)	1 2 3	4 5 6 7	8 9 10	25.00%	

なお，２次試験の受験対策教材として『国連英検 特Ａ級・Ａ級 面談対策』（三修社）が刊行されています。また，特Ａ級・Ａ級で実施される２次試験（面接テスト）の様子を紹介した動画が国連英検のホームページ上に公開されています。

http://www.kokureneiken.jp/about/interviewmodel

国連英検実施要項

（2023 年度時点）

主　　催	公益財団法人 日本国際連合協会 国連英検事務局
問い合わせ先	〒 104-0031　東京都中央区京橋 3-12-4 MAOビル 4 階 TEL 03-6228-6831 ／ FAX 03-6228-6832 http://www.kokureneiken.jp/

※国連英検 D 級・E 級は 2023 年度より開催を休止中。最新の実施情報は国連英検ホームページ http://www.kokureneiken.jp/ で必ず確認すること。

<table>
<tr><th>試験日</th><td>
<table>
<tr><th></th><th>1 次試験</th><th>2 次試験</th></tr>
<tr><td>第 1 回</td><td>毎年 5 月下旬の日曜日</td><td>毎年 7 月中旬の日曜日</td></tr>
<tr><td>第 2 回</td><td>毎年 10 月下旬の日曜日</td><td>毎年 12 月中旬の日曜日</td></tr>
</table>
※ 2 次試験は特 A 級・A 級のみ。</td></tr>
<tr><th>試験地</th><td>■ 1 次試験…札幌・仙台・さいたま・千葉・東京・神奈川・名古屋・神戸・京都・大阪・広島・福岡・鹿児島・那覇の予定

■ 2 次試験…特 A 級：東京・大阪
※特 A 級・A 級の併願者の 2 次試験はすべて東京・大阪で行なわれる。
A 級：札幌・仙台・東京・名古屋・大阪・福岡・那覇の予定
受験会場名，所在地は受験票に明示される。受験地の変更はできない。なお，1 次試験を特別会場で受験した受験者の 2 次試験は，最寄りの試験会場となる。
※開催最小人数に満たない会場は開催を中止する場合がある（1 次・2 次共）。</td></tr>
<tr><th>検定料
（税込）</th><td>特 A 級…13,200 円　A 級…11,000 円
B 級…8,800 円　C 級…5,500 円
※一度納入された検定料は返却できない。申し込み後の変更もできない。
※事務局が申込書を検定料の受領後，受付完了。</td></tr>
<tr><th>併願受験
検定料
（税込）</th><td>特 A 級＋ A 級＝ 22,000 円　A 級＋ B 級＝ 17,600 円
B 級＋ C 級＝ 13,200 円
※一度納入された検定料は返却できない。申し込み後の変更もできない。
※事務局が申込書を検定料の受領後，受付完了。</td></tr>
<tr><th>1 次試験の
開始時間</th><td>A 級　C 級……午前 10 時 30 分（集合時間午前 10 時）
特 A 級　B 級……午後 2 時（集合時間午後 1 時 30 分）</td></tr>
</table>

試験内容

■ 1 次試験

級	試験方法	試験時間
特A・A	リーディング・英作文	120 分
B	リスニング・リーディング・英作文	120 分
C	リスニング・リーディング	100 分

■ 2 次試験

※特 A 級・A 級の 1 次試験合格者および 1 次試験免除者が対象。

※面接シートに事前に所要事項を英語で書き込み，外国人面接官などの質問事項に答える。

※ A 級については会場により Skype 等によるオンライン面接になる場合もある。

※面接の内容は試験実施の品質向上と厳正さを担保することを目的に録音（オンラインの場合は録画）される。

合格発表

合格者には合格カードを発行

試験結果は郵送にて通知。

	1 次試験	2 次試験
第 1 回	毎年 6 月下旬	毎年 8 月中旬
第 2 回	毎年 11 月下旬	毎年 1 月中旬

受験申し込み要項

●併願の場合

午前午後で隣接する 2 つの級を同日に受験することができる。併願を希望する場合は「受験申込書」の併願欄に記入して申し込むこと。

● 1 次試験免除

前回または前々回の 1 次試験に合格し，2 次試験に不合格または欠席した場合，申請により 1 次試験が免除され，2 次試験のみ受験できる。申込書の所定欄にその旨を記入し申し込むこと。検定料は同じ。

受験票

申込書と検定料金の受理後，受験地の会場・所在地が記載された受験票が 1 次試験日の 1 週間前までに送付される。届かない場合は，必ず試験日の 3 日前までに国連英検事務局（03-6228-6831〈代表〉）へ問い合わせること。顔写真 1 枚（4 センチ× 3 センチ）を試験日までに用意し受験票に貼り付けておくこと。試験当日は，受験票とともに身分証明書を持参すること。

受験申し込み方法

書店，郵送，インターネット（PC・スマートフォン）で申し込みができる。
詳細は国連英検ホームページ http://www.kokureneiken.jp/ で確認する。

申込受付期間

第 1 回　3 月初旬～ 4 月下旬　※翌日消印有効

第 2 回　8 月初旬～ 9 月下旬　※翌日消印有効

検定料のお支払い方法

電話で申し込む場合	国連英検事務局へ電話・FAXにて申し込みができる。申し込み受付後「コンビニ支払用紙」が郵送される。
郵送で申し込む場合	国連英検事務局に受験申込書を請求する。 ●支払方法：必ず受験者氏名で銀行または郵便局から振り込む。
インターネット (PC・スマートフォン) で申し込む場合	国連英検のホームページから申し込みができる。 (PC・スマートフォン) http://www.kokureneiken.jp/ ●支払方法：クレジットカード支払い，コンビニエンスストア支払い，銀行または郵便局から振り込む。

検定料の各種支払詳細

振込の場合	**●銀行からの振込** 銀行名：　三菱UFJ銀行　日本橋支店 口座名：　(公財) 日本国際連合協会　国連英検事務局 口座番号：普通口座 0010400 金額：　　該当級の受験料 ※振込手数料は受験者負担。 ※現金・為替は取り扱い不可。 ※いずれも事務局が申込書と検定料の受領を確認後，受付完了。 ※インターネット（PC・スマートフォン）で申し込んだ受験者は，ご依頼人の前に「受付番号」(メールにて通知される) を記入する。
	●郵便局からの払込 郵便局設置の払込書（青票）にて以下の内容を記入の上，払い込む。 加入者名：(公財) 日本国際連合協会 口座番号：00130-7-24670 金額：　　該当級の受験料 ※振込手数料は受験者負担。 ※ご依頼人欄に受験者名，住所，電話番号を必ず記入する。インターネット（PC・スマートフォン）で申し込んだ受験者は，ご依頼人の前に「受付番号」(メールにて通知される) を記入する。 ※払込金受領書は必ず保管する。
クレジットカード の場合	**●インターネット（PC・スマートフォン）からの申し込みのみ可能** 入力フォームにて「クレジットカード払い」を選択し，カード番号，有効期限などを入力する。 ※利用可能クレジットカードは国連英検のホームページで確認のこと。
コンビニエンスストア の場合	●インターネット（PC・スマートフォン）からの申し込みの場合 入力フォームにて「コンビニ払い」を選択すると，払込票が送付される。 ●電話・FAXで申し込みの場合 申し込み受付完了後事務局より「コンビニ支払用紙」が郵送される。 ※全国の主要なコンビニエンスストアにて受験料を支払う。

著者・執筆協力者プロフィール

著　者

髙橋信道（たかはし・のぶみち）
翻訳家。京都大学理学部および文学部卒。国連英検指導検討委員会委員。著書に『国連英検過去問題集特A級・A級』（共著，三修社）他。

長　和重（ちょう・かずしげ）
高崎経済大学講師。敬和学園大学講師。国連英検指導検討委員会委員。著書に『国連ニュースで読む世界』（共著，三修社），『国連英検過去問題集特A級・A級』（共著，三修社）他。

村越亮治（むらこし・りょうじ）
玉川大学准教授。学術博士。国連英検指導検討委員会委員。

Lawrence Karn（ローレンス・カーン）
大妻女子大学特任教授。成城大学講師。学術博士。国連英検指導検討委員会委員長。論文に「Developing English Skills by Reporting on Current Events and World News」（OJSIS），著書に『国連英検過去問題集特A級・A級』（共著，三修社）他。

執筆協力者

服部孝彦（はっとり・たかひこ）
大妻女子大学・同大学院教授。言語学博士。国連英検統括監修官。著書に『国連英検ベーシック・トライアル』（三修社）など多数。

武藤克彦（むとう・かつひこ）
東洋英和女学院大学准教授。国連英検指導検討委員会委員。著書に『国連英検特A級・A級対策［改訂版］』(共著，三修社)，『上級時事英文法』(三修社）など多数。

Paul Underwood（ポール・アンダーウッド）
東洋英和女学院大学教授。言語学博士。国連英検指導検討委員会委員。著書に『CLIL Writing about Global Relations』（三修社）他，英語教育関係の論文多数。

Gordon Myskow（ゴードン・ミスコウ）
神田外語大学大学院准教授。応用言語学博士。国連英検指導検討委員会委員。著書に『EFL Writing in Japan: Theory, Policy, and Practice』（メディアイランド）他，英語教育関係の論文多数。

国連英検過去問題集《こくれんえいけんかこもんだいしゅう》［特Ａ級《とくえーきゅう》］〈2021-2022年度実施《ねんどじっし》〉

2023年8月31日　第1刷発行

編　者　公益財団法人　日本国際連合協会
著　者　髙橋信道　長和重　村越亮治　ローレンス・カーン
執筆協力　服部孝彦　武藤克彦　ポール・アンダーウッド　ゴードン・ミスコウ
発行者　前田俊秀
発行所　株式会社三修社
〒150-0001 東京都渋谷区神宮前2-2-22
TEL 03-3405-4511　FAX 03-3405-4522
振替 00190-9-72758
https://www.sanshusha.co.jp
印刷・製本　日経印刷株式会社
編集協力／大嶋晶代
装丁デザイン／仁井谷伴子

ISBN978-4-384-06073-7 C2082